Teaching English By Design

How to Create and Carry Out Instructional Units

Teaching English by Design

How to Create and Carry Out Instructional Units

PETER SMAGORINSKY

The University of Georgia

HEINEMANN
Portsmouth, NH

Heinemann
361 Hanover Street
Portsmouth, NH 03801–3912
www.heinemann.com

Offices and agents throughout the world

The author and publisher wish to thank those who have generously given permission to reprint borrowed material:

Figure 4.1: "Collage" by Cindy Cotner from *The English Journal*, Vol. 85, No. 5, September 1996. Copyright © 1996 by the National Council of Teachers of English. Reprinted and used with permission.

Library of Congress Cataloging-in-Publication Data
Smagorinsky, Peter.
    Teaching English by design : how to create and carry out instructional units / Peter Smagorinsky.
        p. cm.
    Includes bibliographical references and index.
    ISBN-13: 978-0-325-00980-3
    ISBN-10: 0-325-00980-5
    1. English language—Study and teaching (Secondary)—United States.
2. Lesson planning—United States. 3. Language arts—United States. I. Title.

LB1631.S53 2007
428.0071'2—dc22   2007027050

Editor: Lisa Luedeke
Production: Lynne Costa
Cover design: Shawn Girsberger
Cover illustration: Ryan Lund Neumann
Typesetter: Valerie Levy / Drawing Board Studios
Manufacturing: Steve Bernier

Printed in the United States of America on acid-free paper
16   VP   9 10

Contents

Foreword

If you have read the history of American education with any kind of critical eye, you know that it is a contentious business. Members of the local community, school administrators, teachers, and parents, not to mention national policy makers, often clash regarding the values and specifics of teaching and learning. Over the decades the classroom has, in many ways, been a battleground, and who controls what goes on within those four walls has never been permanently settled. Now, into the beginning of the twenty-first century, the struggle regarding the control of education continues and takes new and interesting forms.

Today, from a teacher's perspective, it might seem that there is good news. Policy makers now tell us that sound curriculum plans and most thoughtful administrative directives, generous funding, and enhanced technological support may not be as centrally important as once thought. The individual teachers and what they do with students in a classroom seem to be a far more potent factor when we consider student learning and student achievement. At the national level—and this is a historical first—the importance of the single teacher is now widely acknowledged as the crucial factor in student achievement.

But the good news is mixed. Despite the rhetoric regarding the influence of teachers on student learning, in the current climate that learning is measured largely through a single piece of evidence: scores on mandated tests. The content of those tests is rarely determined with teacher input and, further, is not individualized to any meaningful extent. Thus teachers, considered so integral to student learning, are in thrall to tests that they did not create and with which they cannot help their students truly demonstrate unique and individual skills. The tug-of-war continues: even with the satisfying and public citation of the importance and necessity of effective teachers, indeed, the national mandate for a highly qualified teacher in every classroom, many policy makers wish to stop right there, maintaining that the individual—though highly qualified—teacher should really not be allowed to shape what goes on in the classroom. She should, more appropriately, solely be the implementer of others' ideas regarding curriculum, instructional strategies, and, the most important thing of all, testing.

A strange time, isn't it? What at first might have seemed to be a victory for the primacy of the influence and importance of the teacher is not really such. We live in a time that hearkens back to what some fifty years ago was advanced as the possibility of a teacher-proof curriculum—as if the only way to ruin a great lesson were to let a teacher implement it. And today, along with mandated standards and high-stakes tests, we also face, in many school districts, required curriculum coverage, scripted instruction, and pacing guides meant to keep those supposedly invaluable teachers—and thus the instruction of their students—in line and on schedule. It is as if education is just too important to be left up to the teachers.

So the very idea of this book, meant to guide and encourage an individual teacher to design instruction, select material, and organize strategies, runs against what some view as a teacher's role in the classroom. For some, a teacher crafting an integrated and coherent curriculum is a dangerous thing, and if you are one of them, this book is not for you.

But I think this book *is* for you and for many teachers, both novice and veteran. Like *Teaching English by Design*'s author, I maintain that no one enters this profession to follow a mandate blindly, to ignore his students and simply read an instructional script or administer prepackaged worksheets, tests, and activities. Most of us teachers are, at heart, creative, inventive, free thinkers, and our aspirations for our students are—appropriately—far beyond delivering a prepackaged curriculum at someone else's behest. Certainly the traditional preparation for our profession encourages thought and reflection, university and college courses, and in some cases, graduate degrees, and time in classrooms observing and practice teaching. In apprenticeship situations, beginning teachers start to learn how to design original lesson plans and activities, how to make sense of student progress and achievement, how to read the professional literature, and how to conduct research in the classroom—in fact, novice teachers learn how, in an educational context, to become thinkers and doers.

As Peter Smagorinsky shows in this book, teacher thinkers and doers have a vision of what can be achieved in the classroom, and they express it most clearly in the act of designing and implementing effective instruction. Learning design principles is part of the best that we can do for our students and in our schools, and if the current climate discourages such, Peter challenges us in this book to think beyond the immediate reality:

> I want you to think about school as it might be, rather than the way you likely know it to be. I am not trying to prepare you to function comfortably within schools as they exist but am trying instead to get you

to rethink what schooling is and how you can make it more authentic, dynamic, purposeful, and fulfilling. (72)

This is vision not of what is, but of what can be. And it benefits all in the classroom—the gifted, the underachievers, the alienated, the complacent. Students who hate school, hate reading, hate writing because they have no control, no place, no freedom, no input can benefit directly from the creativity of individual teacher-designed, student-inspired units and activities. Students who are good at the ways of school but often bored and unchallenged by preset, fragmented curricula can also become energized. This book offers an outline and an inspiration for the great variety of what one intelligent teacher can craft and implement for real and very individual students. In *Teaching English by Design*, Peter Smagorinsky gives us a crafted, cohesive compilation of what we know about teaching and learning—what motivates students and fosters student skill—and shows us how we can use that knowledge effectively. And it is not to the "lowest end of the cognitive ladder" (18) where these units are directed, but to the highest.

Teaching English by Design is a book with big ideas and bigger ambitions. It honors the intelligence of students and the creativity and professionalism of teachers. It deserves to be read, and its ideas, when implemented, will effect big changes in the classroom.

—Leila Christenbury

Preface

In this book I outline a way to plan what David Anderson, English department chair at Hinsdale South (Illinois) High School, calls a *conceptual unit of instruction*. This is a block of time that you devote to a particular topic. Some possible categories for conceptual units are a *theme*, such as progress; an *author*, such as Toni Morrison; a *period*, such as American naturalism; a *region*, such as the British Lake poets; a *reading strategy*, such as understanding irony; and a *genre*, such as the detective novel. If you learn how to plan in units, your teaching will have continuity and purpose for students. You will also relieve yourself of the burden of planning day to day. If your lessons are well planned and interrelated, you will be able to focus on other aspects of teaching in your daily instruction. If you do not plan ahead, each night will require you to think of something new to do for each class the next day, perhaps till after midnight. Not my idea of a good time. To teach well and to stay healthy, after all, you'll need a good night's sleep.

Central Metaphor

To talk about teaching and learning, I employ the metaphor of *construction*. This construction occurs concurrently at two levels. At the teaching level, you will be a builder of curriculum, of a classroom community, of conceptual units. Building requires tools, materials, plans, and methods of building. Your unit design, then, is described as a process of construction that engages you in purposeful, and at times collaborative, activity.

At the same time, your students will be builders. One of my premises about being a teacher is that *people learn by making, and reflecting on, things that they find useful and important*. Your unit design should involve students in the production of things that matter to them. These things are called *texts*. Texts are usually written, but they can also be spoken or nonverbal (art, dance, or a spoken word performance, for instance). Like other kinds of builders, your students will work in a social environment where they'll get frequent feedback on their texts as they construct them.

Think of yourself, then, as a builder of curriculum and as one who helps students learn to build their own texts. This approach is known as *constructivist* teaching. As you might know from your experiences, schools are more likely to rely on what I call *authoritative* teaching. In this approach, the teacher is presumed to be an expert who fills students with knowledge. In asking you to use a constructivist metaphor for teaching, then, I'm asking you to rethink what it means to be a teacher.

Constructivism is a theory; actually, there's more than one version, and for constructivists, each of us constructs our own version, so life in a constructivist world is very open-ended. The brand of constructivism that I embrace, however, is not strictly individualistic. Rather, it requires attention to the environment in which teaching and learning take place. This environment includes the social history of the school and all of the traditions and rituals provided by that history. A school in which English teachers have historically emphasized the cultural heritage of the West, imparted through the structure of the curriculum and the teachers' lectures and discussions (but mostly lectures), provides a set of routines and expectations that are difficult to teach within if you're working from a constructivist perspective.

Further, externally imposed testing mandates both occupy time and suggest a purpose for education that goes against the grain of a constructivist approach. When a set of practices and traditions collude to support authoritarian teaching, the constructivist teacher may take on a fairly lonely project within the confines of the school. Yet I believe that the constructivist approach provides opportunities for students to experience school far more richly than the conventional approach of sitting in class after class, listening to teachers talk, and then getting tested on what the teacher has said. Thoreau wrote in *Civil Disobedience* that "any man more right than his neighbors constitutes a majority of one already" (1998). While it is no doubt arrogant to assume that adopting one educational approach over another makes one "more right" than her colleagues, I agree with Thoreau that there is honor in persisting if you believe that what you are doing is right, no matter how relentlessly others try to make you conform.

Many people believe that theories, including constructivism, have little to do with the classroom and its gritty realities. Arthur Applebee quotes one teacher who, when asked about contemporary literary theory, said that theories are "far removed from those of us who work the front lines!" (1993, 122). Yet I suspect that this teacher could not effectively work in the trenches or on "the front lines" without some theory of what she was doing. Regardless of which metaphor you use to characterize your classroom work (war, gardening, assembly-line production, incarceration, etc.), you have a set of beliefs about what you're working toward, how you should get there, which materials best enable a good trip, and so on. Indeed, the teacher quoted by Applebee conveys many of her beliefs about teaching simply by declaring that she's on the front line, presumably in a war against her students.

What I think that this teacher, and many others, reject is the way theory is presented. Typically, theorists present their ideas through an array of specialized, polysyllabic terms—*interiorization, heteroptia, interinanimation, phallologocentrism,* and other fine words rarely heard in the high school faculty lounge. These terms require the theorists to explicate extensive sets of formal rules and abstractions that they parse by examining the details of endless hypothetical examples. I've done this myself when writing primarily for university-based readers.

Teachers' interests are more pragmatic, and so wading through the technical language and abstract concepts of the theoretical specialist can be daunting and unproductive. As a result, many teachers say that theory is impractical and irrelevant. What I think they're really saying is that *theorists* are impractical and irrelevant, at least to their needs.

In this book I try to present a theoretically grounded approach to teaching without getting bogged down in the task of the theoretician, which is to focus primarily on an elaboration of concepts through technical language. Instead, I present *theory as an extended metaphor,* much as the teacher does in locating herself on the battlefield of instruction. To repeat (and not for the last time): The essence of the theory I've proposed is that people learn by making, and reflecting on, things that they find useful and important. They do so through a process of composition in which they develop goals, locate appropriate tools and materials, develop plans, and construct a text. This text is always provisional; that is, it stands as a temporary statement of meaning that will later be revised—if not in this text itself, then in a new text that builds on the old. Throughout this process of composition, they revise their goals and plans to meet arising circumstances, use new tools and materials as needed, reflect on the emerging text, and reconsider how and why they're making it.

This process enables learners to construct new meaning as they work, both through emerging ideas and those that come through reflecting on the text during production. The learners I refer to include both those we call teachers and those we call students, although I think that their roles can merge in dynamic classrooms. While the texts constructed by learners may reach a point of temporary completion, they are part of an ongoing effort to construct meaning and so may serve as points of reflection for the development of new compositions. Texts, then, are occasions for learning through both the process of composition and reflection on the product: both on its provisional form during composition and on its equally provisional form when completed for school assessment.

All of this composing takes place in some kind of social context. The context of construction has a lot to do with the kinds of compositions and composition processes that are valued and encouraged. The context also includes the way in which you set up your classroom. If you place the seats in rows facing you at the front, you discourage the use of speech as a tool for exchanging and constructing ideas among students. If you allow for multimedia composing, then you open up students' tool kits for constructing meaningful texts. An act or text is rarely meaningful in and of itself. Rather, it takes on meaning through the validating effect of the environment. If a teacher values only five-paragraph themes and a student submits a statue to interpret a novel, then the statue will have no significance or worth in this context, regardless of what the student has learned or how the statue might be appreciated in another context.

There's one other thing that is important in using the metaphor of construction as a theory of teaching. In order for this metaphor to be useful, you need to get fulfillment from doing work. I mean this in several ways. First of all, I mean that what I've outlined in this book will require a lot of work from you. You can't go on cruise control and let the teacher's manual or the curriculum do all of the thinking and teaching for you. Rather, you need to view instructional design as stimulating, intellectually challenging, important work that can potentially put you in the sort of "flow" described by Mihaly Csikszentmihalyi (1990)—that is, an experience so involving that you lose track of time. You need to get satisfaction out of putting a lot of effort into something with the understanding that it will probably result in a provisional product that you'll need to revise—no yellowed lecture notes for you to trot out year after year. You need to enjoy the challenge of aligning goals and practices, of devising activities that students will find engrossing and enlightening, of channeling your creativity into the production of the text that will serve as your unit of instruction.

You also need to be prepared to do work in response to what your students produce. Grading papers takes a lot of time. But it's unlikely that students will learn to write unless they're writing, and it's unlikely that they'll grow as writers without your earnest, engaged response to their papers. There will be times when grading a volume of student writing (or other composing) will be a grind. But the overall satisfaction that you get from participating in your students' growth should overcome whatever time commitment is involved in evaluating their work.

You also need to be prepared to do work alongside your students. Sometimes this means doing a project of the same type that they are doing: writing with them during a writing workshop, keeping a portfolio about your teaching as they keep one about their learning, and otherwise learning in parallel with their learning. Sometimes it means doing a project to understand better how they are learning: studying the effects of your instruction, charting the development of relationships that follow from a change in your teaching, or otherwise systematically reflecting on your teaching. Sometimes it means trying to learn more about your students' lives outside school so that you can teach them in ways that build on their strengths. Becoming an actively reflective practitioner will require an inquiring stance and the time that it takes to enact it. But doing so can make your work as a teacher much more stimulating than it would be if you were to simply pass out the handouts that accompany your commercial literature anthology and grade them with an electronic scanner, year after year, with the same emphasis and information taught and tested regardless of how much the students themselves have changed.

Your students also need to have some kind of work ethic. I think that most students do, but that much school instruction dulls it, at least with regard to schoolwork. I had a sobering experience about halfway through my fourteen years of teaching high school English. I was talking with a guidance counselor about one of my students and lamented that the student just didn't care about school. The counselor paused and then said, "You know, I've been a counselor here for twenty years, and I don't think I've ever worked with a student who doesn't care. They all care; often, they're just fearful, and don't do their assignments because they're afraid to fail at them."

This chance discussion provided me with one of the most important lessons I've learned about students' motivation. I had always taken an individualistic view of motivation: it's something that individuals have that propels them to success. The conversation with this counselor led me to take a more sympathetic view of young people and their motivations. First, I learned that young people's motivations are often intertwined with their adolescent angst and insecurity, often in ways that make them appear unmotivated to adults, including teachers. Second, I began to think about what my students might be motivated to do, even if my English class didn't always capitalize on their goals.

Finally, I began to develop a much more social perspective on motivation, one in which the environment helps to provide motivating features. In doing so I was not relieving the students of personal responsibility or mindlessly trying to inflate their self-esteem. Rather, I began to take some responsibility for setting up my classroom so that their motivations could be realized more easily and for providing activities and goals that my students would be more likely to expend their motivations on. I found that when I involved my students in constructive, productive activity, they would work pretty hard and feel pretty good about what they produced. Of course, this engagement doesn't happen with everything you do. Some things you teach in the English curriculum are not going to light a fire under every student. But you can make an effort to teach so that it happens as often as possible.

My notion of work is not of the nose-to-the-grindstone variety, although there are times when that's what you need to do. Rather, it refers to the labor of love, the transforming potential of authentic, constructive, productive activity. I think that all great teachers love what they do and do it with passion. If they stay up till two in the morning, it's not because they don't know what to do the next day, it's because they're so involved with their work that they lose track of time. When you teach with this kind of engagement and passion, your students will know, and they will show their appreciation and respect in ways that surpass just about any sort of fulfillment that I can imagine.

Acknowledgments

This is the third time I've tried to write this book over the last seventeen years. This ongoing effort serves as a sequel to the book through which I originally learned how to teach: *Dynamics of English Instruction, Grades 7–12* (Hillocks, McCabe, and McCampbell 1971). Steve Gevinson and I made the first effort to update *Dynamics* in 1989 with *Fostering the Reader's Response: Rethinking the Literature Curriculum, Grades 7–12*, which was a summer curriculum project gone wild. I tried again with *Teaching English Through Principled Practice*, published in 2002, which bears some resemblance to the current effort.

Believing as I do that no text is truly original, I have many people to thank. First up: Lisa Luedeke, who opened Heinemann's doors to this new version and has been a splendid editor and colleague throughout my work on this project; and Lynne Costa, my deft and eagle-eyed production editor at Heinemann. My friends from my days at the University of Chicago have influenced just about every idea I've had about teaching. The Chicago group numbers in the hundreds and so would be difficult to list here, but Steve Gevinson, George Hillocks, Larry Johannessen, Betsy Kahn, Tom McCann, and Michael Smith have been my close friends and collaborators for many years and deserve particular recognition and appreciation. I also taught in three Chicago-area high schools from 1976 to 1990, and my many students and colleagues from those great years have helped shaped my view of teaching. In particular, Jane Christino, Dale Griffith, Tim Hull, Art Hutchinson, Carol Mayer, Pat Millen, Tom Mooney, Bernie Phelan, Charles White, and Joe Wolnski were friends who guided me through my early years of teaching and offered both professional and personal support for many years. Finally, my students and colleagues at the University of Oklahoma and the University of Georgia have been great sources of stimulation, with special thanks due to Steve Bickmore, Deborah Brown, Tricia Cameron, Leslie Cook, John Coppock, Elizabeth Daigle, Mark Faust, Bob Fecho, Pam Fly, Peg Graham, Cori Jakubiak, Tara Johnson, Jim Marshall, Cynthia Moore, Sharon Murphy, Cindy O'Donnell-Allen, Patty Reed, Amy

Sanford, Lynda Thompson, Melissa Whiting, Maria Winfield, and Michelle Zoss. And, of course, thanks to my main homies: Jane, Alysha, and David, with Dude and Abby (Whiskers and Luna, RIP).

This book is dedicated to my father, Joseph Smagorinsky, who passed away on September 21, 2005, at age eighty-one. He was one of those great American success stories. His parents were from Gomel, Belarus, which they left during the pogroms (the government-supported "ethnic cleansing" of Jews) during the early twentieth century. He was born in 1924 in New York City and was raised in a Jewish ghetto on the Lower East Side of Manhattan during the Great Depression. Like his three brothers, he worked for his dad's sign-painting business; unlike them, he took a different direction as an adult. He became a meteorologist and, along with his longtime friend and colleague Norman Phillips, was awarded the Benjamin Franklin Medal in Earth Science from the Franklin Institute in Philadelphia in 2003 for "their seminal and pioneering studies" that led to "an understanding of the general circulation of the atmosphere, including transports of heat and moisture that determine the earth's climate." In its recent bicentennial celebration, the National Oceanic and Atmospheric Administration named him as one of the ten most significant figures in NOAA's history, and the organization lists his general circulation climate model as one of the three most important breakthroughs in meteorology in the last two hundred years.

I never had much of a knack for atmospheric physics or any science except the social kind, instead dedicating my career to the teaching and learning of English. Throughout my work I've tried to adopt the qualities that helped to distinguish his life, in particular his integrity in carrying out his career project. Thanks, Dad—I love you, and I hope I've made you proud.

About This Book

Hello! And thanks for buying this book. I know how much these things cost. I hope that by the time you're done reading and thinking about teaching English by design, you'll feel that it was a few dollars well spent.

I've tried to write this book so that it has a strong theoretical basis but doesn't overwhelm you with a lot of theoretical language. Learning to design instructional units is plenty hard, and I want your focus to be on the design principles, not on words such as *ventriloquation* and *heteroglossia*. These might be really cool words, but they probably would make your learning curve steeper on a task that can seem nearly vertical as it is. I've tried to translate concepts into relatively plain language so that your job—learning to design units of instruction—doesn't get sidetracked unnecessarily.

You will probably want to run straight to your computer and bookmark a couple of web pages. First, there's the Virtual Library of Conceptual Units, located at www.coe.uga.edu/~smago/VirtualLibrary/index.html. This resource provides you with a whole lot of examples of the kinds of unit I'm trying to teach you how to design in this book. Each one has been written by a student (or in many cases, by collaborative groups of students) in one of my classes at the University of Georgia, using some version of the book you're reading right now as a guide. Most of them are pretty doggone good, and the best ones to use as models are the ones listed in red. You are welcome to use any ideas from these units in your teaching. Together, they provide a cornucopia of units and lessons within units that should make your teaching a lot more satisfying than it would be if you were simply to teach from the recipe provided in your anthology's teacher's manual.

A second web page to bookmark is the Outlines for Conceptual Units at www.coe.uga.edu/~smago/VirtualLibrary/Unit_Outlines.htm. This page (actually, it's one really long page) will help you sketch out units on many, many topics. I've taught a lot of them myself, which is where a bunch of the materials lists come from; others are units I might have taught if I'd stayed in the secondary school classroom, where I worked from 1976 to 1990 in three Chicago-area high schools.

For those using this book to teach classes in instructional design, an Instructor's Guide is available at http://books.heinemann.com/products/E00980.aspx. This guide provides possible ways to use this book with preservice or inservice teachers learning methods for teaching English.

I wrote this book to help you learn how to design units of the sort you'll find in the Virtual Library. Believe me when I say that designing a unit for the first time will be one of the most challenging things you've ever done. It's very different from writing papers for English classes or other university courses. Designing a unit requires you to take into account a lot of things you might never have thought deeply about but that are essential to producing a unit that you and your students will experience in a positive way. You will need to consider who adolescents are generally and what they can benefit from learning at the age at which you teach them, as well as who the specific adolescents in each of your classes are: how they learn, which versions of English (if any) they speak, what their backgrounds are, and many other factors that are essential to understand in teaching and learning relationships.

You need to think about why you are teaching your particular unit topic and be able to defend that decision to your colleagues, your administrators, your students, your students' parents, and anybody else who takes an interest—for better or worse—in your teaching. You need to identify a set of materials—literature, other writing, film, music, Internet resources—and decide how appropriate they are for your teaching situation. You need to identify how you'll assess your students and how to judge their performance so that you can distinguish between one grade and another when assigning grades to their work.

But that's the easy part. What most people struggle with when learning to design units of instruction is teaching students *how* to do the tasks they are asking of them and designing lessons within the unit that lay out clearly the ways in which they will guide their students through the learning process. You may have never done anything like this before, and it can be daunting. I always have students who think that they'll never be able to complete a unit, but as the Virtual Library shows, almost all of them have. I should confess that the first time I wrote a unit in my master's degree methods class, I got a B– on it. But I stuck with it and eventually got the hang of it. So when you experience frustration, I ask you to accept it as part of the process of learning something new and difficult. And think of how your own students will struggle when you are trying to teach them a new task. You may be familiar with it, but they probably won't be. Work to understand their struggles as they go through the process, and support their learning by designing lessons that gradually move them into new competencies. I hope that this book provides just such a scaffold (dang, that's one of those jargon words) for you as you develop your skills as an instructional designer.

Part I

Teaching with Students in Mind

1 *Students' Ways of Knowing*

Something happened when I was teaching high school that I'll never forget, although to the other people involved it seemed to be a routine, passing moment that was entirely unremarkable. I was standing in the hallway between classes, talking to the English teacher who taught next door. We engaged in the typical brief banter that teachers exchange amid the currents of students going to class, talking, laughing, rummaging through their lockers, and catching their breath before the next class begins. Another English teacher walked by and, seeing my colleague, called across the clamor, "Hey, I'm just finishing up *Death of a Salesman*, and somebody told me that you have a really great test to use with it. Could you lend me a copy?"

"Sure," answered the other, and as the passing period came to an end, we scattered along with the students to start the next class.

The incident seemed so casual that I'm sure neither of the teachers thought anything odd about it at all. To me, though, the idea of teaching something for several weeks and then using an assessment developed by another teacher for other students is fundamentally at odds with everything I understand about evaluation. Testing students in this way involves the following assumptions:

1. There is such thing as a good test that anybody studying a text can take to see how well he's understood it. This in turn carries more assumptions:

    - The text itself stands as a concrete work whose meaning is stable across readers and groups of readers. I refer to this presumed stable meaning as the work's *official meaning*.

    - Anyone teaching the text will inevitably emphasize the official meaning.

    - The test itself stands as an objective measure of students' understanding of the official, invariant meaning.

- Whatever knowledge students construct from the literature beyond the official interpretation is irrelevant in terms of their grade on the assessment.

2. It's fine to teach without any sense of how one will assess the students at the end. This in turn carries the following assumptions:

   - Instruction is about the texts, which have a particular meaning, which can ultimately be assessed by an exam designed by someone who has never seen any of the teaching or learning.

   - There is not necessarily a relation between actual classroom processes and assessment.

   - Assessment does not necessarily need to be related to the unique exchanges that take place among particular groups of students and teachers when discussing works of literature or unit concepts.

Perhaps the utter casualness of the exchange I witnessed, its very mundane character, is what made it so striking to me. The assumptions behind it were so deeply embedded in my colleagues' conception of teaching that the loan could be uncritically secured through a chance meeting in the hallway. And so the exam moved from one file cabinet to another, perhaps still being administered to this day, the meaning of the play remaining stable no matter who teaches the class or who enrolls in it.

My account of this exchange undoubtedly seems harsh. You might be surprised to learn that I liked both of these teachers a great deal and that both had extremely good reputations around the school. And perhaps that's what makes it all so remarkable: that two highly regarded teachers in a high school with a national reputation would view assessment in what struck me as a thoughtless and cavalier manner.

I tell this story to open this chapter because this chapter is about what students know and what teachers grade. Schools tend to have a well-established conception of what counts as knowledge. You will recognize this conception when I describe it, for you have undoubtedly been assessed according to it in most classes you have taken throughout your education.

I don't want to suggest that the dominant values of school are always off the mark or unimportant, even if in significant ways they often are. I do, however, hope to persuade you that you should also assess other ways that students have of knowing things. To do so, I review other ways that people can come to know something. You will probably recognize these other ways, too, although you may be less familiar with their role in formal education.

By designing assessments that take these other types of knowledge into account, you will be teaching in ways responsive to the range of diversity that your students bring to class. In some cases people's ways of knowing are inborn; some of us are born with the capacity to configure space much better than others. In some cases our ways of knowing come from our culture; some cultures promote collaboration while others promote competition. In some cases the source of difference is not so clear; most people agree that men and women tend to see the world differently, although it's never been established whether they are born different or are socialized into different ways of knowing, or whether both factors combine to produce gender differences.

Regardless of the source of difference, your students will most likely exhibit quite a broad range of capacities. Throughout much of their schooling, these diverse students will be forced to fit the Procrustean bed of conventional assumptions about knowledge and assessment. Procrustes was an Attican thief who laid his victims on his iron bed. If a victim was shorter than the bed, he stretched the body to fit; if the victim was too long, he cut off the legs to make the body fit. In either case the victim died. Assessments can be deadly for students, too, when the same evaluation is viewed as a universal fit for all students, no matter what shape they are in relative to the test. If you instead allow for flexibility in the ways in which students can express themselves and come to know the discipline of English, you'll be assessing students on their own terms and through vehicles that suit their strengths.

In school there are relatively few ways in which knowledge is assessed. Let's take something relatively simple, a bicycle, and see how you might know it:

- You might have memorized its different parts and be able to answer questions about them.

- You might know how, from experience and perhaps some instruction, to ride the bicycle across a variety of terrains.

- You might associate the bicycle with your dear grandparent who bought it for you and fixed it when it broke, therefore knowing it through sentiment and love.

- You might know the history of bicycles and this particular type of bicycle's place in that history.

- You may know the rhythms generated by riding it at different speeds and know its potential for producing percussive sounds, especially if you clip cards so that they strike the rotating spokes.

- You may have had significant experiences while riding it and view those stories as central to your identity.

There are undoubtedly many other ways in which you could know a bicycle. If you were to study the bicycle in school, however, it's likely that you would be tested on your knowledge by your ability to identify its parts and their correct functions. It wouldn't matter much if you could actually ride a bicycle or not. You might know how to shift gears appropriately to ride the bike up particular inclines, but if you forgot the names of gear mechanisms you were asked to identify, you would be deemed unknowledgeable about bicycles.

I ask you to open your mind with regard to thinking about what it means to know something. This consideration should take into account a few key points:

- Achievement is a function of what you measure. By this I mean that students are judged to be good or bad, knowledgeable or unknowledgeable, A students or D students, according to some means and focus of measurement. Far too often, those measurements are restricted to students' memory of official and/or factual knowledge. Any other knowledge they have, particularly when it departs from the conventional, is not considered noteworthy when their achievement is measured through a school assessment.

- What you test is what you get. By this I mean that assessment tends to set the terms for what teachers emphasize in instruction. And so when students will be assessed according to their memory of official knowledge, classes will likely be conducted to impress that knowledge on them, through lectures that impart the information or reinforce facts from the reading.

You must consider many factors when developing appropriate assessments. I present these factors in binary fashion; that is, I discuss each by outlining oppositional perspectives on it. I should caution that I often find binaries to be problematic because they involve a false dichotomy. I use them more to outline firm positions on each topic that shed light on how schools work. Rather than view them as bipolar opposites with nothing in between, I see them as points on a continuum, with many possibilities between and outside the boundaries of their differences.

Two Theories of Communication: Transmission and Constructivism

Two theories of communication, transmission and constructivism, will provide a vocabulary for further discussions of assessment. The argument I make here is not new, yet the problem I discuss is remarkably persistent. The problem concerns a paradox of schooling: that the most pervasive assumption about knowledge is the *transmission* view, which conceives of knowledge and communication in superficial ways, while the relatively rich *constructivist* assumptions rarely influence curriculum, instruction, and assessment.

Transmission

There have probably been a number of occasions when you have felt that what you knew was not measured by a school assessment. I still remember a college course I took in classical civilizations where, after reading all sorts of interesting history and literature from early Mediterranean culture and having a reasonable understanding of how these civilizations shaped subsequent history, I found a question on the final exam asking me to identify a classical figure named Bucephalus. Perhaps you don't recognize this character, as I didn't while taking the test. Yet the professor believed that identifying Bucephalus was so significant that it should serve as a measure of my knowledge of classical history. It turned out to be the name of Alexander the Great's horse. Fortunately we were not asked to identify his cat, or I might still be in college.

Such, however, is the way that knowledge in school has typically been conceived and measured: instead of focusing on important concepts, it fixates on labeling their parts, and sometimes it seems that the more obscure, the better. Another example: Not long ago, the certification exam for English teachers in one state asked candidates to identify the name of the frog in Mark Twain's "Celebrated Jumping Frog of Calaveras County." In case you've forgotten, it's Dan'l Webster. Fortunately for you, your future as a teacher probably does not depend on knowing this nugget of information, as it did for the teachers taking that exam.

When test makers pose questions of this sort, they assume that knowledge is objective and static and capable of being handed down intact from one person to another, from text to student, from lecture to notebook and back again to the teacher on a test. When the questions concern the names of horses and frogs, rather than their significance, the test makers appear to believe that any detail will do for testing purposes. Or they might have something in mind that is simply indecipherable, such as when they wrote the true-or-false test item "Huck Finn is a good boy." (Thanks to Alan Purves, by way of Jim Marshall, for this example of assessment lunacy.)

This view of knowledge has been called the *transmission* view. Knowledge is thought to be a stable entity that can be transmitted like a baseball, thrown from one person to another, arriving in the same condition in which it began. And thus a teacher can say in a lecture that in Emily Dickinson's "Narrow Fellow in the Grass," the narrow fellow is a snake, and students can write this fact down. Later, the students can prove they are knowledgeable readers by affirming the serpentine nature of the narrow fellow on a test. Woe unto the student who has constructed the narrow fellow as something else and has the poor judgment to say so on the official assessment.

Schools in general are conducted so as to support a transmission view of knowledge because they tend to follow a top-down model of authority. Administrators make decisions that teachers put into practice. Teachers, though they usually lack schoolwide authority, are the authorities in their classrooms and so transmit their knowledge of facts to students. Students have the option of doing school in ways that lead to success or resisting those ways and being labeled as troublemakers or bad students, or even students of bad character.

To be a success, students show that they have mastered the knowledge that their teachers have provided for them, no matter how useful they find that knowledge or whether they even believe it. Indeed, James W. Loewen (1995), in *Lies My Teacher Told Me: Everything Your American History Textbook Got Wrong*, argues that school textbooks frequently suppress historical facts in order to promote a sanitized, grand narrative of American history. It's also quite common for one commercial textbook to present facts that are different from the facts provided in another. The students' job is to memorize the particular version of history presented in the textbook they study—even though this version might be contradicted in a different textbook and be viewed with skepticism by many historians—and report it correctly on exams.

Students' ability to replicate official knowledge intact is depicted through their grades, a sorting process appreciated by colleges that need ways to discriminate between one applicant and another. The flow of transmission is invariably from teacher and text to student. Students have little say in deciding what is good or bad, right or wrong, meaningful or not meaningful. Their role is to show that they've received the information and can throw it back in the same form. Cynics have used such unseemly analogies as regurgitation or mindless metaphors as parroting to describe the expectations for students under a transmission pedagogy.

Constructivism

Even though schools are widely operated according to transmission assumptions, there are plenty of ways to know something other than to know it according to its official facts, right or wrong. Another view of knowledge falls under the umbrella term *constructivism*. As the word suggests, this idea refers to the notion that knowledge is constructed rather than received through a transmission. Learners draw on a variety of sources for the knowledge they create:

- One is their reading of the codes provided by whatever text they are studying. If, for instance, a student reads or writes a science report on the dissection of a frog (not, presumably, Dan'l Webster), the expectation of the genre would suggest that a material frog existed and was duly parsed as described in the report. If, however, the same student were to read Swift's *Gulliver's Travels* and come across talking horses (not Bucephalus), the literary codes would suggest that the animals not be viewed literally. If a student included an account of a talking frog in a lab report for a science class, the teacher would likely assume it was either an unfaithful science report, one unusual frog, or a work of fiction and likely assign it a low grade because it did not include the proper codes for science reports.

- A second source of constructed knowledge is the learner's personal experiences. While reading *Gulliver's Travels*, someone with personal experience in human avarice might see images of greedy people in her mind. Doing so would infuse the literary characters with a particular and probably idiosyncratic meaning. In contrast, a transmission view would frown on an idiosyncratic reading of literature as a departure from the official meaning and in all likelihood would dismiss the interpretation as irrelevant, unnecessarily personal, or incorrect.

- A learner's attributions of meaning can also be a function of the social context of reading. If, for instance, a class was reading *Gulliver's Travels* in preparation for the Advanced Placement exam, then the teacher's instruction might focus students' readings on AP values. The AP scoring rubrics would provide the guidelines for learning how to read and think about the novel. In contrast, if adult members of a book club were reading it, the reading might be accompanied by wine and snacks, the conversation might include much laughter, the discussion might digress to consider personal experiences with avaricious people or talking horses, and open emotions such as crying would be viewed as appropriate responses. There would be little attention to how to write a high-scoring essay that would please AP judges and more attention to what the readers did and didn't get from the book. The conversation might include a lot of storytelling, rather than a lot of analysis. Similarly, it would be highly inappropriate to respond to Swift's satire in an AP class by bursting into tears except, perhaps, upon receiving a test score. In both cases, the social context helps to determine appropriate responses.

- Finally, the cultural backgrounds of the learners can influence their construction of meaning. Margaret Mitchell's *Gone with the Wind*, for instance, for many years was among the twentieth century's most beloved novels, at least among white readers. Toward the end of the century, however, its depiction of southern gentility came under criticism because of its unproblematic view of slaves. In both novel and film, the slaves are devotedly subservient and regret the fall of the South. This portrayal was accepted for many years by the novel's and film's devoted admirers. The current climate has fostered more critical views of this depiction of the contented slave. *Gone with the Wind* is now read as racist by readers who view its representation of southern gentility as a valorization of oppression. Different worldviews can provide the framework for a different kinds of meaning.

Knowledge construction, therefore, comes as part of a transaction among a variety of factors: the text that the student reads or produces, the personal experiences that the student brings to the situation that contribute to understanding and interpretation, the influences of the environment that suggest appropriate ways to be literate, and the cultural history that provides the values for both the immediate environment and the individual's experiences.

Any assessment ought to provide the occasion for new learning. It is possible that transmission-oriented assessments can allow for new learning, although most such assessments I've seen do not (my enduring knowledge of Bucephalus' identity notwithstanding). Rather, many assessments of this type reduce some pretty splendid literature to a tedious job of memorizing information that's forgotten before long. Most taxonomies of cognition place simple memorization fairly low on the hierarchy and rank inference and generating new knowledge fairly high. Yet school assessment concentrates on rote memorization and location of facts, even in the decidedly ambiguous and symbolic world of literature.

Two Views of Speech and Writing: Final Draft and Exploratory

Related to the transmission and constructivist views of communication are Douglas Barnes' (1992) descriptions of the two kinds of classroom speech:

- *final-draft* speech, which often occurs in conjunction with transmission pedagogies
- *exploratory* speech, which can serve to achieve constructivist ends

Final-Draft Speech

In his studies of classroom interactions, Barnes found that assumptions about knowledge affect the ways in which students speak and write in school. Most readers of this book will understand Barnes' metaphor of final-draft speech. A final draft is the one in which all of the kinks have been worked out, all of the bad ideas rejected, all of the language smoothed over. It has a certainty about it that reflects an authoritative view of the topic. The product is complete and presented for the teacher's approval.

Barnes argues that in too many classrooms, discussions are conducted so that only final-draft speech is rewarded. That is, students are encouraged to participate only when they have arrived at a fairly well thought out idea that they can present to the teacher for approval. Under these circumstances, a lot of students don't say much at all because they are thinking through their ideas and never quite reach that finalized state where their thoughts can be offered for the teacher to approve. By the time they've articulated their thoughts in their head, the discussion has moved along and the contribution is no longer relevant. Rather, the teacher—who has often taught the book or the class a number of times and can provide an authoritative interpretation in reasonably polished form—occupies much of the floor.

This conception of speech is compatible with a transmission view of communication because only finished, authoritative ideas are considered legitimate, and for the most part the teacher is the one who has them. The teacher's role, then, is to provide official knowledge for the students, who demonstrate their expertise by repeating it back as faithfully as possible on assessments.

Exploratory Talk

Barnes argues that classrooms ought to encourage more exploratory talk, in which students think aloud as they work through their ideas. Such talk is tentative, spontaneous, provisional, half-baked, and constructive as students discover what they have to say by voicing their emerging thoughts.

Allowing such talk changes much about classrooms. First of all, it changes the purpose of discussion from transmitting official knowledge to constructing new knowledge. This shift in turn alters the dynamics of discussions. The teacher no longer exclusively holds the floor, but instead orchestrates students' efforts to realize new ideas through exploratory talk. The contributions of speakers needn't be formal and authoritative but can be partial, playful, and experimental. Since ideas are not being offered as finished products for final approval, the discussion allows its participants to inquire and grope toward meaning. These conditions apply not only to the students but to the teacher as well, who also has the opportunity to realize new thoughts and insights through the process of discussion.

The idea of exploratory talk also extends to writing. Although there is now more attention to writing process than there used to be, writing is still not typically viewed as an opportunity to discover ideas through exploratory, tentative expression. A constructivist approach includes informal opportunities for students to write freely as a way to find what they have to say without concern for submitting the finished product for approval. Used in this way, writing serves as a *tool* for learning, part of the student's tool kit for constructivist thinking.

This conception of writing and speech contributes to what some have called a *growth model* of education (see Barnes, Britton, and Torbe 1971; Dixon 1975). In this view, the emphasis of school is on students as well as, and perhaps more than, on subjects. The purpose of the class then shifts from teaching the subject—lecturing on the Victorians, explaining the significance of literary symbols, and so on—to considering how engagement with a domain will contribute to the personal growth of learners. Such an emphasis relies on language as a tool for exploring ideas and creating new knowledge and is less concerned with the knowledge displays inherent to transmission pedagogies that rely on final-draft speech.

Paradigmatic and Narrative Ways of Knowing

Psychologist Jerome Bruner (1986) has argued that there are primarily two ways of knowing, *paradigmatic* and *narrative*. Schools tend to rely on paradigmatic knowledge more than narrative. These ways of knowing are not necessarily tied to transmission and constructivist assumptions about learning. That is, either paradigmatic or narrative knowledge can be constructed or it can rely on presumably transmitted facts. Unfortunately, paradigmatic knowledge is often reduced to knowledge displays for teachers, robbing students of the opportunity to construct new knowledge through scientific procedures. But it needn't be that way.

Paradigmatic Knowledge

Paradigmatic knowledge is the most widely emphasized way of knowing in American schools. It is concerned with rational problem solving and scientific procedures of investigation involving formal verification and empirical proof. The scientific report is an obvious example of how a paradigmatic approach is used in schools.

English classes, however, also include an emphasis on paradigmatic knowledge. The approach to literary criticism known as New Criticism (not so new anymore—it was introduced in the 1930s) was founded on principles of scientific analysis. New Criticism has become well engrained in American schools and the textbook industry. While falling out of favor in universities, it still provides the dominant approach to teaching literature in secondary schools.

Paradigmatic approaches to literature involve any of the kinds of analytic essays typically required in English classes:

- *Comparison-contrast* papers, which involve a comparison of one author with another, one period with another, one novel with another, and so on.

- *Extended-definition* essays, which involve the generation of a set of criteria that define a term and the effort to classify various items according to that definition. Examples might include defining realistic literature and determining if a particular author's work meets the definition or defining an abstract term such as *progress* and judging various actions or conditions (e.g., the frontier society in Thomas Berger's *Little Big Man*) in terms of the criteria of the definition.

- *Analytic* essays, which require the analysis of some aspect of a literary work that follows the conventions of argumentation. Such essays usually involve a major thesis, a set of claims (in school, usually three), and supporting evidence for each claim, often adding up to what is known as the five-paragraph theme—one of those school assignments that is reviled by writing theorists yet ubiquitous in U.S. classrooms. An example might be to analyze Twain's *Adventures of Huckleberry Finn* and identify the (three) human vices that are being exposed through the action in the novel.

The paradigmatic mode accounts for the bulk of writing done in American secondary schools. Because of the emphasis placed on paradigmatic thinking throughout school, it is not surprising or inappropriate that students get considerable experience with paradigmatic writing about literature. Argumentation and analysis are skills that I would expect someone to learn in school, but they are not the only forms of expression students should acquire in English classes.

Narrative Knowledge

Bruner also identifies the *narrative* mode of thought, which gets surprisingly less attention in a field so heavily concerned with stories. Narrative knowledge refers to our effort to make sense of things by rendering them in story. Narrative does not rely on the paradigmatic elements of logic, verification, and rational proof. Rather, it is concerned with verisimilitude, the likeness of truth, the creation of characters and events that represent emotional and social truths but need not replicate them. Believability is the hallmark of well-formed narratives, even while they may contain falsehoods.

Narratives might be evaluated according to the degree of emotional resonance they prompt in readers. It would be plausible, for instance, for a student to write a narrative about a talking frog in a dissection tray, although probably not for a science class. The evaluation of its quality would be based not on whether such a thing was really possible, but instead on the extent to which the frog was able to articulate or represent some truth about the human (or possibly the ranine) condition.

The world of knowledge revealed by narratives is often a different world than that revealed paradigmatically. Dwayne Huebner describes this world as one involving *spiritual* knowledge:

> What are these histories, stories, myths, and poems? They are symbols of moreness, of otherness, of the transcendent—symbols that life as lived can be different. The otherness, moreness, the transcendent is demonstrated in creativity. It shows forth in insight and new understanding, and is anticipated in hope for the future. The symbols may be stories of relationships—of struggle, conflict, forgiveness, love—during which something new is produced: new life, new relationships, new understandings, new forms of power and political control. (in Hillis 1999, 344)

I do not dispute the importance of learning to think logically and analytically in school. This book is primarily a rational (I hope) argument, as is much of my writing. Much of what I know about this kind of thinking I learned in school. My goal in justifying narrative thinking is to argue for an increased role for other ways of thinking and making sense of the world, ways that have been central to sense making throughout history, according to psychologists. Even in a discipline as devoted to stories as English, narrative ways of knowing are rarely allowed as ways *for students* to express themselves.

Gendered Ways of Knowing

In 1936, Trinidadian calypso singer King Radio wrote a song called "Man Smart, Woman Smarter," a ditty covered over the years by such diverse artists as Harry Belafonte, Robert Palmer, Rosanne Cash, the Grateful Dead, the Carpenters, Chubby Checker, Joan Baez, Bruce Hornsby, and even Lucy, Desi, Fred, and Ethel on an episode of *I Love Lucy*. It outlines an age-old question regarding the relative qualities of men and women, one that seems to get more confusing the more we learn about it.

Do traditional school practices favor boys, girls, both, or neither? It depends on whom you ask. Some observers of schools have argued that, as the American Association of University Women (1995) claims, schools shortchange girls. As evidence, they point to the ways in which schools operate according to masculine conceptions of knowledge. Feminist critics point out that the predominant emphasis in school is on paradigmatic knowledge taught primarily through transmission assumptions involving final-draft uses of language. Girls, according to this argument, benefit more from constructivist knowing facilitated by exploratory speech and narrative ways of knowing. Boys, because of their more aggressive and competitive behavior, are more likely to get noticed and called on and are treated more favorably.

On the other hand, there's much evidence to support the view that girls do better in schools than boys. Christina Hoff Sommers (2000), for instance, reports that in comparison with boys, girls get higher grades, are more likely to go to college, take more rigorous academic programs, enroll in AP classes at higher rates, enroll in more high-level math and science courses, read more books, score higher on tests for artistic and musical ability, are more engaged academically, do more homework, and participate more frequently in student government, honor societies, debate clubs, and school newspapers. More frequently than girls, boys get suspended from school, get held back, drop out, get diagnosed as having attention deficit hyperactivity disorder, commit crimes, get involved with drugs and alcohol, and commit suicide. (Girls attempt suicide more often, but boys succeed more often.)

There appears to be no easy resolution to the disagreement over whether school benefits one sex or the other. There does seem to be some agreement, however, that boys and girls experience school differently. I think it's worthwhile, then, to think about gendered ways of knowing to bring an informed perspective to the discussion.

In my discussion of the basic terms of gendered views of psychology, I make one small but significant change. In much of the literature, ways of knowing are distinguished as either masculine or feminine, as the province of men/boys or women/girls. While I agree that women and men are often different from one another in consistent ways, I hesitate to apply these terms so that they suggest absolute differences between the two (or, for that matter, that gender is neatly divided into only two types).

I therefore use the terms *authoritative* and *connected* in place of men's and women's psychological makeups. These terms allow for a discussion of the issues without so strictly dividing the world into two distinct, gender-based groups. I'm sure you can think of plenty of examples of people who do not act in accordance with their gender profiles, while at the same time seeing that these two ways of relating exist, even if they don't always coexist so well. These two types are points on a continuum rather than absolute categories. Most people, I suspect, fall somewhere in between these two extremes.

Authoritative Ways of Relating

People who take an authoritative view of the world tend to take a competitive and aggressive stance toward other people. In a discussion their goal is to win and so assert their greater authority, rather than to compromise, coconstruct new knowledge, or learn more about the other people involved. Their competitive stance suggests a need for autonomy, therefore making collaboration both unnecessary and perhaps even counterproductive. The need for autonomy reduces attention to other people and their needs and feelings, resulting in a lack of connection to others, who after all are competitors.

This de-emphasis on personal connections leads away from empathic and emotional language and toward the language of analysis and abstraction. The point of schooling then becomes to work toward the creation of taxonomies and hierarchies that establish rules that resist contextual considerations. Classroom time is devoted to analysis of literature, emotional responses are discouraged, and the strongest arguments prevail (with strength at times determined by force as much as logic).

Connected Ways of Relating

Connected knowing refers to ways of relating to other people and constructing knowledge that are more collaborative, less competitive, and more likely concerned with the personal relationships of the people involved. Talk that characterizes connected knowing is often

- *tentative*, indicated by hesitations, false starts, qualifiers, politeness, intensifiers, repetition, slow rate of speech, deferential remarks, and tag questions
- *nurturing*, indicated by efforts to encourage the contributions of other speakers
- *connected* with other speakers, indicated by the way in which discussions are cohesive and collaborative
- *indirect*, allowing speakers to establish a rapport and requiring listeners to make inferences

Because of concern for the emotional well-being of others, connected knowers are less aggressive in group discussions and are more likely to support others or coconstruct knowledge with them. Because they are less concerned with autonomy, they are less emphatic about developing universal rules and more interested in understanding how situational factors affect behavior. The acceptance of the tentative possibilities for language is consistent with Barnes' characterization of exploratory speech.

Types of Intelligence

Howard Gardner (1983) has proposed that people have *multiple intelligences* through which they make sense of the world. Gardner's views on intelligence overlap in many ways with the issues I have covered thus far, in particular in his account of how schools take a narrow view of student performance. Gardner takes exception to the ways in which school stresses two types of intelligence. First is what he calls *linguistic* intelligence, the ability to express oneself through language. English teachers, to no one's surprise, share this emphasis on language in most aspects of teaching and learning.

The second kind of intelligence Gardner finds emphasized is what he calls *logical/mathematical* intelligence, most obviously seen in math classes but also evident in the analytic focus of most writing and problem solving. As I have already described, English classes also focus on analytic thinking and writing, often to the exclusion of other ways of knowing the domain (e.g., through emotions, narratives, etc.).

Gardner, following his work as a neurologist and his extensive reading of cultural history, has argued instead that people across time and cultures have drawn on eight types of intelligence to know and act on their worlds. Historically, the linguistic and mathematical/logical intelligences so exclusively valued by modern American schools have figured peripherally in the essential work of other cultures. Among Gardner's favorite examples is the ancient sailor who spent much of his life at sea. The sailor had to know how to navigate ships according to stellar patterns, forecast weather, size up waves, repair and maintain the ship facility, catch fish and preserve foods attained through trade, and have the savvy to barter effectively once on land. The operation of the ship required sailors to employ *spatial* intelligence, which Gardner identifies as the ability to configure space in order to pose and solve problems. Spatial intelligence was fundamental to the survival of sailors and was their most important means of problem solving.

Spatial intelligence is not simply an artifact of an ancient culture, however; it is vital for many in the modern world. Many people throughout the world, for instance, still fish for a living, requiring the same skills as the ancient navigators described by Gardner. Tailors, landscape architects, sports coaches, engineers, artists, and others whose work requires the order of space all rely on spatial intelligence in order to make their way successfully in the world. With the explosion of the telecommunications and computer industry and the resultant emphasis on producing and comprehending images, spatial intelligence will undoubtedly become increasingly important in our society.

Gardner identified other kinds of intelligence through which people have historically understood their worlds and solved problems:

- *Musical* intelligence is the ability to produce or appreciate music. Musicians, music critics, dancers, figure skaters, singing frogs, and others who must understand the use of rhythm, tone, melody, and other aspects of musical expression are blessed with musical intelligence.

- *Bodily/kinesthetic* intelligence is the ability to use the body effectively in order to solve problems. Gardner distinguishes between having athletic skills and having bodily/kinesthetic intelligence; a strong and fast athlete does not necessarily use that physical giftedness in intelligent ways. Rather, a player who can read a playing field well and make the appropriate moves; a thespian who can suggest pathos with the arch of an eyebrow; a massage therapist who has an understanding of the body's needs and an ability to apply appropriate pressure; and others who use their bodies to solve problems possess bodily/kinesthetic intelligence.

- The ability to read and respond to the needs of others is *interpersonal* intelligence. Good teachers, therapists, salespeople, politicians, and others who deal effectively with the public often demonstrate interpersonal intelligence in their communion with people. The whole notion of collaboration is predicated on the idea that people can interact successfully, requiring interpersonal intelligence.

- *Intrapersonal* intelligence is the ability to look within oneself for self-knowledge and understanding. People who are highly reflective have intrapersonal intelligence, including those who seek and benefit from therapy, those who learn from their mistakes, those who practice yoga or meditation, and others who have the ability to come to a greater understanding of themselves.

- *Naturalistic* intelligence allows people to distinguish among, classify, and use features of the environment. Charles Darwin is an obvious example, whether you believe in evolution or intelligent design. I think that a teacher who reflects on the consequences of her teaching through careful selection and analysis of evidence would also qualify. So would students who conduct primary-source research.

Most activities in life require some combination of these intelligences. A building remodeler must have spatial intelligence to know how to reconfigure the space of a household and also the interpersonal intelligence to deal effectively with customers, the mathematical intelligence to operate a budget, and the bodily/kinesthetic intelligence to manipulate tools properly.

As noted, however, it's possible to get through school without being assessed through most of these intelligences. When schools are set up to promote autonomy, they provide few opportunities to employ interpersonal intelligence. When schools focus on analytic thinking, they tend not to provide chances to reflect on personal issues. When budgets are cut, art and music are often early sacrifices. When students are expected to sit quietly all day, they rarely have opportunities for kinesthetic performance.

Summary

In general, school assessment misses the point by ignoring many ways of knowing. A transmission approach is largely predicated on ill-founded assumptions about the nature of learning; schools valorize abstract, static, logical, analytical knowledge at the expense of idiosyncratic, dynamic, protean knowledge; emergent understandings through exploratory uses of speech are discouraged in favor of neatly packaged, final-draft speech that is typically borrowed from elsewhere rather than generated by students; and for the most part, students work at the lowest end of the cognitive ladder, foregoing synthesis and synergy in favor of rote memorization and mimicry. In following such an approach, teachers underestimate what young people are capable of and limit students' school learning to its most reductive, least interesting parts. In place of this method, I urge you to consider the possibilities of teaching students in ways that challenge them to draw on a wide range of their intellectual resources to construct new knowledge and meaning in relation to the English curriculum.

2 *Providing Scaffolds for Student Learning*

It took me so much longer last year to plan [during student teaching]. And I think it was because I was thinking in terms of, many times, "What do I need to teach today?" And I've shifted that now to, "What do my kids need to learn?"

—Sherelle Jones Patisaul, Westside Middle School, Winder, Georgia, from "Integrating Visual and Language Arts," by Michelle Zoss

The notion of an *instructional scaffold*, developed by Jerome Bruner (1975) from Vygotsky's (1978, 1987) views on human development, refers to the way in which experienced and capable people assist others in learning new knowledge and skills. An example would be the way in which an experienced carpenter teaches a novice how to build a cabinet. The carpenter might use a variety of methods to teach the skills of cabinet making: providing information verbally (e.g., explaining why it's important to use safety goggles), modeling (e.g., demonstrating how to strike a nail without bending it), showing how to find resources (e.g., doing comparative shopping by phone), and so on.

As the learner grasps the concepts and learns to use the tools properly, the carpenter begins handing over responsibilities to the novice. This transfer might involve providing feedback and support while the novice begins to apply the concepts (corners should be square) and use the tools (a T-square helps to make a right-angle cut precise). As the novice demonstrates increasing competency, the carpenter allows more autonomy and intervenes only as needed. Ultimately, the novice grasps how to build a cabinet and can work independently.

In learning complex new knowledge, a person benefits from an extended process of using concepts and tools across a variety of contexts: building a china cabinet with glass doors, making built-in kitchen cabinets, making cabinets from different materials, and so on. The novice described previously might learn from the initial building experience how to build a level freestanding cabinet from oak, but might struggle with how to use the softer maple in a confined kitchen space without denting it. Knowledge learned from the first experience might require modification and refinement when applied to the next. Multiple experiences would be necessary in order for the novice to be considered a skilled builder of cabinets. When encountering new circumstances, the novice would benefit from additional support from the carpenter so as to recognize how to adjust knowledge of concepts and tools to new circumstances.

The scaffolding metaphor has its critics, and their reservations are worth noting. Dennis Searle (1984) posed the important question *Who's building whose building?* In other words, the scaffolding metaphor suggests that the person providing the support will lead the learner toward the best possible construction. Searle raises questions about the extent to which a teacher's decisions are always in the students' best interests. He suggests that it's possible that students have entirely different needs and purposes than those served by the kinds of constructions that the teacher has in mind. He also critiques the conventional notion of the teacher as someone who teachers rather than learns. Critics of authoritarian approaches to schooling maintain that teachers ought to learn through the process of teaching. The teacher's notion of a building, then, can potentially change through her engagement with learners and their ideas about what needs to be constructed.

This criticism is important to keep in mind when teaching. You should always ask yourself, Whose building is being constructed here? Whose needs will it serve? Who is learning what through this kind of construction? Are there other possible ways to envision and build this text?

Searle is not the only critic of the scaffolding metaphor. Anne Haas Dyson (1990) finds it to be overly rigid and too focused on the teacher as expert. She suggests the metaphor of *weaving* instead, which she finds more flexible and democratic. A literal scaffold on a building provides a supporting framework for the structure and the builders who work on it. Both the building and scaffold are inert and immobile. Teachers and learners, however, are alive and animated. They are responsive to one another and so need to be both sensitive and adaptable. They mutually influence one another, which Dyson sees as a central reason for adopting the weaving metaphor, in which a common product emerges from overlapping, joint activity. While the teacher often leads, she does so with careful attention to the child's progress; further, she remains open to the idea that the student may come up with an approach to learning to which a more impervious scaffold might be insensitive.

A final concern about the scaffolding metaphor is that it suggests, if we apply the analogy strictly, that one scaffold is enough: a single scaffold serves to support the building, the building goes up, the scaffold comes down, and everyone goes home. If teaching and learning were so easy, we wouldn't need all these books about education. When people learn through guided activity, scaffolds are continually being built, modified, adapted to the learner's growing understanding, or cast aside and replaced with something more appropriate in relation to the learner's conceptual and practical progress.

An instructional scaffold therefore needs to be more organic, more protean, and more supple than a building scaffold. Scaffolds must be amendable to change as the learner grows. Teachers, then, must also be learners as part of this process, in terms of what they discover about the students and their learning, about their own teaching, and about the possibilities for ways to manipulate the material that is the subject of the learning. The scaffolding metaphor shouldn't be taken too literally. It needs to be reimagined in order to serve as the kind of learning support that is available in the constructivist classroom.

Learning Procedures for Learning

Since the 1970s (see, e.g., Bransford 1979) many educators have emphasized the importance of teaching *procedural knowledge*—that is, knowledge of how to do things. To return to the example of learning about bicycles: I would need to have strategies for remaining balanced, attuning my legwork to the speed I desired, applying the brakes without flying over the handlebars, and otherwise knowing how to operate the bike safely and efficiently.

As noted in my review of transmission approaches to education, however, much school instruction is centered on students' learning of *declarative knowledge*: the ability to repeat information provided by someone else. For bike riders, declarative knowledge would consist of knowledge of the names of each part of the bicycle, even if they did not know which way to push the pedals. In English class, instruction based on declarative knowledge is evident in grammar lessons in which students identify parts of speech in someone else's sentences, in writing instruction in which students label and then try to imitate the parts of model essays such as the five-paragraph theme, and in literature instruction in which students are assessed according to their recall of facts that the teacher believes are important.

An emphasis on procedures is focused more on ways to do things. It is thus more generative and constructive. A generative approach to learning grammar might come through sentence combining, in which students join given clauses and phrases into new sentences that are syntactically complex (see, e.g., Strong 1994). A writing teacher, instead of focusing on the traits of finished products, would focus more on how to render ideas and content knowledge into a given kind of text. Teachers of literature would concentrate on learning strategies such as how to generate images for reading, how to interpret a symbol, and how to recognize and interpret irony.

These efforts are consistent with the idea that for assessment purposes, students should have the opportunity to interpret or produce something new, rather than be tested on what they have already covered. And so, instead of reading *Animal Farm* as part of a unit on animals as symbols and then being tested on their recall of the teacher's explanation of which pig represents Trotsky and which represents Stalin, the students would use their knowledge of how to interpret an animal as a symbol by reading a fresh literary work, such as Walt Whitman's "Noiseless Patient Spider" or Daphne du Maurier's "Birds," and writing an interpretation of how the animals function symbolically.

A Process for Instructional Scaffolding

There are many constructions of what an instructional scaffold is and is not; one teacher's scaffold might be another teacher's wrecking ball. I don't pretend to have *the* definitive idea of how to go about supporting students' learning. I do offer one general approach that is compatible with the idea of designing conceptual units and that is attentive to students' need for procedural knowledge. This approach relies on instruction that begins with a teacher's introduction of a concept or procedure through accessible materials, has the students work initially on learning the concept or procedure in small groups that enable exploration and error without penalty, and ultimately has the students working independently as they are weaned away from the teacher's and fellow students' support.

Let's look at examples of instructional scaffolding of students' learning in two areas. In the first scenario, the teacher shows her students how to use an all-purpose tool, the double-column response journal, to promote literary understanding. In the second, the teacher instructs students in a writing procedure to write comparison-contrast essays. Both involve a sequence in which the students move from learning procedures through teacher-supported activity using familiar or accessible materials, to applying the procedures to new materials with peer feedback in small groups, to performing independently with unfamiliar materials of appropriate complexity for the students at this point in their development.

Double-Column Response Log

I am indebted to Cindy O'Donnell-Allen, whose senior English class I observed for a year, for this approach to using response logs. While Cindy didn't invent response logs, she developed a way of teaching students how to use them that was very effective. Cindy wanted to promote students' sense of agency and felt that one way to help students achieve it was to use response logs as a tool for learning different ways of thinking about literature. She did not want them to rely on her for their interpretations, which she felt would do them little good once they left her class.

Rather, she wanted them to develop both a stance that they were competent and insightful readers and a set of strategies for pursuing their insights and questions. Based on her years of teaching, however, she found that her students had been conditioned to answer their teachers' questions rather than pose inquiries themselves. They therefore needed to be taught different kinds of questions to ask, particularly the sort of open-ended questions rarely posed to them in school. They also needed to be taught the specific format of the response log, which was used infrequently in her school district.

Ultimately, she wanted to have the students produce a reading log according to specifications something like the following:

Keep a reading log in response to the literature we are studying during this unit. To keep your log,

- Divide each page with a vertical line down the center.
- On the left side of each page, record significant passages from the literature you read.
- On the right side, across from each passage, include at least one question of each type for each work of literature studied.
  - Ask *open-ended questions* that would help you understand the passage better.
  - Give your personal *response* to the passage (i.e., any thoughts you have in connection with it).
  - Give your personal *evaluation* of the passage.
  - Think through a possible *interpretation* of the passage.

  Three rules:

1. Remember that your journal does not need to follow the conventions of textbook English. Rather, the purpose is to think about the literature without worrying about the form your thoughts take.
2. Turn in your response log every two weeks. I will read your log and respond to your comments. If you make an entry that you do not want me to read, place an *X* at the top of the page and I'll skip it. Really.
3. Keep in mind that *I am required to share any thoughts or suggestions of violence, suicide, substance abuse, family abuse, or other harmful behavior with the school counselors.*

A lot of teachers stop at this point. That is, they think of a good assignment, present it to students, and then wait for the results. Cindy was very careful, in contrast, to support the students' initial efforts at maintaining their reading response logs, which was a new genre of writing for them. As a result, simply making the assignment and collecting the logs was insufficient. She needed to think about how to structure and sequence the students' experiences so that they would learn how to keep them as she intended.

The first consideration in providing learning scaffolds is to think about what is involved in using them, in this case, what it takes to keep a reading log. For many students, writing in a double-entry response log requires them to reorient themselves both to reading and to writing. As school readers they are not accustomed to being asked what they think about the literature; they are conditioned to seeing literature as the basis for a memory-based test. They thus need to learn not only the form for the log but the social practices that produce it. These practices include taking an inquiring stance, using writing for exploratory purposes, understanding the importance of taking risks, and realizing that some schoolwork will not be penalized for being incorrect.

Given that students are likely unaccustomed to responding to literature in generative and constructive ways—by posing questions, responding according to their personal experiences and dispositions, evaluating the work according to their own criteria, and constructing an interpretation—they also need to learn how to generate these responses in the context of the double-entry log. Cindy thus set for herself the responsibility to help students reposition themselves in relation to their school reading and teach them how to respond in these personal, idiosyncratic, open-ended, generative ways.

The sequence that she followed involved the following general stages, which I illustrate with examples from her double-entry reading log instruction:

1. The teacher introduces a skill, strategy, or procedure to the whole class. This introduction includes

   - a clear explanation of the nature of the task (e.g., what a reading log is and why they're keeping it)

   - explicit information about the expectations for what the students will do (e.g., using the log to pose particular kinds of questions and try to answer them)

   - modeling of how to make reading log entries, using accessible materials so that the students can clearly follow the explanation (e.g., taking a literary selection and thinking out loud while formulating reading log entries)

2. The teacher then asks students to work collaboratively on a similar kind of problem, using accessible materials so that they can succeed in their initial learning (e.g., they are provided with an accessible work of literature and, in small groups, pose a set of reading log questions about it).

3. Students get feedback on these initial efforts. This feedback can come from peers (e.g., groups exchange and critique one another's efforts) and/or the teacher. If the teacher provides the response, she needs to collect the work and respond to it by the next class session.

4. Students get the critiques back. If the class is ready to move forward, they can then begin with a reading log entry that they keep individually, which in turn gets some kind of feedback from peers or the teacher. If the initial log entries do not come close to expectations, the small-group stage might be repeated.

To summarize: The sequence Cindy used went from *teacher modeling* in a *whole-group* setting, to *small-group practice* with immediate *feedback*, to *individual application* of the procedure. This sequence is a good example of one kind of instructional scaffold. If applied rigidly, a teacher might move along before students are ready, so one characteristic of a flexible scaffold is that you are attentive and sensitive to how the students are performing and adjust your teaching according to what they need. A second characteristic of a flexible scaffold is that the teacher does not simply expect students to do things as modeled, but encourages them to generate new ideas about how to do the task. The purpose, then, is not to get students to mimic the teacher faithfully but to use the teacher's modeling as an opportunity to learn a new way of thinking about something.

I have spoken with a number of educators who would find this fairly direct instruction in making reading log entries to be overly explicit and not liberating enough for the students. In the sequence of instruction I have described, it's clear that the teacher is imposing a value on students; that is, the teacher is specifying a stance toward literature and procedures for taking that stance. Some critics would accuse her of being hegemonic here by imposing her view of literature on students. They would say that she is requiring students to be reflective readers, even if that isn't their inclination or preference. And they're right; that's what the teacher is doing.

I justify my imposition in terms of what I think is deficient in most school instruction. When I saw Cindy go through this sequence of teaching students *how* to engage in response, I was impressed with her understanding that students would have difficulty inventing their own procedures for asking questions. She assumed that they would benefit from being taught some ways of generating open-ended questions to provide themselves with richer reading experiences. It's true that she decided whose building would get built. But I'm convinced that, for too many students, the lot might still be vacant if she hadn't.

There are occasions, then, when it's beneficial for you to impose an agenda on students and teach them how to do a particular thing in a particular way. Primarily, it's important to do so when there's a good way to do something that they would be unlikely to think up on their own.

Comparison-Contrast Essay

The comparison-contrast essay is a staple of secondary school writing instruction. One website establishes its importance by saying,

> We can really understand only those things that are familiar to us or similar to things we already understand, so comparing and contrasting the unfamiliar with the familiar is one of the most important techniques for writing. You can, and probably do, use comparison and contrast to describe things, to define things, to analyze things, to make an argument—to do, in fact, almost any kind of writing. (Cogdill 1997)

People voting for one candidate against another, picking one jar of pickles instead of a competing brand, deciding which Harry Potter novel they like best, selecting the best movie of the year, or engaging in countless other kinds of decisions go through a process of comparing (finding similarities) and contrasting (outlining differences) in order to make the best choices for themselves. Small wonder, then, that this kind of essay has become established in the writing curriculum.

A common method for teaching the comparison-contrast essay is to provide students with a model essay and have them label its parts. At the website from which I took the previous quote, readers see a set of sample outlines for different organizations for an essay comparing and then contrasting corsets and foot binding, both of which are ways to restrict a woman's body, to which I simply say, ouch. Readers are provided with sample outlines and charts that reveal what the basic structures of the essays would be—for example, introduction, similarities (or differences), differences (or similarities), conclusion. They do not, however, teach inexperienced writers *how* to produce these parts of the structure. Following is one way to strengthen students' understanding of how to generate ideas for the purposes of comparison and contrast and ultimately write comparison-contrast essays on their own.

In this approach, which I learned from George Hillocks (see Hillocks, McCabe, and McCampbell 1971; or more recently, Hillocks 1995, 2007), the teacher designs activities through which students work initially in small groups on a task-oriented problem. Their activity in solving the problem leads them to develop procedures inductively for how to solve problems of a similar type. They then use these procedures to work through increasingly complex problems of a similar nature, beginning in small groups and gradually weaning themselves toward independent performance.

Ultimately, I'd like my students to be able to compare and/or contrast two things of a fairly complex nature. In literature units, the culminating task might be to write an essay comparing and/or contrasting two constructs or characters central to the unit concepts: two utopias in a unit on utopias and dystopias; two movements such as realism and naturalism; two writers within a genre, such as William Wordsworth and John Keats among the British Lake poets; two symbols such as the river in *The Adventures of Huckleberry Finn* and the river in *A Separate Peace*; and so on. I would not want my students to write their first comparison essay at such a formidable level, however. Rather, I'd want them to learn procedures for comparing and contrasting by working initially with familiar, accessible materials—not, I hope, corset and footbinding.

I would begin, then, by having the students do the following:

1.   Get in a group of three to five and brainstorm for two things to compare and contrast. Following are some possibilities:

- Two athletes or athletic teams. Pick two that are reasonably similar, such as two goalies or two gymnastics teams; don't choose an ice hockey goalie and an equestrian rider, or a jai-alai team and a bowling team.
- Two restaurants. Pick two of the same type, for example, two Mexican restaurants or two pizza parlors.
- Two social groups in your school.
- Two musical groups of relatively similar types, such as two gospel choirs or two calypso bands.
- Two TV shows or movies of the same type, such as two "odd couple" stories or two police dramas.
- Two clothing stores of the same type, such as two department stores or two military surplus stores.
- Other comparison of your choice.

2. Think of areas in which you can compare and contrast the two items. For instance, let's say that your parents play music by both the Beatles and the Rolling Stones around your house. You have acquired their music for your own collection and so are familiar with both groups. You decide to compare and contrast them because you wonder which is the better band. What *categories* might you use for points of comparison? These categories should be aspects of musicianship that are important to you. You might, then, rule out eye color because no matter what color their eyes are, their music still sounds the same. Categories that matter could include songwriting ability, singing ability, virtuosity on their instruments, influence on other musicians, and longevity in the music business. What areas of comparison can you think of for the two items that you are focusing on?

3. Think about how your two items measure up in each of the areas of comparison you have identified. For the Beatles–Rolling Stones comparison, the groups might be evaluated as follows in each of the five areas outlined above:

Songwriting Ability

Beatles: Lennon and McCartney the primary songwriters; early in career, recorded rhythm and blues songs by other writers; toward the end of the band's life, often the songs had nonsensical lyrics; wrote many classics

Rolling Stones: Jagger and Richards the primary songwriters; early in career, recorded rhythm and blues songs by other writers; wrote songs that generally made sense; wrote many classics

Singing Ability

Beatles: All four members sang; Starr rarely sang lead and had a not unpleasant voice; Harrison sang more often and was OK but too nasal; Lennon or McCartney sang most leads and had strong voices; McCartney best on "pretty" songs; great harmonies

Rolling Stones: Jagger sang lead on all songs; sassy, edgy voice; not always quite in tune; decent harmonies

Virtuosity on Their Instruments

Beatles: McCartney had to overdub Starr's drumming on later, more complex material; McCartney played multiple instruments; great ensemble sound; few long guitar or keyboard solos; great rhythm

Rolling Stones: strong musicianship across the board; Jagger played some percussion but mostly sang; changed personnel following death and other turnover so musicianship varied

Influence on Other Musicians

Beatles: Often thought to be the world's most influential rock group; pioneered theme albums copied by the Who, Jethro Tull, etc.; early leaders in incorporating Eastern music; leaders in psychedelic rock

Rolling Stones: Known to many as the world's greatest rock and roll band; mostly a rhythm and blues band who borrowed from black U.S. performers; sexuality mimicked by other bands; among the first to use elaborate showmanship in their live acts (makeup, lights, smoke, etc.)

Longevity in the Music Business

Beatles: The group disbanded within ten years, but its music is still popular; Lennon was murdered at age forty; Harrison died at age fifty-eight of cancer; McCartney still recording; Starr still recording

Rolling Stones: Still together after over forty years; Brian Jones died a "death by misadventure" at age twenty-seven shortly after quitting the band; Jagger and Richard were constants, with periodic turnover at other positions in the band; drug addiction affected the band's durability; individuals took leave from the band for solo projects and substance abuse rehabilitation

4. For the two comparison items you have selected, think of examples you can give for each in all of the categories you have identified. Then, begin to assemble this information into a written comparison. After looking over your notes, you might discuss them with your group or freewrite about the similarities and differences between the two things you are comparing and contrasting. You should also begin to think about the conclusions you could draw from your inquiry. For instance, for the Beatles–Rolling Stones comparison,

you might develop the thesis that the two groups are both highly influential and talented, but that you prefer the Beatles because they were more innovative in developing new directions for rock and roll music, while the Rolling Stones mainly stayed within the rhythm and blues genre for more than forty years.

This sequence should help the students to learn *how* to conduct a comparison-contrast inquiry: selecting well-aligned items for comparison and contrast, identifying categories for comparison, and thinking of examples for each item in each category. As a result of this process, they will develop procedures for conducting similar inquiries in other areas. Note that the instruction begins with attention to content rather than attention to form, with particular focus on how to manipulate and think about the content.

Next, students can begin drafting essays based on the information that they have assembled. They might work in relation to the following guidelines:

1. The thesis you developed previously—for example, that the Beatles and Rolling Stones were both popular, influential bands but that the Beatles were more innovative because their music grew beyond their rhythm and blues roots—could provide the basis for an introductory paragraph to an essay comparing and contrasting two items.

2. Next, try to develop a paragraph for each area of comparison. For example, if you were comparing the Beatles and the Rolling Stones, you might start by comparing and contrasting them according to their singing ability. However, instead of just listing the illustrations from your notes, think of examples that would support the major points you are trying to make. You might say that because all four Beatles could sing, they were able to produce better harmonies than the Rolling Stones and so had more flexibility with their song arrangements, which allowed them to develop more complex songs. By doing so, you are providing evidence in support of your thesis that the Beatles were a better band because their sound took new directions over time. When possible, give specific evidence to support your claims, such as that the Beatles' harmonies and multiple singers gave their albums a divergent sound, while the Rolling Stones' reliance solely on Jagger gave all of their music a similar sound. Further, provide a *warrant*—that is, an explanation (often beginning with "Because . . .") of why the evidence supports the claim.

3. Finally, draw some sort of conclusion based on your comparison and contrast, possibly developing the ideas you stated in your thesis. You might conclude, for instance, that songs recorded by the

Rolling Stones across four decades all have a very similar sound, while songs recorded by the Beatles during the 1960s show a radical change from derivative rhythm and blues to highly sophisticated acid rock, incorporating influences from multiple cultures and sources.

Once again, the task focuses on content; issues of form are treated as ways to present and make sense of the content. At this point, each student proceeds to write an essay based on the information assembled and organized. You might want to adjust this plan and have the students write this initial essay on familiar material in the small groups as a way to provide immediate feedback as the students discuss how to present the information and evaluations in essay form. The choice you make reveals your sensitivity to the students' need for scaffolding at this point in their writing development.

One brief but important point is that the process of thinking about and organizing this comparison actually helped me to refine my previous thinking and to generate new ideas about these two groups. I had always liked the Beatles better than the Stones, but here, because I was forced to articulate my ideas for this comparison, I pushed myself to explain why and in the process generated new thinking. This process is central to the idea of *writing to learn*: people often use writing as a way to discover what they have to say. This idea is very compatible with the emphasis on exploratory speech and writing in the classroom, and it supports the belief that writing consists of more than simply transferring ideas from the head to the page. Rather, writing—and the talking that accompanies writing in this teaching approach—may also serve as a way to generate new ideas through the process of articulating one's thoughts.

After writing their drafts, students should have opportunities for formal feedback from their peers. A small-group feedback session can provide them with both response to their writing and an opportunity to develop their critical reading skills by critiquing their peers. To set up this stage of the scaffold, you might give instructions of the following sort:

> After you have written a draft of your essay, get back in your small group to share your writing. Proofread the essays of your groupmates, pointing out passages that you feel are strong and suggesting ways to improve the writing, particularly with regard to the writer's use of evidence to support each comparison and contrast. One way to evaluate the writer's use of evidence is to see if there is a *warrant* in which the author explains why the evidence supports the claim. Pay careful attention, too, to the writer's conclusions and how well they are supported by the evidence in the presentation. Make comments in the margins of the draft wherever you feel they would be helpful, and write a summary evaluation at the

end of each draft you read. Feel free to discuss the essay with the writer and other members of the group.

Following this feedback session, each student should have received a critique from several classmates. Based on their suggestions, the author then produces a draft to be submitted to the teacher.

This sequence should prepare the students for a more sophisticated comparison-contrast essay. It's possible that they would benefit from exploring an intermediate topic before taking on the task of comparing and contrasting such complex constructs as naturalism and realism; perhaps they might compare and contrast two writers within one movement, such as Stephen Crane and Jack London within the naturalism genre. In teaching extended definition, Johannessen, Kahn, and Walter (1982) take students through twelve different activities, from relatively simple classification games to definitions of terrorism, freedom of speech, cruelty to animals, and courageous action—perhaps more of a time commitment than you could make given the testing mania of current schooling, but a meticulous approach to teaching the process.

Perhaps you will have all or some of the preparation done in small groups; perhaps you will go straight to an individual assignment. It really depends on how much support you believe that your students need in order to stretch their thinking and abilities without overwhelming them with too great a leap. As you can see, instructional scaffolds require a great deal of judgment and decision making on the teacher's part; you can't simply go through a lockstep set of activities without evaluating students' response and progress and making adjustments in your plans. You thus provide the support that proponents of scaffolding advocate without the rigidity that concerns its critics.

Summary

Ideally, you would provide instructional scaffolding any time you taught students how to do a new task: read ironic literature, write a narrative, produce compound and complex sentences, and any other process that requires new kinds of complex thinking. Unfortunately, the overall school culture works against such process-oriented teaching and learning—anthologies must be read in their entirety, tests must be taken, skills must be taught (if not learned). But consider the long-term effects of simply giving and grading assignments, as opposed to giving assignments and taking responsibility yourself for how well students complete them. Personally, I would rather have students really learn how to do a few things in school than cover many things superficially and with little lasting effect. The task for teachers, then, is to balance what the school absolutely requires that they do with what they can create time for and accomplish—taking more time, certainly, but making that time well spent.

3 *Alternatives to Teacher-Led Discussions*

Teacher-led discussions, usually of literature, are a staple of much English class instruction. Many observers of English classrooms, however, are not entirely satisfied with how discussions work. Some critique the common IRE pattern, in which a teacher *initiates* with a question or remark, a student *responds* briefly, and the teacher then *explains* or *elaborates* a preferred answer in much greater detail. Such discussions position the teacher as the one whose ideas about the reading set the direction for what follows, with students providing cryptic answers that the teacher then incorporates into a minilecture, or perhaps a maxilecture.

Jim Marshall (in Marshall, Smagorinsky, and Smith 1995) found that while teachers often state that they seek to have free-flowing "jam sessions" in which students riff and improvise in harmonious interaction, in actual practice the teachers more typically control the floor in ways that limit students' contributions. In the classes he studied,

> teachers used their responses to students' contributions to weave the discussion as a whole into a coherent and sustained examination of two or three general topics. Students' contributions . . . were most often repeated, questioned, or elaborated upon in ways that pulled them into the ongoing discussion. The discussions stayed "on track" largely because teachers used their responses to students' remarks as occasions for making transitions from one turn to another, from one question to another. The teacher ultimately controlled the direction, the pace, and the organization in most of the discussions . . . observed. (55)

Even in "discussions," then, teachers tend to control the talk, and students speak largely in response to what teachers say, with few of their contributions requiring little more than recall of information from the text and most of their remarks being swept up into the teacher's *explication* de texte. Significantly, such a pattern provides students with little opportunity to pose questions of their own; their role is relatively passive. Students tend to speak only in those spaces that teachers leave open for them, primarily in response to the teacher's queries, and these queries tend to steer the class toward a conventional interpretation of the sort established by university professors and the authors of literature anthologies (who are often, of course, university professors).

A number of excellent books provide strategies for teachers to change these patterns; in particular, I recommend McCann and colleagues' *Talking in Class: Using Discussion to Enhance Teaching and Learning* (2006) and Adler and Rougle's *Building Literacy Through Classroom Discussion* (2005). The following activities, very few of which I designed myself, provide alternatives to teacher-led classroom discussions. Some of these vehicles have been around for ages, others have been recommended to me by teachers I know, others I've picked up along my professional travels. All have the potential to shift responsibility for interpretation from the teacher and teacher's manual to the students and to encourage students to work at the level of synthesis rather than recall. As a result, the discussions ask more of students, challenging them to respond in complex ways to a literary work, as I'm sure the author would hope a reader would do.

I have divided these discussion formats into three varieties: student-generated whole-class discussions, task-oriented small-group activities, and student-led small-group discussions. My goal is to outline a set of possibilities, without going greatly into detail on any. You can google (yes, that's now an official verb) most of them for a more detailed understanding or to find variations that teachers provide on how to employ them.

Student-Generated Whole-Class Discussions

Student-generated whole-class discussions involve the whole group but rely on students to produce the content of the discussion. This approach enables teachers to monitor the discussion in the manner to which they are accustomed, without weaving in the broader interpretive text that Jim Marshall found so limiting to students' participation and construction of meaning.

Fishbowl

A fishbowl puts a small group of students in the center of the room, surrounded by their classmates and teacher, and has them initiate a discussion. Strictly speaking, only the students who are inside the fishbowl should be involved in the discussion. The rest of the class listens to their discussion—attentive at all times, of course. Students who wish to enter the discussion may, at any time, get up and tap out one of the fishbowl discussants and replace him in the center of the class. A fishbowl discussion may proceed for as long as the teacher decides it's working. The teacher's role is to monitor the proceedings from the perimeter, perhaps encouraging students to tap out others at periodic intervals.

Fishbowl discussions, when they work well, provide an exploration of the literature that, while having continuity, benefits from fresh blood as new students enter the discussion. Given that the activities are conducted entirely by the students, they have the potential to move outside the boundaries of conventional interpretation and allow the students to discuss the literature on their own terms.

Informal Writing as the Basis for Discussion

One way to start a discussion that arises from students' engagement with the text is to begin a class with students writing informally in response to a reading. This informal writing might come as part of routine writing in journals or reading logs, or it might more simply serve as an occasional way to help students find what they want to talk about in response to a text. This approach is quite simple, with the teacher asking students to write about their engagement with a text—in terms of observations, questions, interpretations, attention to language, areas of confusion, and so on—for a period of perhaps five to ten minutes, and then asking the students to volunteer their writing as a way to generate discussion. The trick is to make sure that the discussion stays true to these interests, instead of reverting to the teacher's orchestration of an official critical interpretation of the reading.

Put an Author on Trial

In one of my favorite novels, *At Swim-Two Birds*, by Flann O'Brien, the narrator is a young man who is writing a novel about an author whose characters rebel against him because they do not like what he is having them do. Complicated stuff indeed. Students who do not like an author's or narrator's deployment of characters may put the author or narrator on trial, prosecuting her for crimes against the characters. To do so, a student would have to be able to defend the author or narrator, while a prosecution would have to be able to mount a convincing case against her. Other students may serve as witnesses, as wronged characters, as characters believed to be well crafted, and so on.

Talk Show Format

Most students are familiar with afternoon talk shows: Oprah, Montel, Ricki, Jerry, and many others who've come and gone with the cathode rays. Students can discuss literature using a talk show as a basis (though Jerry Springer programs get tedious before long, often before they begin). In doing so, they combine their parodic skills with their insights about literature to pose questions, play roles of characters who visit the show, and perhaps invent new roles (narrator, author, outsider) who can shed light on the literature.

Text Rendering

In text rendering, each student picks out one word, one phrase, and one sentence from a text. The selections should be those that the students find especially compelling, provocative, or meaningful. They then sit in a circle, and for the first round, each reads his selected word; then each student in turn reads the selected phrase; and finally, each student reads the selected sentence. Following this reading, the students pose questions or comment on the selections in a general discussion.

Task-Oriented Small-Group Activities

A task-oriented small-group activity usually begins with an assignment identified by the teacher that involves the construction of a new text in response to a literary work. Students use their imaginations to build collaborative interpretations that result in material products.

Graphic or Material Productions

Anthology Built Around a Central Theme

Literature, by and large, centers on various themes—courage, gender roles, loss of innocence, and countless others. Students can express their response to the theme that they find in their literary reading by collecting materials that are familiar to them that illustrate those themes. Their anthology might consist of songs, film clips or reviews, art, literature, magazine articles, video games, photographs, diary entries, and other personal belongings or collected items. By discussing what might go into their anthology, groups of students must consider the literary themes and how they are present in their experiences.

Board Game

The traditional elements of literature—plot, setting, character, theme, and perhaps others—are usually taught as labels. An alternative way to cover these elements is to have students create a board game based on a literary work. The board itself provides the setting for the action; the pieces represent the various characters; the path along which they travel symbolizes the plot; the characters' means of negotiating the board indicate their capabilities; the game's goal is related to the literature's theme. The games can serve a variety of purposes: students can play the games and consider how well they map onto the story and its action, or the games can serve as springboards for discussion, such as the ways in which the board/setting affects the ways in which characters may act. (Thanks to Tanya Martin for suggesting this activity.)

Body Biography

Cindy O'Donnell-Allen (2006) adapted an idea from an *English Journal* article (Underwood 1987) to create one of the most popular and effective activities I know of: the body biography. Students work in groups to fill in the outline of a human body with images and language that depict the experiences and relationships of a literary character. Cindy had students use butcher paper to construct life-sized images; I have also had students prepare their body biographies on overhead transparencies. The assignment she provided to students following their reading of *Hamlet* was as follows:

> For your chosen character, your group will be creating a *body biography*—a visual and written portrait illustrating several aspects of the character's life within the play. The body biography should:
>
> - review significant events, choices, and changes involving the character
> - communicate the full essence of the character by emphasizing the traits that make her/him who s/he is
> - promote discussion of the character
>
> The body biographies should include
>
> - a review of significant happenings in the play
> - visual symbols
> - an original text
> - the character's three most important lines from the play

Cindy also recommended that the students be deliberate in the placement of the body biography elements and what their placement indicated about their relationships, employ the character's spine symbolically, depict the character's distinctive qualities and flaws, use color as a symbol, consider additional symbolic possibilities, use formula poems to reveal significant aspects of the character's experiences, consider both the surface and inner dimensions of the character's psyche, and indicate important changes that the character underwent during the course of the story.

If students present their body biographies to the class, the series of presentations constitutes a sort of jigsaw through which a portrait of the whole text emerges. It is also interesting to see how a given character is viewed both from her perspective and that of other characters. The availability of multiple perspectives on each character provides a richer portrayal than does a single depiction from the character's point of view.

When reading a long work such as a novel or play, students can construct body biographies at several points during their reading. By producing a series of interpretations, the students can represent changes in the character over time. Ultimately, these depictions can serve as the basis for students' analyses of character development over the course of the literary work. In a sense, they would be interpreting their evocations of the work as they sought to understand the character's evolution.

Homebody

One evening I was discussing body biographies with a group of master's degree students that included Helene Halstead, Valerie Pflug, Scott Reed, Maggie Taylor, Mimi Voyles, Allen Witt, and Chris Woodward. Scott suggested that students might draw the house in Gabriel García Márquez's *One Hundred Years of Solitude*, given the role of the house as the central location in the novel. We also discussed perhaps creating a website depicting the house, with the viewer being able to click on each room in order open a new window detailing that room, with additional clicks providing further windows about items found in the room.

We eventually settled on the idea that any dynamic location could serve as the basis for such a drawing. Many literary works, we realized, indeed were centered in houses—Hawthorne's *House of the Seven Gables*, Shakespeare's *Hamlet* (one's home is indeed one's castle), Williams' *Glass Menagerie, Streetcar Named Desire*, and *Cat on a Hot Tin Roof*, and many more. A different central location might be the river in Twain's *Adventures of Huckleberry Finn* or the baseball field in Kinsella's *Field of Dreams*.

As with a body biography, the idea is to take a basic framework (a house shape) and depict what happens within it—both literally and through symbols. And as with body biographies, producing a series of such interpretations can help students interpret and understand the changing role of a setting over the course of a literary work.

Coat of Arms

When creating a coat of arms for a family in a literary work, students must pay careful attention to how the family is positioned in society in order to represent the family's history symbolically through the elements of the coat of arms. For our purposes here, I use the traditional elements of the Scottish coat of arms:

- The *shield* includes the primary symbol (in Scottish heraldry, often a cross) for the family.

- The *helmet* symbolizes a specific class such as barons or earls. It is usually depicted from the side, with the visor closed.

- The *crest* is the plume or emblem on top of a knight's helmet. It might symbolize something about the character of the family, for example, their determination to preserve the family's values.

- The *ribbon* and *motto* (aka *torse*) are displayed above the entire coat of arms, and/or at the bottom of the shield, containing the family name. It is usually the same color as the shield background and also includes the color of a metal (silver or gold).

- The *compartment* is a piece of solid land that the coat of arms rests upon.

- The *mantling* is a cloak that shields battle armor from the sun. On a coat of arms, mantling appears in conjunction with a helmet and may appear as a leafy, swirled form that flows around the coat of arms. Mantling is the main color in the coat of arms and is lined with a metal (silver or gold) color.

Having students produce a family's coat of arms would be especially interesting for literature that relies on family or social group dynamics: the Montagues and Capulets of *Romeo and Juliet*, the families of the Socs and the Greasers in *The Outsiders*, and many others. This activity might work well to help students synthesize their knowledge of a family that recurs in literary works, such as the Snopes family in *The Hamlet*, *The Town*, and *The Mansion*, by Faulkner. Perhaps students could produce a coat of arms that they place strategically in a homebody.

Concept Map

A concept map is a diagram or other graphic way of representing relationships in a reading. The idea is to identify and represent a central concept in the literature and establish how characters, themes, events, and other aspects of the story are related to that central concept and to each other. The central concept might be at the top, with relationships proceeding downward, or it might be in the center, with relationships radiating out from it.

A concept map can have a fairly technical appearance—for example, labeled boxes placed in relation to one another, connected by lines and/or arrows to suggest the flow of authority between and among characters, settings, or some other aspect of the literature. Or it can take a more creative appearance. Students may, for instance, use a symbol of some sort—a tree, a river, a question mark, a galaxy—for their basic outline and depict relationships in the form of fruit on a tree, stars in the galaxy, and so on.

Concept maps, as the name suggests, help students to think at the conceptual level rather than the literal level required in much classroom discussion. They need to understand how a literary work's elements stand in relation to one another, who has control over whom, who is responsible to whom, how a setting creates possibilities and limitations for characters, and so on. Students may produce their maps on overhead transparencies and present them to the class as a way to see how each group grasped the literature and as a way to stimulate further discussion.

Mandala

A mandala is an ancient form of representation that uses a circular form filled with symbols and images (see, e.g., www.mandalaproject.org). I have used mandalas as a way for students to evaluate my class; they created mandalas that represented what they understood my class to be about. Students can create mandalas that symbolize literary characters or events, generally as a culminating activity through which they synthesize their understanding of a complex set of ideas.

Planning a Movie Based on the Text

Students may enjoy considering what might be involved in bringing a literary work to the big screen. To do so they would need to consider how to cast the story, who might direct the film, how it would be costumed, and so on. They could ultimately prepare a poster of the sort found in movie theatre lobbies depicting the leading characters in a pose that represented the film's primary themes.

Political Cartoon

Political cartoons provide a pictorial satire, usually accompanied by brief verbal observations by characters or the cartoonists. Students can work in groups to create a political cartoon that lampoons some aspect of the literature they are reading; this activity would work particularly well when studying satirical works.

Webquest

A webquest is the product of an Internet search that produces links to pertinent information on a given topic. It provides a medium through which to conduct an inquiry, with the goal of acquiring, integrating, and using information located through the search. Webquests are described in detail at http://webquest.sdsu.edu and other sites. They can introduce or supplement student research into particular authors, literary periods or movements, historical periods that provide the setting for literature, or other information that may inform students' engagement with literature. When done in collaborative groups, webquests provide a vehicle for discussion as the students make sense of and organize their understanding of their topic.

Four-Square Activity

A four-square activity begins with students taking out a sheet of notebook paper and folding it into . . . you guessed it, four squares (actually, rectangles). They can either do this individually or in small groups. I have heard of several versions of how to fill in the spaces but will give only one here for purposes of illustration. In the upper left-hand corner, students draw a picture that represents their understanding or depiction of some part of the literature they are reading. In the upper right-hand corner, they write an explanation of their drawing, using language that they might use when talking to a friend. In the lower left-hand corner, they analyze their illustration, using language that they might use when talking to a teacher. In the lower right-hand corner, they write a found poem (described later) derived from the original language of the literature. Their four-square response then serves as the basis for small-group discussions, followed by a whole-class discussion centering on the issues raised through the activity.

Memory Box

At the beginning of the 1962 film version of *To Kill a Mockingbird*, as the credits roll, a box is shown in the background that contains significant items from the story: Atticus' eyeglasses, jacks, marbles, crayons, and other things. Presumably they are symbolic; Atticus' glasses, for instance, might represent his vision. For their own interpretive efforts, students could work in groups to create memory boxes for characters from literature and have their classmates interpret what the contents might symbolize. Through the creation and interpretation of memory boxes, students would engage in discussions of the symbolic meaning of the literature.

Collaborative Writing

Found Poem

A found poem consists of words found in one text and rearranged in a new text to form a poem. The idea behind using a found poem for literary analysis is to have readers focus on the language that they find most significant, meaningful, and important in a literary work they are reading, extract it, and create a poetic work of their own that distills the meaning that they find in the original. When produced in small groups, found poems serve as a vehicle for reading carefully and discussing what language is most critical to representing the meaning that they find in literature.

Parody of an Author

By writing a parody of an author, students must first study the author's style, including common themes, representative language, syntax, perspective, typical settings, and other characteristics that distinguish the writer. It is often a good idea to start with parodies that are relatively simple and accessible, such as television commercials or programs, and use them as scaffolds for writing a more literary parody. Students often have fun when parodying something with a seemingly incongruous vehicle, as David Ragsdale's students did in parodying Reginald Rose's *12 Angry Men* as *12 Angry Cheerleaders* (see Ragsdale and Smagorinsky 2005).

Narrative Written from a Different Character's Perspective

Textbooks often cover the issue of narrative perspective by having students label whether a narrator is omniscient, first person, and so on. A more complex approach to understanding the role of narration is to take a scene from a literary work and rewrite it from a different speaker's perspective. In order to do so, students need to discuss the different ways in which various characters experience the scene. Further, they need to discuss and identify a character's personality, experiences, perspective, role, ways of speaking, and so on in order to depict how that character would relate a scene from the story.

Sequel to Literary Work

One way to understand a narrative is to consider what might happen afterward. An interesting small-group activity is to write a sequel to a literary work. Doing so requires students to engage in prediction, which reading researchers have found to be a critical comprehension strategy. In order to make a good prediction, readers need to have a clear understanding of what they have read so far. They need to recognize text structure and how it sets the stage for what follows. They should understand what a character has done in order to predict what he will do next. By writing a sequel, students need to synthesize their comprehension of what has happened and imaginatively project what could conceivably happen in the next stage of literary events.

Student-Created Study Guides

I learned about student-created study guides by observing Cindy O'Donnell-Allen's high school English class. Study guides are usually created by teachers to help direct students' attention to what the teacher believes the students ought to know. Student-created study guides require kids to engage in the sort of analysis that teachers go through in order to design study guides: reading the work carefully, considering what matters, and posing questions about it. Cindy required students to

- create a title for each scene
- write a summary of the scene
- list and describe each character's function in the scene
- select and respond to what they saw as the most significant conflict and quotation from the scene

These study guides could serve a variety of purposes. The process of creating them requires the sort of careful and thoughtful reading that teachers always hope to promote among their students. The study guides could further serve as the basis of class discussion—students could trade study guides with other groups and complete them, or volunteer questions and observations from their own study guides to initiate and sustain whole-class discussions. The guides could also provide the substance for exams and the preparation students make for them.

Performances

Freeze Frames

A freeze frame provides students an opportunity to choose an event or scene from a literary work, decide why they consider it important, design a new interpretation of it in a new (perhaps contemporary) setting, title it, and perform it. Their classmates' role is to figure out which part of the literature they are interpreting, following which the performers explain their decisions, which may stimulate further student-led class discussion. This activity allows students to discuss the literature in their own language, reconstruct the events in terms of their own experiences, and translate the author's language and themes into their own rendition.

Oral Interpretation of Literature

An oral interpretation of literature consists of a dramatic reading of a segment or entirety of a literary work. Even if the work provides only a single speaker, a group of students may participate in the planning and production, being involved with lighting, costumes, and other aspects of the performance. In order to succeed as an oral interpretation, a reading should elicit the emotions and ideas suggested by the text through such devices as vocal tone and volume, costumes, props, and other elements of the performance. The process of planning the oral interpretation should involve the students in a careful analysis of both the speaker's perspective and personality and the context in which the presentation occurs.

Student-Led Small Group Discussions

Student-led discussions ramp up the degree of responsibility that students take for the success of the class as a whole and of the individual sessions during which they take an authoritative role. As the following array of possibilities illustrates, the forums through which they lead discussions are myriad and enable widespread participation in the class' construction of meaning.

Single-Session Discussions

Jigsaw

Jigsaws consist of two stages of small-group activity. First, students form in home groups consisting of about five students each (assuming about twenty-five students in the class—my apologies if you've got more). The teacher then provides five topics for discussion based on the day's reading. Within each home group, each of the five students volunteers for one of the five topics so that each will be in a different discussion group. The students then move from their home group into one of five new groups, each organized around one of the discussion topics. For a given amount of time, each group discusses its topic. Then the students return to their home groups, with each member now an expert on one of the discussion topics. The home groups then engage in discussions of each of the five topics, each led by its expert group member.

Ranking Activity

A ranking activity requires students to assign a value on some aspect of various characters as they stand in relation to one another. For instance, when I taught *Death of a Salesman* to high school juniors, we did so in the context of a thematic unit on success. Toward the end of the play, I used a two-stage ranking activity. In the first stage, the students worked in small groups to rank the main characters (Willie, Linda, Happy, Biff, Bernard, Howard, Uncle Ben) from most materialistic to least materialistic. They then ranked the same characters from most admirable to least admirable. The students were often surprised to find an inverse correlation between their rankings; that is, they found that the characters they judged to be the most materialistic were the ones they considered the least admirable. The ranking activity helped them to clarify their own beliefs about materialism, and I often found that students, on their unit-end evaluations, said that the activity had caused them to reconsider their materialistic values.

Discussion Web

Discussion webs (Alvermann 1991) build on Lyman's (1981) "think-pair-share" approach to discussions. In a discussion web, the teacher provides students with an open-ended question that they think about for a minute before finding a partner to pair with to discuss their response further. These pairs then join with another pair of students to form a small group, in which they continue their discussion. Ultimately, a spokesperson for each group shares the group's deliberations with the whole class.

A discussion web may serve as a prereading discussion forum (e.g., prior to reading Ken Kesey's *One Flew Over the Cuckoo's Nest*, to consider a question such as What does it mean to be "crazy" in today's society? How does society react to people it thinks are crazy?), or as an intermediate discussion forum (e.g., to discuss the symbolic implications of the Chief's hallucinogenic dreams), or as a way to synthesize a whole reading (e.g., to consider Kesey's intentions in crafting the respective fates of the Chief and McMurphy at the novel's end). The benefit is that students consider these questions without a teacher's direction. As a result, more students participate, students have greater agency with their interpretations, and the possibility exists that students have the opportunity to see meaning in the literature that a conventional reading overlooks.

Long-Term Discussions

Book Clubs

Book clubs are similar to literature circles (see next section), without the structure of the assigned roles. Like literature circles, they are predicated on student choice of literature, student direction of the discussion, and regular meetings. Book clubs are described in detail in a number of publications, including McMahon and Raphael's *Book Club Connection* (1997), Faust et al.'s *Student Book Clubs* (2005), and O'Donnell-Allen's *Book Club Companion* (2006).

Literature Circles

Literature circles (Daniels 1994) are small groups of students who discuss literature of their choice, taking on specific roles to do so. They meet on a regular schedule in groups of four or five, all of whom have read the same book; different literature circles within the same class may read different books. The roles are as follows:

- The *discussion director* gets the discussion started, makes sure that everyone contributes, and is responsible for posing questions if the discussion slows.
- The *literary luminator/passage master* draws group members' attention to memorable or important sections of the text and reads them aloud.
- The *connector* makes associations between the world of the text and the world of human affairs.
- The *illustrator* draws pictures that depict action from the novel.

A number of teachers I've worked with have said that they develop additional roles as appropriate for their students.

Summary

As you can see, there are a number of alternatives to conventional teacher-led discussions of literature. I have found that students appreciate approaching literature through a variety of structures, tasks, and activities, which alleviates the tedium that they have unfortunately come to expect in school. More important, however, by engaging in these activity-oriented, student-centered means of discussion, students become more active agents of their learning and rise to a higher level of expectation for their engagement with literature.

4 *Planning the Whole Course*

The end is where we start from.
　　　　　　　　　—T. S. Eliot

Recall the story with which I opened Chapter 1: After several weeks of discussing a play, one teacher borrowed another teacher's exam to administer. This chapter explains how to plan your assessment *before* teaching rather than after, to reduce the likelihood of disjunctures between what your students learn and what you grade. You will establish a clear, tangible goal for your teaching and for students' learning and in the process will identify what you need to be responsible for in your teaching.

In a sense, then, you'll be planning backward—that is, you'll think about the end point first and then use that goal to plan the path of instruction. To me, this is an excellent way to ensure that your teaching and assessment will be well aligned and that students will find your classes purposeful and helpful in accomplishing the unit goals.

I approach instructional design by focusing first on the whole year. By thinking of the whole year before I design individual units in detail, I am searching for overall coherence in the students' experiences in my class. I hope to plan so that our discussions and inquiries over the course of the year involve what Applebee (1996) calls *curricular conversations*: the overarching concepts that allow for extended explorations of key ideas and that provide continuity across the various units. By mapping out my master plan for the year at the outset, I help to establish a sense of unity for the more particular decisions I make during the planning and teaching of the individual conceptual units.

Sophomore-Year English Curriculum

For the purposes of illustrating curriculum development, I have designed a hypothetical curriculum for the sophomore year in high school. One of the design features I would like to stress is that *the culminating projects can be produced by any student, regardless of perceived ability*. This is because the students are using prior knowledge as the basis for constructing new knowledge.

The projects allow students to reconstruct the material they transact with in class so that they learn something new. All students, except perhaps those with severe learning disabilities, are capable of doing this.

The Yearlong Curriculum: Overarching Concepts and Assessments

We will first consider what might serve as overarching concepts for the whole year. These themes are often suggested by the title of the course you are teaching. If you teach British literature to high school seniors, for instance, your identification of an overarching concept will be limited by the range of literature afforded by the curriculum. Often the overarching purpose for English classes in grades 7–10 is less clearly specified than it is in grades 11 and 12. In grades 7–10, the curriculum often consists of a set of skills to be learned.

Because the curriculum typically lacks a thematic focus, you often have the latitude to identify one yourself, even if your anthology or curriculum may constrain your decision making. Here I have tried to identify overarching concepts for the sophomore year that are feasible in terms of the kinds of options I typically see in schools. Even if my choices are not possible everywhere, they should serve to illustrate the design processes I'm advocating. You should ask yourself, After a year of engaging with literature and related arts, producing writing and other texts, and learning about uses of language and other forms of communication, what kinds of culminating texts can my students produce to show what they've learned? And in particular, How is this learning related to a set of concepts that have recurred in our engagement with the year's materials? And finally, How can I ensure that new learning takes place through the process of constructing these culminating texts?

In thinking about what your students will produce for this culminating assessment, you might also think about what *you* could produce as a way of helping you understand your own learning during the year. Some teachers produce their own version of the texts required of students, in order to synthesize their own learning during the year. In other words, you might want to demonstrate to your students that you, too, are in the process of learning, and create a culminating text to share with them.

Such a stance would reinforce a constructivist perspective because it would mean that texts, including literary texts, are continually open to reinterpretation and do not have a static, official meaning. You would also show that your engagement with the kids and the literature has caused you to change and learn, reinforcing the idea that educational processes should promote the construction of new meaning for both teachers and students. If you take this stance, you will likely surprise your students, who are probably accustomed to authoritative instruction in which teachers serve as experts of a stable knowledge base. I think that in school, there are not nearly enough of these surprises.

Considerations in Curriculum Planning

Because the sophomore year does not usually have an official guiding theme, it is up to the teacher to establish one, possibly through negotiation with students and/or colleagues. For the sophomore curriculum, the literature anthology—in conjunction with whatever mandates are issued by the state, country, district, school, and department—will constrain your choices. In all likelihood, your anthology will be organized according to literary forms: poems, short stories, drama, a Shakespeare play, nonfiction prose, and possibly a short novel. If you wish to teach so that your instruction is responsive to overarching concepts, these forms are insufficient as guiding principles. You'll then need to develop a set of overarching concepts beyond what's offered through your anthology. In addition, you'll probably end up teaching the selections in an order quite different from the way in which the anthology presents them.

Types of Overarching Concepts

I use the term *overarching concept* to describe related sets of ideas that unify a whole curriculum. Overarching concepts may include, but are not limited to, the following types:

- *Theme*: A theme provides a recurring idea, question, or topic that is developed across a series of units. An example for an American literature curriculum would be *Whose perspective provides the American outlook?* For the British literature curriculum, a theme could be *How is the evolution of British literature a reflection of the social worlds in which authors from different eras lived?*

- *Strategy*: A strategy reinforces a particular way of approaching reading and/or writing. Broadly speaking, a strategy could encompass *attention to learning processes*. More specifically, it could focus on a particular skill such as *understanding narrative perspective* in texts that students both read and produce. Tenth-grade students' experiences with literature, then, might be guided by the question *Who is the speaker in each text, and how does the speaker's perspective contribute to the way in which the story is told?* This question might have a number of subquestions, such as *To what extent is the speaker trustworthy and reliable?* and *How would a different speaker tell the same story?*

- *Stance*: A stance is a perspective taken toward living and learning. Some educators view schooling as an arena in which to foster a stance toward life, such as being imaginative, caring, thoughtful, inquiring, critical, or inclusive. An overarching concept for the tenth-grade curriculum might be *How do I position myself in a school with so many different social groups?*

- *Aesthetic Awareness*: Aesthetic awareness turns students' attention to questions of how to evaluate the quality of experience and of artistic forms. An overarching concept for the sophomore curriculum could be *What criteria help me distinguish quality literature from literature of lesser quality?*

Each of these questions is open-ended and amenable to idiosyncratic interpretation and construction by the unique students in your pluralistic class, and thus each is open to a constructivist approach to teaching. The questions are quite different from those that are likely to emerge from a transmission perspective, which might seek to have the students master a body of knowledge such as the characteristics of the Western cultural heritage, which is often the curriculum suggested by anthologies. A teacher working from this perspective might pursue the question *What characterizes Western civilization, and how are these traits evident in the literature we read?* Presumably, this question would have a fairly clear, unambiguous answer—perhaps students considering this question would be able to explain whether or not Huck Finn is a good boy or, if not explain it, at least repeat the teacher's determination of whether it's true or false.

Let's look at one type of overarching concept that could serve to unify the sophomore curriculum and then consider a set of other overarching concepts that could provide other conversational threads for the course. Students might find it tiresome to have a single emphasis for a whole course, so it's wise to provide a set of overarching concepts rather than just one.

One Possible Theme: Negotiating Thresholds

When you look at what high school sophomores tend to read, you'll notice that much of the literature concerns some kind of transforming experience, often emerging from a conflict. This emphasis can serve as the basis for an overarching theme such as *negotiating thresholds*. This theme concerns the manner in which tenth graders are on the border between adolescence and adulthood, peer-group values and home values, and other critical junctures in their lives that require a decision about which direction to take.

A rationale for this overarching theme could come from the findings of developmental psychology, which sees this age as one of identity formation. If the school or community is experiencing problems with inappropriate negotiations of these thresholds—bullying, discrimination, harassment, fighting, gang involvement, and so on—then these factors could also figure into the rationale.

The theme of negotiating thresholds could suggest a series of units through which students would read and produce texts dealing with some of the key conflicts they'll face in their midteen years. For our hypothetical curriculum, the following thematic units would serve this purpose well:

- coming of age
- conflict with authority
- gangs, cliques, and peer pressure
- discrimination

Keep in mind that thematic units are only one of several types of unit you can develop. For my hypothetical curriculum, I designed four other units for the year's activities. They represent some of the other types of conceptual units I outlined previously and additionally include the open-ended approach to instruction known as a *workshop*.

- heroic journey (genre)
- Shakespeare: *Julius Caesar* (works of single author)
- writing workshop
- reading workshop

A Shakespeare unit is often required in the sophomore curriculum, with *Julius Caesar* typically included in the literature anthology. The Shakespeare unit is therefore a somewhat pragmatic choice, though it is also highly defensible from other perspectives. The unit on the heroic journey is compatible with the theme of negotiating thresholds because the genre involves the hero's overcoming of a series of obstacles in the course of the quest.

A writing or reading workshop is an open-ended block of time in which students have the opportunity to write or read on topics and in genres of their choice, with the teacher serving as resource. The teacher also writes or reads along with the students. Because they involve a complex set of managerial skills, I do not devote extensive space to workshops in this book. Rather, I recommend you consult other books that explain their operation in detail (e.g., Atwell 1989, 1998). Workshops can fit well with other overarching concepts you might identify for your whole course, and can be appropriate when emphasizing the stance of *self-determination*.

To provide students with varied formats and focuses, it would make sense to distribute and sequence the units across the year as follows:

First Semester

coming of age

writing workshop

discrimination

heroic journey

Second Semester

> gangs, cliques, and peer pressure
>
> reading workshop
>
> conflict with authority
>
> Shakespeare: *Julius Caesar*

This distribution places one workshop, two units on negotiating thresholds, and one unit from a different type of concept in each semester. It places Shakespeare at the end of the year, a good location given the play's likely difficulty for many students and their maturity as readers over the course of the year. This variation in focus and format should help keep students as stimulated as students can be, even while they explore recurring ideas.

Other Possibilities for Overarching Concepts

Following are overarching concepts of three types—strategy, stance, and aesthetic awareness—that could conceivably complement the negotiating thresholds theme. You would never use all of these focuses for a single course. Rather, you would identify a few to provide conversational continuity for your class across the various units.

Strategy

Understanding narrative perspective. When he taught high school English, Michael W. Smith made narrative perspective a recurring issue in students' engagement with literature (see Smith 1991). He believed that understanding literature was dependent on understanding who told the story. Central to this knowledge was the ability to recognize a narrator's limitations and how those limitations affect the narrator's reliability. Holden Caulfield in *The Catcher in the Rye*, for instance, has a uniquely jaundiced view of his world that prevents him from seeing many of his own flaws. Smith identified a set of questions that recurred in each unit of instruction, providing his classes with an overarching strategic approach, regardless of the topics covered in the units.

Cultural modeling. Carol Lee (2000) has argued that teachers can build on students' cultural resources when teaching them to become literate in a particular domain. For many students, school is already well aligned with their cultural resources. School, as many critics have pointed out, is conducted according to the norms of the white middle class. As a result, white middle-class students tend to be well matched to the expectations that schools have for successful performance.

Lee has argued that students from other backgrounds also bring plentiful cultural resources to school. Because the curriculum focuses on Western history and literature, and on middle-class speech patterns, these resources often go untapped. Her primary interest is in African American students and their rich uses of figurative language in their daily speech. Lee has argued that teachers can do two things to help African American students have more fulfilling experiences in school:

- include more literature by African American writers to allow for clearer connections to the speech and experiences of African American students
- explicitly draw attention to figurative properties of African American English to help provide students with strategies for understanding literature, not just by African American writers but by any writers who use figurative devices

A teacher who uses cultural modeling as an overarching strategy routinely finds ways for students to reflect on and analyze their own cultural practices, particularly their uses of language. Formal knowledge of these language practices then serves as essential knowledge in students' experiences with literature that employs similar devices.

Dramatic images. Another strategic approach that could govern a whole course would be to teach students a range of strategies for helping them visualize literature. Images can be created in a variety of ways. Jeffrey Wilhelm and Brian Edmiston (1998) have described a number of strategies through which students can enact sections of stories in order to help them visualize how characters might interact and to help them make inferences about why they think and act as they do. Others have identified various approaches to using art and drama in ways that help students both represent their understanding of literature and develop new understandings through the process of interpretation. Wilhelm (1997) argues that these approaches are particularly helpful for students who resist reading. He has found that their resistance comes largely from frustration over how to make sense of texts and that among their chief problems is a difficulty evoking those texts through images.

Stance

Critical literacy. Some observers of school advocate what they call *critical literacy* taught through *critical pedagogy.* Critical literacy aims to teach students about power relationships, particularly when one group or class of people has advantages over another. Critical pedagogues try to get their students to examine their own class status and to see how their communities and nation privilege some groups of people over others. Teachers who emphasize critical literacy as an overarching stance routinely have students ask questions about who has power and why. This question can be directed to virtually any kind of human relationship, including

- the school (e.g., which kind of people make decisions, which are in subservient positions, etc.)
- the classroom (e.g., who speaks about what, whose opinions are likely to be favorably rewarded, etc.)
- the characters in the literature (e.g., how characters of different class, gender, and race are portrayed by writers of different class, gender, and race)
- the traditional literary canon (e.g., authors of which class, gender, and race get privileged status; which topics and themes get privileged status)
- society as a whole (e.g., how class, gender, and race are implicated in power relationships in society)

Self-determination. Some teachers believe that education should be geared toward helping students determine who they are and what their purposes are. The role of the teacher is to provide the environment in which students work, without overly specifying what that work is or which standards it should meet. Teachers who embrace this belief would employ the most student-oriented approaches described in this book: negotiating the curriculum with students, using book clubs or literature circles to discuss novels, establishing writing workshops, and so on.

Multicultural awareness. The term *multiculturalism* is quite the rage. I use the term *rage* in two senses: it is a fiercely advocated trend in colleges of education and many school curricula, and it has caused outcry and equally fierce opposition among those known as traditionalists, those who wish to preserve schools as they have been in the past. While a traditionalist would wish to preserve the literary canon, a multiculturalist would wish to diversify it to include more women; authors of color; gay, lesbian, bisexual, and transsexual authors; and authors from traditionally underrepresented nations and cultures. Multicultural concerns would perhaps include a heavy dose of critical literacy, critiquing established norms and questioning why things are as they are. There would be a strong effort to read authors from diverse backgrounds and to consider the ways in which different cultural practices contribute to different worldviews.

Aesthetic Awareness

Beauty, truth, goodness. Howard Gardner, in *The Disciplined Mind* (1999), has argued that education ought to be concerned with the ancient considerations of inquiring into what is beautiful, true, and good. If a teacher were to adopt this as an overarching concept, students would continually ask a set of questions when considering literature: By what criteria do I distinguish the aesthetic quality of a text? What eternal truths does the literature suggest? What notion of virtue does the author promote? What does it mean to be good, true, and beautiful?

Summary

My review here is hardly complete. A number of other worthwhile goals for schooling have been identified by others that could serve as overarching concepts. The goals that you identify for a whole course will be determined by a variety of factors. I do not advocate any one over any other, but instead encourage you to think about the importance of having a limited set of overarching concepts to serve as the conversational thread across a whole course of study. How you arrive at them (e.g., through your own choice, through negotiation with colleagues, through negotiation with students) and how you put them into practice are questions that deserve considerable thought. Equally important is determining how you will assess your students' learning at the end of the course.

Assessing Students for a Whole Course

One overarching concept for the sophomore course I have designed is the theme of negotiating thresholds. I have already provided a brief rationale for this theme. With an overarching concept serving to provide continuity across the units, you must next consider what students will do at the end of the course to synthesize their understanding of the year's work. You may need to think in terms of semesters rather than years, depending on how your curriculum is set up and on how many students transfer classes at the semester break. My reference to a year's final exam, then, might need adjustment depending on how your school is organized and conducted.

I have identified a set of possible culminating texts for a whole course of study. It is not likely that you would use all of them for a single course; my goal instead is to identify a possible range of assessments. The following assessments help students *synthesize their knowledge* from the year and *construct new knowledge* through their process of producing them:

- Assessment of the students' own learning about learning through a *portfolio*. This kind of assessment would fit well with an overarching *stance* of *self-determination*, with the portfolio helping students determine what they have learned and what they have learned it from.

- Assessment of the students' understanding and evaluation of literary form through their writing of an *extended definition of good literature*. This kind of assessment would fit with Gardner's emphasis on *aesthetic awareness* and belief that students should consider the *beautiful, true, and good*. In this assessment, students would apply these considerations to the question of what counts as quality literature.

- Assessment of the students' learning about the year's overarching concept through a *multimedia project* synthesizing knowledge gained from the year's engagement with texts and classroom activities. This assessment would combine the course's attention to *negotiating thresholds* with a course-long emphasis on the *strategy* of *generating dramatic images*.

- Assessment of the students' understanding of the literary texts through an *essay analyzing literary characters' changes* in relation to the overarching concept. This assessment would take a *paradigmatic* approach to understanding the theme of negotiating thresholds.

- *Assessment developed by students* based on their own construction of the purpose of the course. This assessment would fit with the *stance* of *self-determination*.

As you can see, each of these assessments provides an opportunity for students to learn something new in a different arena. Through the portfolio they can learn about how and what they have learned. Through the extended definition they can learn how they evaluate literature. Through the multimedia project they can generate an image that both shows their learning and enables them to learn something new about the year's work. Through the analytic essay they can learn more about the literature they have studied.

Again, doing all of these projects for a single course—particularly if students do them earnestly and in detail—would probably be more than they could manage without shortchanging some. Rather, these assessment types illustrate possible ways in which you can use a final exam to enable students to construct new meaning through engagement with the course's overarching concepts and the materials and activities through which they have explored them.

Portfolio

One kind of culminating project that serves any curriculum well is the portfolio. Portfolio assessment is borrowed from the world of the arts, where artists use a collection of representative works as a way of showing their prowess to galleries, customers, art schools, and other venues for their work. The idea is that rather than having each and every effort evaluated, an artist (or student) works at a variety of projects—some of which are abandoned or turn out poorly, others of which turn out well—and then chooses the best products for evaluation. This conception of assessment assumes that not all work is intended to be graded and that evaluation should focus on the work that best represents the artist's ability.

In education, the idea of a portfolio has been adapted rather than adopted wholesale. Indeed, there are a number of different ways in which a portfolio can be assembled. For the culminating project for the sophomore curriculum, I focus on a kind of portfolio called the *process portfolio*. A process portfolio is unique in that its purpose is to encourage the students to reflect on their learning processes, rather than to feature their best work (which is the artist's approach, known as a *showcase portfolio*). A process portfolio gives students the opportunity to go through their year's work and select artifacts that demonstrate key learning experiences. A key learning experience is not necessarily reflected in a polished, final product. In a process portfolio, the *exhibits* may include

- something that received a poor grade, yet through which the student learned something about the topic, the importance of good work habits, and so on

- a rough draft for a piece of writing, rather than the final draft, if the rough draft served as an occasion for significant learning or if the rough draft received feedback that contributed to new understanding

- an abandoned effort, if the abandonment came about through an important realization

- a text produced by someone else, if through reading that text the student gained critical new insights

In other words, the purpose of a process portfolio is to trace and reflect on significant learning through the exhibition of key learning experiences, even if those experiences are reflected in rough, unfinished, or polished texts. A showcase portfolio, in contrast, features the student's best work as a way of demonstrating the most successful *products* of learning.

The process portfolio assignment might look like this:

Throughout the year you have had a lot of experiences with literature and other art forms. In response to these texts, you have produced a variety of pieces of writing, art, and other forms of expression. Presumably you have learned something about yourself, the literature, how to write, how to read, and other things.

Your culminating project for the year is to prepare a portfolio in which you present things you've produced that have resulted in your most valuable learning. We will call these things *exhibits*. The exhibits you present do not need to be your best work. Often we learn the most from our rough drafts, our frustrated efforts, and other experiences that do not yield our best products. *You will not be graded on the quality of the exhibits that you include.* Rather, you will be graded on how carefully you reflect on what you learned from producing them.

Your portfolio should include the following:

- Title page with name and date.

- A minimum of eight items that serve as your exhibits. You must include a minimum of one exhibit for each of the eight units we studied. Your portfolio may include additional exhibits if you wish.

- A written statement that identifies and discusses significant learning based on each exhibit, consisting of a minimum of two hundred words.

- A longer *synthesis paper* in which you discuss how these artifacts as a whole reveal what you've learned this year about both yourself and the material we have studied, consisting of a minimum of one thousand words.

If you plan to use a portfolio assessment of any kind, students need to know this at the beginning of the year so that they can save their work. Let students know that if they don't save their work, they may do poorly on the final evaluation for the course, which will require them to reflect on something from each unit studied. You might need to weave instruction in reflective thinking into each unit, stressing to students that they need to save at least one exhibit from each unit for their portfolios. You might want to provide models of successful portfolios, particularly if students are not required to produce them elsewhere in your school. You could use these models throughout the year to help students assemble their portfolio materials as they work on each unit. Doing so would also reinforce the constructivist, reflective emphasis of your teaching during the process of each unit.

Extended Definition of Good Literature

Elliot Eisner (1985) has argued that one way to know something is through an understanding and appreciation of its form, what he calls *aesthetic knowledge*. To Eisner, it's important to understand how things are made, how their ultimate form suggests meaning, and how the aesthetics of art enhance the quality of life.

Eisner's attention to aesthetic knowledge can be taken several ways. To a transmission-oriented teacher, it might imply a duty to explain to students the aesthetic aspects of literature—Shakespeare's metaphors, the rhyme scheme he employs in particular kinds of verse, and other aspects of form—and then assess students' knowledge of them on a test. As you can imagine, I recommend minimizing this kind of attention to literary form, limiting it to whatever formal knowledge that students find useful in making sense of literature. If you simply lecture students about the difference between synecdoche and metonymy without engaging them in literary reading in which they find this distinction useful, and then give them a test in which they match terms to definitions without using them in some productive way, they will likely forget the distinction soon after the exam.

It would be much more effective to let aesthetic knowledge serve as one of the overarching concepts for a course of study. Imagine that, instead of taking the typical textbook approach of memorizing a technical vocabulary and adopting the values of literary critics in evaluating literature, students developed criteria for evaluating the quality of literature. If constructing this definition became a goal of instruction, then you would need to devote classroom time to discussing the relative merits of different literary works. Students are rather quick to express their opinions on whether they like a text or not. Rare is the teacher who hasn't heard "This book's boring!" or "What a stupid story!" or some similar point of view in response to a text. Such comments are seldom treated as legitimate in classrooms, where the typical response from the teacher is to ignore or suppress negative evaluations of a piece of literature and discuss it anyway.

Yet such comments could serve as the starting point for helping students articulate what they see as qualities in literature (and the lack thereof). Why is a story boring? What makes literature interesting? Is it possible for a boring story to be a good work of literature? Can literature that someone finds personally offensive still be quality literature? Is it possible for different people to have different conceptions of what counts as good literature?

If these questions are routinely asked during literary discussions, and if you consistently help students formulate their opinions into criteria for a definition of quality literature, then you are helping them to develop a formal understanding of what they think good literature is. You will need to provide instruction in how to write extended definitions as part of your writing instruction as well. If you are effective in both of these areas, then you might be able to ask students to do the following on a final exam:

Throughout the year you have read a variety of texts: poems, short stories, plays, novels, essays, songs, and more. You have undoubtedly liked some of these better than others. For your final exam, write an essay in which you explain what distinguishes quality literature from literature of lesser quality. To do so, provide the following:

- a set of *criteria* or rules that state clearly what each literary quality is

- for each criterion, an *example* from literature we have read this year (including literature you have read on your own) that illustrates the rule at work

- for each criterion, a *counterexample* from literature we have read this year (including literature you have read on your own) that comes close to meeting the conditions of the rule, but falls short in some way

- for each example and counterexample, a *warrant* that clearly explains why the criterion is or is not being met

- for your whole argument, a *counterargument* expressing the viewpoint of someone who might disagree with you

- for the counterargument, a *rebuttal* in which you defend your position

This final exam suggests the need for a constructivist classroom with an aesthetic focus and reliance on exploratory talk. The final evaluation is primarily logical and analytic—that is, paradigmatic—yet the year's activities can include a variety of approaches to thinking about what makes good literature. The purpose of the class is established from the outset, allowing students to work confidently toward a worthwhile goal. They are engaging in a practice central to their domain: the construction of criteria for evaluating literature.

Those criteria might vary from student to student; one student may decide that literature ought to be primarily entertaining, another might feel it should ring true emotionally, another might feel it should make a statement about the human condition, and so on. The assessment of their knowledge will be based on how effectively they construct their argument, rather than on how close their opinion is to the teacher's or to that of professional literary critics.

I should also be clear that in order for students to write effective extended definitions, they need the sort of supported instruction illustrated in Chapter 2. In addition to focusing attention on quality criteria throughout the year, you should also provide instruction in *how to write extended-definition essays*. This instruction might involve the same sort of sequence illustrated in the example of teaching comparison-contrast essays in Chapter 2. In other words, you would start with the evaluation of things with which the students are familiar: the qualities that distinguish a good Mexican restaurant from a bad one, a good hip-hop artist from a bad one, a good hair salon from a bad one, and so on.

Students might begin their analyses in small groups, discussing good and bad cases and generating criteria (e.g., a good Mexican restaurant serves food that is fresh, textured, and spicy), examples (e.g., La Cazuela always begins each meal with a bowl of warm, crisp, and salty tortilla chips and a zesty salsa), counterexamples (e.g., La Fiesta's nachos consist of soggy tortilla chips that usually flop and dump the runny contents in the diner's lap), and warrants (e.g., because La Cazuela's chips always remain crispy no matter how much salsa, guacamole, bean dip, lettuce, tomato, or cheese you load them up with, it is a superior Mexican restaurant that takes pride in its presentation of fresh food). They would go through this process to generate a series of criteria to define what distinguishes an exceptionally good Mexican restaurant from a lesser establishment. Students could write either group or individual papers, get feedback, revise, and so forth in order to sharpen their definitional skills. Through such scaffolding, and continual attention to the generation of criteria and supporting evidence for the evaluation of quality literature, students would be well prepared for writing their final exam essays.

Multimedia Project

A third kind of culminating project enables students to reflect on how they have changed personally through their engagement with the year's reading and activities, with special attention to the overarching concept (e.g., negotiating thresholds). The year's activities have presumably included considerable reflection on the themes of the individual units that have contributed to the development of the conversation surrounding this theme. Students might, for instance, have kept a journal in which they reflected on their own conflicts with authority, experiences with peer groups, coming-of-age experiences, and so on. They might have written personal narratives describing such experiences. They might have produced art, music, and/or drama depicting their experiences. In other words, if this theme has consistently served as the conversational thread running through all of the units, then students should be conversant in thinking about how their own lives have changed in relation to the changes they have seen in literary characters.

These reflections can be brought together in a multimedia project, produced in a form of the students' choice. It might be a personal narrative in which the students recount and reflect on key experiences through which they have negotiated thresholds. The narrative could be either a conventional written story or rely on other artistic tools, including the capabilities offered by computer software. It could be a song that depicts threshold experiences, perhaps recorded and/or performed. It could be a drama, written and/or performed. For artistic students, it could be a sculpture, painting, or other rendition. And, of course, it could combine a range of media and genres of the student's choice (see, e.g., Romano 1995).

Such an assignment might look like this:

> Throughout the year we have read a series of texts that concerned the theme of *negotiating thresholds*. Undoubtedly, like the literary characters, you have negotiated thresholds yourself in the last year or so. You entered the class fresh out of ninth grade and now are prepared to become a high school junior. During this time you have gone from being among the

youngest students in the school to being among the older half, bringing about changes in expectations, peer groups, relationships with adults, cultural groups, and many other things.

For your culminating project for the year, your assignment is to produce a text that in some way depicts how you have personally negotiated significant thresholds during the year. You have had many opportunities to reflect on such experiences during previous units of study. For your culminating project, select one significant experience, or one set of related experiences, and use your project to depict how you have changed.

Your project can take any form you choose. Some possibilities include

- a written narrative about a significant experience or set of experiences
- a narrative about a significant experience or set of experiences, produced in a different form (song, computer graphics, cartoon series, drama, or other medium)
- a work of art that depicts the experience and how you have changed; be prepared to explain how the work of art accomplishes your goals
- a text that combines any of these forms and others to depict your changes

This type of project enables students to reflect on how their schooling has helped them realize personal growth. The major disadvantage is that it is not easy to assess; in fact, many teachers avoid projects of this sort because they feel it's hard to grade them objectively. I recommend grading it as you would a portfolio, focusing on the extent to which the student has accounted for change (or lack thereof). Some teachers find that in order to assess these projects fairly, they need to ask that some products (e.g., a sculpture) be accompanied by an oral or written explanation.

Analytic Essay

The assessments thus far have focused on the students and how they have learned about their own learning, their development of aesthetic criteria, and their personal changes in relation to the year's overarching concept. Teachers may also feel the need to assess students on their understanding of the literature studied. Often these assessments require students to answer questions about their memory of facts from the literature: whether Ponyboy was a Greaser or a Soc, whether S. E. Hinton was a man or a woman, whether Dan'l Webster was a frog or a toad, whether Huck Finn was good or bad.

Such assessments, while being easy to grade and presumably objective, are questionable because they require the repetition of superficial knowledge and do not enable students to construct any new meaning during the process of assessment. I advocate instead some kind of extended writing, which is more likely to encourage complex thinking through which students can synthesize and extend their knowledge (see Langer and Applebee 1987). To write an extended essay on the year's worth of literature centered on the theme of negotiating thresholds, students might respond to the following:

> During the year you have read about a great many characters negotiating a variety of thresholds, some successfully, some not. For your final exam, your task is to write an essay in which you select three literary protagonists from our year's reading and explain how effectively each one negotiated a significant threshold in the literature. Each protagonist should come from a different unit of study. To do so, you will need to
>
> - describe the threshold being negotiated (e.g., a conflict between two social groups, a conflict between two sets of goals, a change between two stages of maturity, etc.)
> - describe the conflicts involved and why the situation is problematic for the protagonist
> - describe how the threshold is negotiated
> - evaluate whether the threshold is well negotiated or not
>
> From your description of these three protagonists' experiences, draw a conclusion about how to negotiate a threshold. In doing so, make sure to refer to all three protagonists and contrast their negotiations.

Evaluating this kind of final exam will take you much longer than it takes to grade an objective test. You can't take these essays and run them through a scanner, then compute the grade by adding up the number of correct answers. Rather, you have to read them carefully and apply some kind of evaluative criteria, likely involving a complex set of factors: the detail of the reviews of the protagonists' experiences, the fidelity to some kind of language standard, the insight of the synthesis at the end, and so on.

Extended writing gives students the opportunity to develop their writing skills, synthesize personal and textual knowledge, and construct new knowledge through their reflection on the year's experiences and engagements with literature. In my view, providing them with this opportunity more than makes up for whatever additional time you must spend grading them and whatever consequences come from risking subjectivity in your evaluation.

Assessment Developed by Students

Another way to approach a final assessment is to dedicate class time toward the end of the course to having students generate tasks and questions through which their engagement with the course can be evaluated. This kind of assessment fits well with a teaching approach in which students help to plan the curriculum, with any approach that falls within a constructivist perspective, and with the overarching concept of self-determination. It relies on students to reveal what they have learned through their identification of authentic tasks and projects that will demonstrate how they have constructed the purpose of the class. Students could either generate a menu of tasks, projects, or questions or negotiate a classwide project. You could then ask them to develop a scoring rubric through which their work would be evaluated and possibly allow them to participate in the evaluation themselves.

Taking this approach requires a key role for the teacher, that being to ensure that students generate tasks that meet both their own sense of authenticity and the school's notion of rigorous assessment. Students need to know that if they design a frivolous assessment, then you have a responsibility to the community to replace it with something more fitting. You might need to identify a set of guidelines for student-designed assessments. You might specify, for instance, that the culminating text must

- account for material from each individual unit of study from the course
- synthesize knowledge across the various units
- meet the expectations of some literate community
- reveal a construction of new knowledge
- communicate effectively with the specified audience

You might identify other requirements, depending on the particular experiences you and your students have had within the course. If, for instance, your overarching concept is designed to address a community-wide problem such as environmental contamination, students might submit their final exams to the city mayor or other official. Doing so would both provide them with an opportunity for social action and give them an audience for their exams beyond the teacher.

Students could follow any one of a number of processes to design this assessment. They might start by generating possible tasks in small groups, and then explain them to the whole class, with the teacher serving to orchestrate the discussion. Once each group has presented its ideas, the class as a whole can negotiate some kind of agreement on which one would serve as the most fruitful opportunity for a final assessment. Another possibility would be for the class to generate a menu of projects from which individual students or collaborative groups could choose.

This activity is a departure from the other assessments reviewed in this chapter in that the specific mode of assessment is developed at the end, rather than the beginning, of the course. It does meet the spirit of the general approach, however, in that it is responsive to the content and process of the instruction that have led to it. What distinguishes this method is that the students determine what is significant about the class and identify assessment vehicles through which they can synthesize their understanding and create new knowledge.

Culminating Texts for Teachers

I have referred to the ways in which teachers can produce texts during the year to construct meaning from their teaching. Following are some possible ways in which you can compose a text that contributes to your own learning and shows others how you have changed through your teaching.

Work That Parallels Student Work

One way to reflect on your teaching is to produce the same kind of culminating text that your students are working on. This approach would work best, I think, on open-ended projects such as keeping a portfolio, producing a multimedia text that synthesizes your experiences and understandings, or maintaining a journal or log in which you do a naturalistic study of your own teaching.

Portfolio

If you were to keep a process portfolio, your exhibits could include student work that taught you something about your teaching, feedback on unit evaluations, excerpts from a log you've kept on your teaching, articles or books that you read that changed your teaching, or other artifacts through which you learned how to be a better teacher. As with students' process portfolios, the purpose would be to reflect on what you've learned, rather than to showcase your best work. Students will undoubtedly be interested in knowing what you learned from teaching them and how you will teach differently as a result of their experiences in your class.

Multimedia Project

You could also produce some kind of creative or multimedia project that represents what you've experienced and learned through your teaching. A good example of this comes from Cindy Cotner, who, for a graduate course I was teaching at the University of Oklahoma, created a collage that synthesized her understanding of what it means to be a teacher (see Figure 1). A reproduced version of her collage was published in the *English Journal*, the leading journal in the field for teaching ideas. Producing some kind of creative work that represents your teaching experiences might fascinate your students and help them view artistic composing as more legitimate in school.

Teaching Log

If your students are keeping journals or reading logs, you could also maintain a teaching log in which you reflect on your teaching. Through

Figure 1   Collage by Cindy Cotner

a teaching log you can identify problems with your instruction and think about how to make appropriate changes. You can think about how a unit is working and whether it works better for some students than others. You can think about classroom dynamics, school politics, curriculum debates, media views of education, or other issues that affect how you contemplate your work. A number of excellent books have been published that feature teachers reflecting on their own practice. This reflection often begins with the kinds of observations that teachers make in teaching logs.

Systematic Reflection on Teaching and Learning

Ethnographic Experiments

Luis Moll (2000) has recommended that teachers conduct inquiries into what he calls the *cultural resources* of students by getting to know students and their families outside school. His work in the Tucson area is designed to bridge the cultural gap between middle-class white teachers and the working-class Mexican American students they teach. These students often do poorly in school yet engage in sophisticated cognitive lives at home and in the community. Moll's idea is for teachers to get a better understanding of students' competencies outside school and adjust instruction so that the students can build on these strengths and resources in their classroom work.

This work entails getting out into the community and observing students and their families at work. You might not feel comfortable inviting yourself into the homes of your students and watching them eat dinner, and that's understandable. There are, however, arenas in which you may feel more at ease, such as community centers, public parks, after-school programs, and other centers of public activity. You might coach a youth sports team, get involved in Scouting, or otherwise participate in community life so as to better understand the strengths of students that aren't so apparent in school.

Moll also believes that communities will develop greater respect and trust for teachers if they cultivate these sorts of relationships. Students will then be more likely to trust that a teacher's decisions are in their interests and be less likely to resist both the system and its individual teachers. Community studies of this sort work best, he finds, when they are conducted by teams of teachers. Working in a team allows for the sharing of ideas and impressions, collaboration in the development of new teaching approaches, and support for one another's efforts. Conducting ethnographic experiments is obviously a lot of work and would place great demands on your time. They have, however, the potential to help you teach in ways that recognize and take advantage of strengths your students have that are typically overlooked in schools.

Frame Experiments

In *Teaching Writing as Reflective Practice*, George Hillocks (1995) argues that teachers can learn a great deal about their teaching by conducting frame experiments, that is, by adopting a disposition about teaching that involves continual inquiry into the consequences of teaching methods. These might involve comparative studies, such as teaching two classes differently and contrasting student work produced in response to the two approaches. They might involve experimenting with new methods—using more drama, using small groups in different ways, trying writing workshops—and taking careful notes on the changes that result in your classroom. The idea is to make a systematic effort to study the effects of your teaching methods on students, using whatever means of inquiry are at your disposal.

Studies of Classroom Relationships

In *Inside City Schools: Investigating Literacy in Multicultural Classrooms*, Sarah Freedman and colleagues (1999) report on a project in which a group of teachers studied the ways in which relationships played out in the classrooms in response to changes they made in their teaching. Unlike Hillocks, who was interested in how teaching affects students' schoolwork, the teachers working with Freedman were concerned with how to set up strong classroom communities. In a typical study, a teacher in an urban, multiracial school would assign literature that focused on racial conflict and observe how relationships among students changed as a consequence of classroom discussions and activities. For teachers interested in the relational aspects of schooling, this approach can reveal the kinds of feelings that often simmer beneath the surface of classroom order.

Electronic Conversations

Another activity you can engage in is to subscribe to a professional *email list*. Usually email list discussions are organized around topics. The topics can be very broad, such as NCTE talk, which is simply about teaching English and can cover any issue raised by its subscribers. It can be more focused, such as teachers applying whole language (TAWL), or more focused yet, such as gay, lesbian, bisexual teachers of speakers of other languages (GLESOL).

Participating on such a list can provide you with a broad-based conversation that's unavailable in any single school. It helps you see what teaching conditions exist in other schools, how teachers approach problems from other perspectives, and how you can form professional networks to help you grow as an educator. You could prepare an email list portfolio in which you print out contributions that you found provocative and reflect on how they've helped you rethink your teaching. Students would be interested to know that you view yourself as part of a larger community of inquiry and that your experiences with them are central to your identity as a person.

Summary

The first step in designing a cohesive constructive curriculum is to think about the big picture—your approach to the course as a whole—and about how students can demonstrate their learning in relation to that theme at the end of the course. If you conceive of the purpose of a whole course, the individual sections—the units that you design—will make more sense to students both in and of themselves and as they provide continuity across the school year.

Part II

Teaching Writing Within a Unit Design

5 Goals for Conventional Writing Assignments

The next step in designing your curriculum is to set goals for the individual units that contribute to the course-long conversation about the overarching theme. Once again, I plan backward in thinking about assessment—that is, I think first about what kinds of culminating texts students could ultimately produce from engagement with the material in each unit. These texts will then serve as goals when planning the path of instruction. They also serve as the texts that I will assess in order to give students grades for the class.

Constructing Units, Constructing Texts

Throughout this book, I have used metaphors of *construction* to help illustrate processes of teaching and learning. I would like to extend that metaphor now to illustrate how to think about planning unit goals and the instruction that leads to them. I encourage you to think of your classroom as a *construction zone*, to borrow an analogy suggested by Dennis Newman, Peg Griffin, and Michael Cole (1989). To work within this zone, you should begin with some kind of plan.

If you were building a house, you would undoubtedly begin by envisioning what the house would look like when you were finished. You might even draw or build a small model of that final product to help you see your ultimate goal during the process of construction. You would also prepare a blueprint, a detailed set of plans that would help you build the house according to a set of specifications.

Having this model and blueprint provides you with a goal and a plan for realizing it. It does allow for flexibility, however, depending on circumstances that arise. If your plans call for a skylight, yet you learn during construction that softwood trees drop debris on the house, you might abandon the skylight idea. If you are building the foundation and unearth a subterranean spring, you will probably move the house to a different site on the lot or change the blueprint to allow the water to flow through the house. If your work crew comes up with an idea on how to route the plumbing more efficiently, you might change some of the infrastructure design. If your goals change, then you will adjust the blueprint and model accordingly. You might, for instance, meet and marry a gourmet cook and decide to change from a standard kitchen to a deluxe design.

In other words, beginning with a sense of your outcome, and with a design for realizing it, does not lock you into a rigid plan. Rather, it provides you with a goal and a pathway that you can adjust in response to changing conditions. Following your plan regardless of intervening events can cause your house to slide into a sinkhole. However, if you try to build a house without any idea of what it's supposed to look like, your stairway to the second floor might let out in the middle of the bathroom. And so planning ahead may seem burdensome, but it can help everyone arrive in what they mostly agree to be a good spot.

My task, then, is to envision what students will be working toward as a consequence of their engagement with the unit texts and activities. These goals will come in the form of culminating texts that I will assess. The construction metaphor applies simultaneously to two things. One is the design of the unit itself. The other is the texts that students will build in relation to the unit. Both of these are goal-directed acts that require the use of tools and materials.

Both teachers and students produce texts whose ultimate form will be assessed. In other words, just as a homeowner or building inspector eventually evaluates the quality of a new home, you will ultimately be responsible for saying how well your students construct their culminating texts. In turn, your students will form judgments about the way in which you have designed your text: the conceptual unit.

Conceptualizing Your Unit Focus

All of the planning you do in a unit will occur in terms of the unit focus. You will need to consider the question, Whose unit of study is this, and who gets to decide what it is about? Conventionally, a teacher is the primary decision maker in the classroom. In this tradition, the teacher picks the unit topic and decides what's important for students to learn about it. The teacher then fashions goals, assessments, lessons, activities, and so on so that students can make progress toward grasping the unit concepts. Taking this approach, the teacher needs to think through the concept under study and plan carefully so that students can explore the key issues in a detailed and connected way.

For instance, in a unit on discrimination, you might think through what it means to discriminate, perhaps starting with examples from your own experiences or from the media. When a parent prohibits a seven-year-old from watching a PG-13 movie, is this discrimination? When a teacher tends not to call on a student who earnestly makes embarrassing statements, is this discrimination? When a person who gets swindled out of money says he has been gypped, is this discrimination against Gypsies? Your consideration of a broad series of examples will help you identify what you think is important to understand about discrimination and plan instruction appropriately.

Setting Goals

In Chapter 1 I reviewed a great range of ways in which students could know something. As you might imagine, it would be very difficult to provide opportunities for assessing all kinds of knowing in each and every unit. Rather, you should try to provide diverse assessments over the course of the whole year. For any individual unit of instruction, you should provide a more limited set of major assessments. In other words, for each unit of instruction, you should identify a small set of culminating texts for students to produce. If you choose these texts wisely, the kids will have plenty of work on their hands, and not just busywork, but significant construction of new and important texts, knowledge, and meaning.

This chapter and the next focus on identifying the major graded texts that students produce during a unit. As a teacher you will be responsible for grading both major assessments and the smaller assignments that lead up to them. To return to the construction metaphor, you will evaluate not only the finished house, but also some (not all) stages of building. For now we will concentrate solely on planning the major culminating texts that students will work toward, often occupying the latter portion of the unit. In so doing, we are thinking about what the house as a whole will ultimately look like.

Conventions and Alternatives

Buildings, like academic knowledge, tend to be constructed through the use of conventional tools. To drive a nail, most carpenters use a hammer. To divide a board in two, most use a saw. School, too, has its conventional tools. Students are likely to write with a pen, pencil, or keyboard and to write on paper. And as I reviewed in previous chapters, in school they most typically use these tools to take notes and write correct answers on exams or to write analytically.

But in constructing buildings and doing school, you don't always follow the established conventions. To get from the ground floor to the second floor of a house, most people would build a straight staircase, or perhaps one with a single right-angle turn near the bottom. But you could also build a spiral staircase, put in an elevator, furnish a firefighter's pole, install exterior vines for climbing in and out of windows, or leave a trampoline by the front door. Most people wouldn't choose these options; they can envision only a house with a straight staircase. But the fact that straight staircases are conventional does not mean that there aren't other ways of getting to the second floor and back.

Schools act in similar ways. There are certain established ways of doing things that often make alternatives hard to see. These well-established methods are deeply ingrained in our ways of conceiving of school, because school was that way when we were kids and has been that way for generations. Under such conditions, it's hard to imagine other options. If things were different, then it just wouldn't be school. What's so difficult to see is that these ways of schooling were developed in response to a different set of circumstances than what exists today and might not fit today's conditions so well.

James Wertsch (1991) illustrates this kind of problem by describing the history of the typewriter keyboard, known as the QWERTY keyboard because of the position of the first keys on the top row. Most people assume that the layout of keys is designed to make typing easier. If you have grown up using computer keyboards rather than typewriters, you probably couldn't imagine any other reason for arranging keys.

Actually, the opposite is true: The QWERTY layout is designed to *slow down* a fast typist. When typewriters were first invented, they were not electronic. The image of a letter on the page came about when a typist struck a key, which was attached to a wire with a letter on the other end. This letter was propelled forward to strike a thin ribbon containing ink, which in turn struck the paper and impressed the letter on it. If a typist went too fast, the wires would get all tangled up. And so the keyboard was arranged to make typing somewhat clumsy and therefore slower and less likely to jam up the typewriter.

In spite of many advances in technology, the QWERTY keyboard has endured, even though most word-processing programs have options that enable you to switch to a more efficient arrangement. We just can't imagine it any other way, and we even assume that the structure is designed to make things better.

Conventions of schooling can act similarly: there are ways of doing things that are part of school, and if we do them differently it just doesn't seem like school anymore. If we envision alternatives, they seem to lack legitimacy because they're different from what we know and are comfortable with. We assume that the established ways of schooling are the best and most efficient ways to educate students, because that's how we've always known them to be.

I want you to think about school as it might be, rather than the way you likely know it to be. I am not trying to prepare you to function comfortably within schools as they exist but am trying instead to get you to rethink what schooling is and how you can make it more authentic, dynamic, purposeful, and fulfilling for both students and teachers. Doing so requires you to think of alternatives to what is conventional.

I used the ways of knowing outlined previously to think of culminating texts that students might produce for different units in the sophomore-year curriculum. Think of yourself as a house builder: Would you build the same house for all people, regardless of the size of their families, their living priorities, the weather conditions that would affect the house, their age, and other factors? Probably not. An unmarried computer programmer on the Florida coast and a married Amish couple with five children and four dogs in northern Pennsylvania would require different abodes. Similarly, different students have different needs that can be met through studying English in your class. Our challenge, then, is to plan assessment so that it allows students of different makeup and background to have the same opportunities for success, for living well.

Although I distinguish between conventional and alternative assessments, both follow the constructivist principles outlined in this book. I am not providing information on how to develop objective tests that ask students to repeat information, distinguish Bucephalus from *Mugil cephalus* (the flathead mullet, in case you're wondering—probably never mounted by Alexander the Great), or otherwise memorize and repeat things that they will soon forget. All of the assessments that follow engage students in the synthesis of previously learned knowledge and the construction of new knowledge. Even though they are nearly ubiquitous in schools, the common means of assessment—true-or-false questions, multiple-choice questions, matching problems, fill-in-the-blank statements, and short-answer questions—play no role in the kind of instruction I outline in this book. If I were to hire you to build my house, I'd watch you work and look at how well some of your completed houses withstand wear and tear, rather than ask you if it's true or false that clapboard siding insulates better than vinyl, especially when the answer might be "It depends."

In producing these texts, your students will inevitably demonstrate their knowledge of characters' names, literary events, and so on. They will do so, however, in service of thinking in complex ways, rather than in the low-level cognitive task of memorization. In advocating a constructivist approach, I am not saying that factual knowledge is unimportant. I am saying rather that students will forget the facts if they don't put them to good use.

Unit Goals as Unit Assessments

I discuss assessment in three chapters. The first identifies what I think of as conventional kinds of assessment. These assessments fit well with the typical structure of school, emphasizing detached analysis of texts that maintains a distant stance from the topic.

Chapter 6 identifies a range of alternative assessments, providing opportunities for learning through exploratory, narrative, connected, multimedia or multigenre, unconventional, and creative modes and forms.

Finally, in Chapter 7 I review ways of evaluating student work produced in response to these prompts.

In making this distinction between conventional and alternative assessments, I am not saying that an analytic paper is never creative, exploratory, and so on. I hope indeed that conventional schooling provides avenues for dynamic engagement with texts and other people, even though many studies of classrooms say that it does not. My distinction between conventional and alternative assessments is based on the findings of recent research in human development, cultural psychology, rhetoric, intelligence, semiotics, gender, and other fields. This research has provided legitimacy, if not widespread acceptance, for considering a broader range of texts and learning processes than English classes customarily provide.

In describing these assessments, I focus primarily on the final form that they will take. In Part III of this book, I shift my attention to the teaching and learning processes that lead to the production of these forms. Traditionally, teaching has focused primarily on the proper look of a final product, without teaching students procedures for creating them. Here, we will first consider what we are working toward and then think about how to teach students how to get there.

Even though I am beginning by describing the ultimate form, it's important to understand that, as they say in architecture, *form follows function*. In other words, the form is not simply a set of things to produce. Rather, the component parts of something like an argument serve the social purpose of persuasion. And so it's important to stress during instruction that the production of a *claim* in an argument is not just something to do so that an essay will get a good mark from a teacher. Rather, it's one part of what people do when trying to convince other people of a point they want to make.

At the same time, some aspects of form are indeed arbitrary. The placement of commas, for instance, varies depending on which set of conventions a writer follows. But back to the broader issue that writing according to convention or genre is a form of social action: Students are often taught issues of form without being provided with good reasons for following them. In requiring students to write five-paragraph themes, for instance, teachers place great emphasis on form—even, in some versions, the specific number of sentences in each paragraph. Why? Because that's what the teacher will grade on, often because that's what's required in the composition textbook, or by the district curriculum, or by the teacher's memory of being taught that way when she was in high school.

I'm asking you to shift attention to the social purposes for writing according to the conventions of particular genres. Why produce an example to support a claim? Because without an example, the claim may be difficult for a reader to understand, or the claim might not persuade the argument's readers. Why link the claim and example with a warrant? Because in order for an argument to be persuasive, the reason that the example supports the claim needs to be unambiguously clear and as convincing as possible.

And so, the criteria I present for writing a good argument (the final form that you will assess) come from learning how to engage in the social action of argumentation. One thing to keep in mind is that not every context calls for the same approach to argumentation. A serious scholar writing for other serious scholars, for instance, usually takes a relatively dry, unemotional approach, elaborating on each point in excruciating, at times tedious, detail. Such an approach might not be persuasive to everyone; some might find it so laboriously meticulous that it ends up being unpersuasive, in part because they dismiss the scholar as a pedantic drone.

In contrast, arguing on a TV talk show usually requires a participant to outshout opponents, listen as little as possible, and employ whatever tactics it takes to get across a simple position, often known as a talking point (or more appropriately, yelling point). Viewers who like to see a good show, to see their opponents treated as dimwits, and to have their opinions verified without the burden of excessive thinking might find their preferred contestants to be triumphantly convincing, even if the aforementioned scholar would consider their exchanges to be anything but persuasive arguments. And so form definitely follows function, even if in school form tends to be an end in and of itself.

When you think about unit goals, you need to keep in mind *both the final form and the social action that produces it.* If you focus on form only, then you run the risk of overlooking the social purposes that the form serves. It's very important to know textual features for particular kinds of writing (or other text)—that is, to know the distinct traits that go into an argument, a response log, a book review, and so on. It's equally important to know that these traits are more than just parts to produce. They enable writers to meet particular social goals. *It's vital, then, to stress the social purposes of any texts that you evaluate, particularly the ways in which they enable writers to communicate with particular groups of readers.*

Each assessment discussed here includes a set of elements. First, students are presented with a description of the general task (to write a personal narrative, to write a literary analysis, etc.). Beneath the statement of the general task is a set of bulleted items. These items serve five primary purposes:

1. to provide students with a clear set of parameters for producing their texts

2. to provide students with an understanding of how their work will be evaluated

3. to provide the teacher with a set of goals to guide his teaching

4. to identify for the teachers what he needs to teach students how to do

5. to provide the teacher with criteria to guide his assessment

The assignments do more than simply tell students what to do. They also outline responsibilities for you in your teaching.

The following assessments fit within the overriding values of school yet can be produced in ways that students find meaningful and that enable them to engage in significant social action. Thinking analytically is a key skill not only for school success but for participating in many of society's activities and professions. It certainly ought to be central to any language arts program offered in school, although I strongly believe it should not be the only kind of thinking and writing evaluated in school. All of the assessments involve some kind of analytic or argumentative writing. Writing of this sort is widely assigned in school and used on high-stakes assessments that involve writing, although it is often reduced to five-paragraph themes both in classrooms and on assessments (see Hillocks 2002; Johnson et al. 2003). As many observers of classrooms have said, instruction in five-paragraph themes, while perhaps teaching some lessons about paragraphing and thesis and support, too often focuses on the production of a form rather than the generation of ideas. *Engagement with content* should be the primary consideration in writing instruction, with attention to form coming later. To borrow an architectural phrase, form should follow function. Yet function should have a form in mind.

Extended Definition

One kind of conventional form that students can learn to produce is the extended definition. Extended definitions serve as the basis for most laws and governing rules, as well as for any kind of scientific classification. Consider, for instance, someone proposing a law to control sexual harassment in the workplace. In order to enforce such a law, you would need to define what it means to harass someone, what it means for that harassment to be of a sexual nature, and what it means to do this in a workplace. You would need to define these terms so that, as clearly as possible, a set of independent observers (e.g., a jury) could say with some certainty whether a particular action was or was not an act of sexual harassment in the workplace. Having a carefully worded, specific, and well-illustrated definition is particularly important in potentially ambiguous cases.

Thematic literature units can provide opportunities to work at developing extended definitions. Often they center on topics such as progress, loyalty, success, justice, courageous action, and other aspects of culture and character that require definition in order to be understood in literature. In our sophomore curriculum, the unit on discrimination would be a good place to include instruction in writing extended definitions. Writing an extended definition of discrimination could help students think through what it means to act in discriminatory ways.

Some literature might present blatant cases of discrimination, such as the legally instituted racism described by Richard Wright in his autobiography *Black Boy*. Other cases are less clear. Through the process of defining and illustrating discrimination, students can help clarify for themselves how to evaluate social interactions they personally engage in and those they observe in their day-to-day lives, the news media, and other sources.

A unit on discrimination could feature sustained attention to the question of how discrimination is defined and illustrated, with classroom activities including personal writing, discussions of literature, and efforts to consider the two in terms of one another. You would also need to provide formal instruction in how to define abstract concepts. I briefly reviewed one approach when talking about criteria for distinguishing a good Mexican restaurant from one that is not so good; a more detailed sequence is described by Johannessen et al. in *Designing and Sequencing Prewriting Activities* (1982). You could provide the following prompt for a culminating text in which students would define and illustrate what it means to discriminate:

> Throughout the unit we have considered the effects of discrimination on both the person who discriminates and the person who is discriminated against. We have looked at questions of discrimination in a variety of situations, using examples from current events, from your personal experiences and observations, and from literature. In some cases, there has been disagreement on what counts as discrimination. Your task is to write an essay in which you provide an extended definition of discrimination. To do so, include the following:
>
> - a general introduction in which you provide an overview for your definition
>
> - a set of *criteria* or rules that state clearly what discrimination is and is not
>
> - for each criterion, an *example* from literature, current events, or your personal experiences that illustrates the rule at work; at least half of your examples must come from the literature studied in class
>
> - for each criterion, a *counterexample* from literature, current events, or your personal experiences that appears to meet the conditions of the rule yet that lacks some essential ingredient; at least half of your counterexamples must come from the literature studied in class
>
> - for each example and counterexample, a *warrant* that clearly explains why the rule is or is not being met

- for your whole argument, a *counterargument* expressing the viewpoint of someone who might disagree with you
- for the counterargument, a *rebuttal* in which you defend your position
- conventional grammar, spelling, punctuation, and usage throughout your essay
- evidence of having written at least one rough draft that has been submitted for peer evaluation

I should reiterate that these bulleted items serve a variety of purposes. The most obvious purpose is to inform students of what they are responsible for and what you will grade. They also specify a set of responsibilities for you as a teacher. If you are going to grade something, then you need to teach students how to do it.

You might want students to narrow this topic so that instead of defining discrimination broadly, they define it under more particular circumstances. If the texts focus on issues of race, gender, physical handicap, physical appearance, or some other more specific topic, you could provide the opportunity for students to define discrimination in these arenas alone. Doing so would help to make the task more manageable. Given that many adults have difficulty making such distinctions—for instance, the National Organization for Women's (at present) unresolved challenge to the Augusta National Country Club's (home to the Masters golf tournament) men-only membership rule—it seems reasonable to help young people narrow the topic to a single area that they find accessible and can get a handle on.

Literary Analysis

Literary analysis is, for many English teachers, the bread and butter of writing instruction. In most cases, however, students are evaluated on their ability to write an analysis of a literary work already studied in class. Under such circumstances, students inevitably rely on the teacher's interpretation to form the substance of their own analysis. They are evaluated, then, on their skill at reproducing the teacher's analysis to the teacher's satisfaction and the low-level cognitive work that such mimicry entails.

This approach does not serve them well as a tool for analyzing new literature. Indeed, it suggests that the teacher's role is to provide a good interpretation for students to replicate on the assessment. Consider, however, what would happen if students were evaluated on their ability to analyze a work of literature that they have never seen before. Not only would this approach evaluate their independent analytic abilities, but it would suggest to the teacher that the purpose of instruction is to teach analytic skills rather than to provide a preferred interpretation, no matter how insightful.

In other words, it shifts the focus of instructional attention from declarative knowledge to procedural knowledge.

Let's say, then, that in the sophomore unit on coming-of-age literature, the teacher helps students see a common pattern in such stories. Coming-of-age stories typically provide some illustration of a protagonist's immature behavior at the outset, move to a critical experience that results in a major realization, and conclude with a transformation to more mature behavior by the end. Class activities could focus on seeing how protagonists negotiate the threshold of this critical experience and thinking about what kinds of transformations they undergo. As part of this literary analysis, students could engage in reflection on personal transformations they have made following from critical experiences, thus recognizing this pattern in their own lives.

The teacher could then evaluate students' ability to recognize and interpret this pattern with an essay based on a choice of literary works, none of which has been covered in class. Their task is then to identify and analyze the transformation that they see in the independently read story, possibly through a culminating text produced in response to this prompt:

From the literary choices provided, read one work of literature and write an essay in which you analyze the protagonist's coming-of-age experience. In your essay, make sure that you

- provide a general thesis for the paper, explaining the protagonist's primary transformation during the course of the story

- describe the protagonist's immature behavior at the beginning of the story, including specific examples from the text

- describe clearly the key event that causes the character to change; in doing so, explain why this event, rather than others in the story, causes the protagonist to come of age

- describe the significant changes taking place in the protagonist following the coming-of-age experience, including specific examples from the text

- draw a conclusion about how people change as a result of significant events and how these changes can be considered as a coming-of-age

- follow rules of conventional grammar, spelling, punctuation, and usage throughout your essay

- give evidence of having written at least one rough draft that has been submitted for peer evaluation

Argumentation

Argumentation is another staple of school writing, a common form of writing in many professions, and the way in which most conflicting points of view come into contact. In order to prove your point, you need to argue it; that is, you need to

- have a thesis (e.g., a belief that conflict between peer groups in school must be resolved)

- support it with a set of claims (e.g., that antagonism has increased, tension is greater in hallways, there is less unity at school functions, administrators have taken steps to provide greater security, etc.)

- back each claim with evidence (e.g., that fights have grown more frequent, students self-segregate in the cafeteria, some students have posted hateful websites, administrators have hired additional security guards, etc.)

- anticipate a counterargument (e.g., that the problem is not so great because for the most part, students in the school are safe; that the school cannot afford the cost of yet more security guards; that increased security guards make the school a hostile environment for learning and socialization)

- rebut the counterargument (e.g., that the problem must be addressed before a crisis takes place, rather than after it happens)

Even if you never become a lawyer or serve on a political talk show panel, knowing careful argumentation can help you see clearly on issues you care about yet over which people disagree.

Many different parts of the English curriculum can serve as opportunities for instruction in argumentation. Students can argue for interpretations of literature or for ways to view literary movements. For the sophomore curriculum, the unit on conflict with authority is a good occasion for students to argue for a particular interpretation of a character's actions. Once again, they will do so with a literary work that is new to them, rather than one that the class has already discussed. And once again, your role as teacher then becomes to teach interpretive and argumentative strategies, rather than to provide good interpretations. The students could write their arguments in response to the following prompt:

From the literary choices provided, read one work of literature and write an argument in which you analyze the protagonist's conflict with an authority figure. In your argument, evaluate the protagonist's approach to resolving the conflict. In producing your argument, make sure that you do the following:

- provide a governing *thesis* in which you explain the conflict and provide a general evaluation of the protagonist's actions

- support this thesis with a set of *claims*—that is, the reasons that support your interpretation

- back each claim with *evidence* from the story

- anticipate and explain a *counterargument*, which is a disagreement with your interpretation

- rebut the *counterargument* with additional reasons in support of your argument

- follow rules of conventional grammar, spelling, punctuation, and usage throughout your essay

- give evidence of having written at least one rough draft that has been submitted for peer evaluation

Research Report

Another conventional kind of assessment found in school is the research report. Such reports are produced in many disciplines and professions, and they often are required in school curricula. A good report on a significant topic can make an important contribution to people's knowledge about issues that matter to them. These reports are focused on facts but use the facts in service of constructing knowledge about a topic.

In English classes, students could write research reports on issues related to the unit concept they are studying. The Shakespeare unit from the sophomore curriculum, for instance, could involve students in doing library research on the historical context of *Julius Caesar*. This research could serve a variety of purposes: evaluating the historical accuracy of the play, learning more about particular characters of interest, informing an understanding of the play's plot, and so on.

For the discrimination unit, students could conduct research on the civil rights movement, the women's suffrage movement, or any variety of discrimination battles waged in local, U.S., or world history. By sharing these reports with their classmates—orally, through a website, or through other avenues—students could provide a good context for discussing questions of discrimination that arise in the literature.

Research reports tend to follow a particular written formula in schools. This traditional means of presentation was established before other media became available to students. I think that, in circumstances where resources allow, teachers ought to take advantage of opportunities that students have to use computers, videos, and related technologies to produce their research reports. The form of the report, then, might vary if students have the capability to produce a documentary film instead of a written report.

A research report might be written in response to the following prompt:

> We have been studying questions of discrimination in the literature we have read and in your personal knowledge of the world. For your culminating project, produce a research report on some historical instance of discrimination. The topic may be of international significance (e.g., apartheid in South Africa), important in American history (e.g., the denial of women's right to vote), or of local or community interest (e.g., a skateboarding restriction on community sidewalks). Your report should meet the following requirements:
>
> - You may produce it in any form of your choice: writing, film, interview recordings, computer graphics, and so on, or any combination of these forms.
> - The report should be guided by some perspective you take on the issue.
> - If written, your report should include a minimum of one thousand words (roughly four typed pages).
> - If produced in some other medium or combination of media, your report should require at least a ten-minute presentation.
> - Your presentation should exhibit some clear organizational pattern that follows from your report's thesis.
> - The information you provide must come from a minimum of five sources and may include secondary sources (i.e., sources such as books or encyclopedias that someone else has written and that you take information from) and/or primary sources (i.e., sources that you personally investigate, such as interviews you conduct, observations you make, or documents you study).

Summary

Conventional assessments of the sort usually outlined in state and district curriculum guides do not need to be reductive and needn't make school learning an exercise in memorization, testing, and forgetting. By working paradigmatically in conventional genres, students have rich opportunities to learn about themselves, social history, literary themes, and other illuminating topics. The key is to focus on content over form initially and to teach procedures that students may use to guide their own inquiries.

6 *Goals for Unconventional Writing Assignments*

Now we'll take a look at some alternative kinds of culminating texts that can form the basis of assessment. While seldom assessed in schools, they are every bit as legitimate in terms of how people think, act, communicate, and represent meaning throughout society.

Exploratory Thinking and Writing

Previously I reviewed Douglas Barnes' (1992) views of exploratory and final-draft uses of speech. Much of what you evaluate in school will be final drafts. One problem with schooling in general is that is focuses on these final products without providing opportunities for students to engage in—and be rewarded for—the informal, tentative, experimental processes that lead to them. Following are four kinds of exploratory work you can evaluate: portfolios, journals, rough drafts, and student-generated questions about literature.

Portfolio

The *process portfolio* is a tool through which you can evaluate students on what they have learned about their learning during your course, often through reflection on exploratory texts they have produced on their way to more formal products. You could also use portfolios in individual units.

Course-Long Portfolio Preparation

I earlier proposed that a process portfolio could serve as one of the final evaluations for a whole course of study. If you make this choice, you need to attend to portfolio preparation during each unit of study. For each unit, students should identify exploratory work that has generated significant new learning and include it in the portfolio they are preparing for the course as a whole. You won't evaluate the exhibits that students select until you evaluate the whole portfolio; that is, you won't have students turn these in for grades during the individual units.

You could, however, periodically devote class time to having students discuss which of their exploratory efforts have been significant learning experiences, and work with them on the process for preparing a reflective statement for an individual exhibit. In this way, you would be readying students for their course-long portfolio throughout the year or semester, giving exploratory work attention and value in everyday instruction.

Portfolios for Individual Units

Following the ideas of the course-long process portfolio described in Chapter 4, you could have students keep shorter portfolios for individual units of study, or perhaps for each marking period. These would require more frequent selections of exhibits gathered from a more limited pool of possible items.

Journal

Students can also keep journals in which they think through their engagement with the unit topics, with exploratory writing serving as the medium for their thinking. Writing used this way can serve as a tool for discovering new ideas. Journals come in a variety of forms, such as personal journals, reading logs, and dialogue journals.

Personal Journal

A personal journal is an open-ended opportunity for students to write whatever they think or feel in response to the unit's content and processes, however they might be experiencing them. Ideally, the journal will involve a strong component of reflection, of thinking through ideas and emotions, of developing a personal response to the unit. It should not simply summarize readings or discussions. You can make reflection part of the requirements of the assignment and include attention to reflection in your assessment.

Many educators believe that *getting to know their students* is essential to teaching effectively, and that all good teaching starts with efforts to get students to reveal important things about themselves. Journals, memoirs, and other introspective writing are often used not just for the purpose of having students reflect on their experiences but for the purpose of enabling teachers to learn more about their students' lives.

Some people find such reflection to be invasive. Some parents, for instance, protest strongly when teachers require introspective writing. They say that a student's personal life is of no importance in learning an academic discipline and is none of a teacher's business. Some students are very private and don't wish to produce writing on personal topics that others will read about.

While not solving all problems, and perhaps creating new ones, journals may serve as useful tools for many teachers and students for thinking through their ideas about a topic. One solution is to make them optional, so that students who benefit from them will have the opportunity, while students whose families discourage introspection in school will not be caught in a conflict. You could present the journal as follows:

> Keep a journal in which you think through thoughts and feelings that you have in response to the material we study, the class discussions and activities that we engage in, and any other experience you have with the unit topic. The following issues will be factors in the way I grade your journal:
>
> - Your journal does not need to follow the conventions of textbook English. Rather, the purpose is to think about the class without worrying about the form your thoughts take.
>
> - Do not simply summarize literature we read in the class. While you need to refer to these texts, the primary purpose of your journal is to think about your response to them, rather than to provide summaries of what they say. In other words, your journal should focus on how you have engaged with the literature.
>
> - You are welcome, though not required, to reflect on personal issues that occur to you in relation to your consideration of the literature.
>
> - Your journal should include a minimum of five hundred words of writing (roughly two typed pages) per week. For each entry, put the date of the writing at the beginning.
>
> - Keep in mind that *I am required to share any thoughts or suggestions of violence, suicide, substance abuse, family abuse, or other harmful behavior with the school counselors.*
>
> - If there are any pages in your journal that you do not want me to read, please mark them with an *X* at the top.

These last two items raise one of the trickiest questions about journals: how to treat issues of confidentiality. You want students to write honestly in their journals, yet they know you will read them. You are also often obligated to report destructive behavior to parents and/or school authorities. Students need to know how you are going to read their journals and what you will do with certain kinds of information. Often, students use assignments like this as a way of asking for help when they don't know of any other way.

Reading Log

A more structured kind of journal, with a more specific purpose, is the reading log. I described double-entry reading logs in Chapter 2 when illustrating instructional scaffolds. Reading logs can also have a less structured appearance, with students simply writing in exploratory ways in response to the literature. The purpose of such journals is to encourage students to attend carefully to the language of the literature and to read reflectively, pausing to think about particular passages before moving along, or perhaps reading longer sections and writing about the text in retrospect. A reading log could follow from a prompt like this:

> Keep a reading log in response to the literature we are studying during this unit. To keep your log,
>
> - Write informally in response to the literature read for class. Your writing may come in response to anything you find interesting, puzzling, compelling, challenging, or otherwise worthy of your consideration. Feel free to pose questions without answers; think through your ideas through the process of writing; rant, rave, or respond in whatever way best helps you to think about what matters to you in the literature.
> - Write a minimum of three entries for each work of literature studied.
> - Remember that your journal does not need to follow the conventions of textbook English. Rather, the purpose is to think about the literature without worrying about the form your thoughts take.
>
> Keep in mind that *I am required to share any thoughts or suggestions of violence, suicide, substance abuse, family abuse, or other harmful behavior with the school counselors.*

Dialogue Journal

A dialogue journal is a journal shared by two or more people, where they carry on a discussion about a shared topic. In this case, the discussion is conducted through written exchanges, and the topic is the unit they are studying. Traditionally, dialogue journals have been handwritten, with students physically handing over the journal to their partner(s) when they have finished their conversational turn. These partners could conceivably include anyone who's interested in participating, such as the teacher, parents, and students who are not enrolled in the class.

Dialogue journals can also be kept through electronic mail, without the unwieldy problem of carrying the journal around and handing it to one another at the completion of a turn. Electronic dialogue journals can also include any number of participants. The idea, in any case, is to provide a forum for discussion beyond what the classroom offers.

A dialogue journal might be prompted as follows:

> With at least one other person, maintain a dialogue journal in which you discuss the issues raised in class. You may keep your dialogue journal in a regular writing notebook, or you may provide printouts of a discussion you maintain over email. In keeping your dialogue journal, remember the following:

- Your journal does not need to follow the conventions of textbook English. Rather, the purpose is to think about the class without worrying about the form your thoughts take.

- Do not simply summarize literature we read in the class. Your discussion should include questions, analysis, reflection, and evaluation. It should be evident that you are learning something new through your dialogue.

- Make sure that you include attention to each text studied in the unit.

- You are welcome, though not required, to reflect on personal issues that occur to you in relation to your consideration of the literature.

- All participants in your dialogue journal should make roughly equal contributions.

- *I am required to share any thoughts or suggestions of violence, suicide, substance abuse, family abuse, or other harmful behavior with the school counselors.*

Rough Drafts

Another way to evaluate exploratory thinking is to have students turn in rough drafts of their work. You can do this in several ways.

For each piece of extended writing they do, students could be required to produce one or two rough drafts. For each of these drafts, they could get in small groups to evaluate one another's work and provide recommendations for improvement.

An alternative is for them to turn these drafts in to you for feedback. You could also have students seek a reader from outside class, including their parents or other significant adults or knowledgeable readers. Keep in mind that in school, teachers are almost exclusively the evaluators of students' work. Having students write for others can help them learn about the notion of audience, which many rhetoricians stress is essential to effective writing and communication.

When students turn in final drafts, have them staple all outlines, notes, drafts, and feedback to the formal version that you will evaluate. This way, you can track their progress and ensure that they are working at extended composition with their writing. Evaluating these drafts should merely consist of making sure that students have done them. If the goal is to allow preliminary work to be exploratory, then putting a grade on its quality is questionable.

Asking Questions

Students rarely pose questions in school. Observers of classrooms have found some rather astonishing things about how frequently students initiate inquiries of their own. In one study, for instance, students asked, on the

average, one question each month. Most questions students ask are procedural, such as how long a paper should be or if they may go to the bathroom. It's hard to imagine establishing a school culture based on principles
of inquiry and constructivism when students so rarely pose the questions
that guide their learning.

Simply telling students to ask questions is often frustrating because they
have been conditioned to view school as a place where every question has
a correct answer. In school, then, when you ask students to ask questions,
they often come up with questions that sound a lot like the ones you'll find
at the end of their textbook chapters: Which character did what? What was
the name of the character who did such and such? The mirror they provide
for schooling is not one I find attractive to look into.

One way you can evaluate students is to teach them to ask questions. I
see this as an issue of exploratory talk because they will need to talk about
the texts in order to generate their questions, and the questions they pose
ought to inquire into the open-ended territory that exploratory talk helps
them investigate. For now, I will simply give an example of how to present
this challenge to students. Later I will give a better idea of how to prepare
students for doing it.

I created this assignment for the study of *The Outsiders* in a unit on gangs,
cliques, and peer-group pressure, but it can easily be adapted to any unit. The
assignment is somewhat unique in that, instead of evaluating students on
their construction of meaning after reading, it places the job of literary discussion entirely in their hands. After many years of leading class discussions
myself—relying on my own clever questions to guide our analysis—I shifted
this responsibility to students. I still led some discussions, but primarily for
the purpose of helping them develop procedures for leading their own. I then
provided them with an assignment such as the following:

> To discuss S. E. Hinton's *The Outsiders*, the class will organize into six
> small groups, with each group being responsible for leading a discussion
> of two chapters of the novel. Each group will be responsible for conducting
> a class discussion on its chapters for one full period. To lead your class,
> you may adopt any format you wish: regular English class, nonviolent talk
> show, town hall meeting, courtroom, or other mode of your choice. Your
> discussion should involve all of the following:
>
> - Each group member should take a roughly equal part in leading the
>   discussion.
>
> - You should make an effort to include each other class member in
>   your discussion.
>
> - The questions you pose should not ask for factual information
>   from the story, unless those facts serve to help explore open-ended
>   questions (i.e., those without a single correct answer).

- The questions you pose should include at least one of each of the following categories:

  inferences about characters or events within the text (e.g., Which character do you believe that the author has the greatest sympathy for? Why?)

  generalizations from the text to society at large (e.g., Where in our school do we see characters like those in the novel?)

  the *effects of literary form or technique* (e.g., Why is the novel called *The Outsiders*?)

  the *purpose of a particular event* in terms of the text's meaning (e.g., What do you think is the most significant point in the novel? Why?)

  evaluations of the literature (e.g., What parts of the story do you like best and least? Why?)

  emotions that students have in response to the story (e.g., Did anything in the novel make you angry? Please explain.)

  personal connections to the story (e.g., Which character from the novel do you most identify with? Why?)

- During the discussion, you should also work at getting students to elaborate on their initial comments.

Narrative Knowing

Recall Jerome Bruner's (1986) contention that narrative knowing, while typically overlooked in schools, has just as crucial a role in human history as paradigmatic knowing. Much literature is presented around some kind of story, one that portrays something about the human condition. Often readers relate to literature by recounting a personal story that parallels the issues depicted in the literature. One thing that students can do, then, as a way of engaging with the unit themes is to write, act, or otherwise produce a personal narrative in which they relate a significant event from their own lives. For the hypothetical sophomore curriculum I have developed, these events would involve the negotiation of a threshold, with particular attention to one of the unit concepts.

Let's say, for instance, that the students are studying the unit on conflict with authority. Their task might be:

Write about a personal experience in which you had a conflict with someone in authority. The authority figure might have been an adult (a parent, teacher, coach, etc.) or a peer in an authority position (a team captain, student government leader, etc.). Through your narrative, you should convey the following:

- your relationship with the person with whom you came in conflict
- the nature of your conflict
- how both you and the other person viewed the conflict
- if you resolved it, how; if you didn't, what happened
- what you learned through the experience

You do not need to explain these things in this order and don't need to announce or label any of them (that is, you don't need to have a paragraph beginning, "My relationship with so-and-so was . . ."). Rather, you should, at some point in your narrative, relate these things in some way.

Connected Knowing

Previously I reviewed ways in which schools do not provide many opportunities for relational or connected learning. Here I suggest a few ways in which you can plan assessments that take connected knowing into account.

Collaborative Learning

One way you can be responsive to connected knowers is to provide opportunities for collaboration on graded work. For instance, you can allow students to conduct their research reports (see page 81) or creative and multimedia projects (see page 59) in teams. You can also plan to include collaborative learning in the activities that lead to the production of culminating texts.

Affective Response

Attention to students' emotional responses to literature is also minimized in schools. Through the use of journals, student-generated discussions, narratives, and other kinds of assessment, you can increase the opportunities for students' affective responses to literature to be included in your evaluations of their schoolwork.

Exploratory Learning Opportunities

Connected knowing is often associated with tentative, exploratory learning. I have reviewed a number of possible ways to allow for exploratory expression in assessed schoolwork: journals, student-generated discussions, process-oriented writing instruction, and so on.

Multimedia or Multigenre Productions

Gardner's (1983) work on multiple intelligences suggests that students ought to have opportunities to generate knowledge through texts and processes that move beyond conventional schools' emphasis on analytic writing. Much of this chapter provides ideas on how to extend students' opportunities for response and interpretation beyond detached analysis. I would also argue that students ought to be able to work in media other than writing. Some of the most remarkable work I have seen from high school students has come through multimedia productions, including art, music, dance, live or videotaped performance, and various combinations of these modes and others.

I should add that some rather intriguing multimedia productions do not necessarily reveal deep engagement with the literature. In one class I observed, for instance, a student baked a cake and decorated it in the fashion of a story's setting, and the class then ate it. It was never clear what the student had learned from this process, although the cake was mighty tasty. You might want to ask students to either write or verbally present an explanation of their project's significance in order to help you evaluate it.

My own studies of multimedia composing present compelling evidence that multimedia compositions can provide a powerful medium for high-level engagement with literature (see O'Donnell-Allen and Smagorinsky 1999; Smagorinsky 1991, 1995, 2001; Smagorinsky and Coppock 1994, 1995a, 1995b; Smagorinsky and O'Donnell-Allen 1998a, 1998b, 2000; Smagorinsky, Zoss, and O'Donnell-Allen 2005). They can also serve a very important function in students' interpretive process, helping them generate images of literature that can then form the basis for a response or interpretation.

Here is one very open-ended assignment that you can adapt to a variety of units.

> You have read a complex work of literature in Shakespeare's *Julius Caesar*. To show what you have learned through your engagement with this play, create an interpretive text in any form of your choice: collage, painting, poetry, music, drama, sculpture, performance art, or other textual form. You are also welcome to combine forms to produce your text. Furthermore, you may use different forms within a form—that is, you can include a gravestone with epitaph, a haiku, a song, an encyclopedia entry, a movie review, and so on, all within a single interpretive text. Keep the following in mind when producing your text:
>
> - It should in some way depict your understanding of the play. This understanding might be about any of the following:
>
>   the play's characters and their actions and relationships
>
>   how the play has helped you learn something about yourself and your world
>
>   Roman history
>
>   Shakespeare as a playwright
>
>   other topic of your choice

- It should make some kind of reference to the play, even if it focuses on you and your current world.

- You may produce your text individually or in a group of any size up to five.

- You will have two class periods in which to work on your text and must do all additional work outside class.

- You must prepare a three- to five-minute presentation of your text to the class in which you explain its significance and what it says about your understanding of the play.

Unconventional Genres (for School)

Another type of assessment is to have students write (perhaps in combination with other media) in genres that are not ordinarily produced by students for school. The following list is hardly exhaustive and is intended primarily to prime the pump of your imagination. When making assignments, you need to identify the traits that should be involved in such texts, specify what they are, and make yourself responsible for teaching students how to produce them.

Book or Film Review

Movie reviews are available through a variety of media, with newspapers, television, and the Internet providing countless examples of the genre. Students could study the genre and its elements and produce reviews of texts they read in class. This kind of assessment might be particularly useful if you choose a book club arrangement for a unit or if you have opportunities to publish the reviews for other students to read.

Guide Book

Students could also produce a guide book. In a unit on peer groups, for instance, students could write a guide book for incoming students. The book would review the different social groups among the student body. The book could include pictures, descriptions, interviews, and other ways to characterize the different groups inhabiting the school. I would caution students that they should try to present each group in a fair and respectful manner; students are often tempted to portray groups they don't belong to in unflattering ways.

Letter to the Editor

Students could write letters to the editor of a publication in which they express their opinions on some topic of importance to them. This task might follow from instruction in expository or persuasive writing, but students could see that letters to the editor often lack the formality of the kinds of analytic writing they learn to do in school. If you've read many letters to the editor, you know they also often lack any semblance of thoughtful logic. By having students read one another's letters to the editor and respond to them, you may help them avoid producing the kinds of rants often published in newspapers.

Children's Book

Students could produce a children's book related to the unit's theme. For the unit on *Julius Caesar*, for instance, students could retell a scene from the play, presenting it in the style of a set of children's books that they study. The assignment could conceivably bridge two different units, with students producing their book in the form of a parody.

Other

My intention here is to help you think about alternative kinds of texts that students could produce, rather than to provide you with an all-inclusive list. The possibilities are virtually limitless. I'm counting on you to think of others. One of my former students, for instance, had her students design the covers for hypothetical compact discs, with themes related to the literary themes they were studying. I was delighted to hear of her idea, for it meant that she was taking the principles from her preservice education and using them to generate new ideas about teaching.

Creative Writing

Students can also generate creative work of their own, produced in a variety of forms. By creative writing, I mean works of poetry, fiction, drama, and other fictive modes. I also assume that any other kind of writing that students do can include creative elements. Following are two examples.

Writing Related to the Unit Concept

Students can produce a poem, play, story, and so on, that concerns the unit concept. They might, for instance, produce some kind of literary work that includes a conflict with authority. You could either have students produce a particular form (poem, story, etc.) or leave the assignment open-ended, allowing them to choose their own medium or combination of genres.

Evaluating creative writing has proven to be difficult to many teachers who find it too subjective to assess. As a result, they don't assign it. Eliminating creative work from the curriculum because it's hard to grade, however, can limit the ways in which students learn through their engagement with literature and other texts. Instead of disallowing open-ended thinking and writing, you should think of open-minded ways to assess it. The following assignment is one way to specify assessment criteria without compromising the open-ended manner in which students may proceed:

During the unit we have read a variety of literary works concerned with the theme of conflict with authority. Now it is your turn to write one. Using a medium of your choice, or a combination of media, produce a literary work that includes a conflict with an authority figure. In producing your literature, keep in mind the following:

- You may use any literary form or combination of literary forms.

- You may supplement your writing with other media: graphics, sound, movement, and so on.

- Your text should in some way involve a conflict with an authority figure.

- While you needn't resolve the conflict (many conflicts go unresolved), you do need to show in some way the aftermath of the conflict and its consequences.

Genres

Students can also produce literature in a particular genre. In the sophomore unit on parody, for instance, they can both study parodies and create them. An assignment that George Hillocks thought up long ago still works quite well. The idea is for students to study a writer with a distinctive style, such as Edgar Allan Poe or J. D. Salinger. After characterizing that style, the students parody it with a kind of text that provides a humorous contrast, such as a children's story or nursery rhyme. Following a careful reading of Poe's style and characterization of his tendencies—dark images, macabre themes, recurring terms—students could retell Humpty Dumpty, Jack and Jill, or another children's story using his style. The prompt for students might appear as follows:

Take a Mother Goose rhyme or other children's story and retell it in the style of Edgar Allan Poe. In your parody,

- remain faithful to the main elements of the children's rhyme or story

- tell the story in a voice that uses elements of Edgar Allan Poe's narrative style, including:

  common themes

  typical sentence structures

  recurring words

  method of narration (e.g., first person)

  narrative perspective

- exaggerate these elements so that they are clearly recognizable and humorous

Summary

My focus on detailing assignments is only part of the story. Each bulleted item in each assignment is also an assignment to myself: I have a responsibility to teach the students how to produce the elements I'm asking for. I focus on this attention to process in later chapters, but I first turn to a vexing question for teachers: how to evaluate open-ended student work.

7 *Responding to Student Writing*

The issue of responding to student writing received a lot of attention in the 1980s (see, e.g., Anson 1989; Freedman 1987) but has not been the subject of great attention lately—at least, among people who write about such things. Teachers, on the other hand, deal with this issue every day. Several considerations figure into the ways in which you read and respond to the work that students do, both during their composing processes and when they submit papers for a grade.

In-Process Response

Before the 1970s, most response to student writing came solely from the teacher, and only at the end of the final draft that students would submit for evaluation. One great contribution of the process movement was the idea that students benefit from feedback as they work, rather than just at the end. This shift is not simply organizational but implies a change in philosophy about learners. By providing in-process feedback to writers and other composers, teachers become more oriented to the growth of the learners than to the perceived quality of their final products. This shift is consistent with the constructivist approach I encourage in this book, in which the goal is to help learners understand how to produce the most satisfying and communicative text and, in the process, develop in terms of both their literacy skills and sense of self.

The exact nature of the composing process can be difficult to characterize. I could argue, for instance, that I began writing this book in 1976 when I first began teaching, and that I've gone through thirty years of prewriting, including two formal, if provisional, versions (Smagorinsky 2002; Smagorinsky and Gevinson 1989). Or I could say that I began as a college sophomore when I was tested on the identity of Bucephalus and rebelled against factoid-oriented teaching. Or, perhaps it all started when I was in high school and a friend and I produced a photo documentary on migrant workers in New Jersey and Florida (which required a spring-break trip to this remote research site). Perhaps instead I began this project when, as an elementary school kid, I developed a cartoon series, "Pooh-Cat the Polecat and Pee-Wee the Squirrel," the adventures of whom I'm sure are still in my mom's attic somewhere.

For school purposes, "prewriting" often has an official beginning and end, circumscribed by the teacher's allocation to time to this "stage" of the writing process. I use quotations around these terms because in practice, they are not so discrete. At the moment, for instance, I'm writing off the top of my head, based on what I know from years of teaching, and thinking about teaching, English. But perhaps something will occur to me as I write that will serve as the basis for something I write later. (So far, no such luck.) It's possible, then, that I'm not only writing but also prewriting. And the parameters of that experience are difficult to establish, in that I may have begun this thought twenty years ago and may never complete it, at least to my satisfaction. So much for *stages* of writing.

My point here is that attention to learning processes makes for very untidy conceptions of teaching. If we think of meaningful compositions as provisional texts in a long-term project of making sense of the world, then what students write for school may or may not contribute to that effort. If students' lives outside school are considered irrelevant to textual interpretation, then I imagine that school writing is mostly irrelevant and disruptive to that quest for meaning. If a lifetime of prewriting becomes available for students in their school compositions, then classrooms may provide more fulfilling experiences for young people. If this book has made sense to you so far, you will likely agree with this proposition. If so, then you may find the following ways of responding to student texts as part of their composition process to be useful.

Response at Conception

One way to enable students to get feedback and to explore ideas collaboratively is to have them work initially in small groups on a problem similar to the one that they will later approach in greater complexity, perhaps independently. Let's say, for instance, that you have designed a thematic unit on loss of innocence, with J. D. Salinger's *Catcher in the Rye* serving as the unit's major work. Among your unit goals is the composition of a parody of Holden Caulfield's narration. Most students are familiar with parody through their experiences with the media: *Saturday Night Live* sketches and films by *SNL* alumni, Weird Al Yankovic songs, films that spoof various genres, and other performances that they have enjoyed and shared with friends.

Using their prior knowledge as a basis, and providing some information about the features of parody—emphasis on typical traits, exaggeration— you can have students work together in generating a topic for a parody and planning how to carry it out. At this stage, students might focus on something brief and distinctive, such as TV commercials for trucks, technical schools, finance companies, deodorants, or other commonly advertised products. (I tend to discourage beer commercials, even if they're fun and easy to parody, just to keep the parents at bay.)

By working collaboratively on an open-ended problem of this sort, the students get immediate feedback on their ideas. At times this feedback might be corrective; at times it might be a coconstruction of an idea; at times it might be supportive. The point is that at this early stage in students' efforts to try something new, they work in a setting in which they may engage in exploratory, experimental, playful discussion through which they mutually arrive at ideas that they put into practice. Further, they receive immediate feedback on everything they say from the other members of their group. By including such opportunities throughout the composing process, teachers build response to composing into students' efforts during their work.

Response to Drafts

Peer Feedback

Another in-process opportunity for response to student compositions is to provide peer feedback following the completion of a draft. Many people advocate using a small-group response session so that students may critique one another's work. There are two advantages to this approach. First, students get feedback on their compositions that helps them in the next draft. Second, students get experience as critical readers that may help them in reading and revising their own work.

Response groups may be conducted in a number of ways. One way is simply to have pairs of students exchange their work and provide each other holistic evaluations, either through marginal commentary or writing conferences. The same approach can work with larger groups, with students reading and evaluating more than one composition.

You might also assign particular reading roles. Let's say that you've taught a unit on the British Lake poets, and among the students' tasks is to write an argumentative essay interpreting a poem such as Keats' "Ode on a Grecian Urn." After supporting their understanding of both how to interpret such a poem and how to write a critical argument, you could have students produce a draft of their interpretive essay. You could then organize the students into groups of roughly four and have them evaluate in turn three qualities on which the paper will be assessed. They can go through the following procedures, which perhaps you've written on the board or provided on a handout:

1. Each student passes his paper to the person on the left. After receiving a classmate's paper, each person reads for a specific quality such as general argumentative structure, including the presence of an overall thesis, a related set of claims, and examples from the poem and/or other British romantic poetry supporting each claim.

Each critical reader makes marginal comments to help the writer sharpen the argument according to this criterion.

2.   Students rotate their papers again to the left so that each is reading the paper written by the person she is sitting across from. Again, the students have a specific responsibility, this time critiquing the paper for the degree to which the claims are orchestrated to support the general thesis and to which the evidence convincingly supports the claims. Again, each reader makes marginal comments.

3.   Students rotate their papers to the left a final time. For this reading, they evaluate for coherence, including the writer's attention to form and mechanics, transitions between paragraphs, and other qualities that contribute to a fluent presentation.

4.   Students then receive their papers back and have an opportunity to discuss their papers with one another before beginning their next set of revisions.

This approach might require some training and practice, particularly if students are unfamiliar with responding to one another's compositions. Students also do not always provide mature advice to one another, so you should caution each writer to evaluate the feedback and incorporate only that which he judges to be valuable.

Writing Conferences

Writing conferences are simply meetings between a teacher and a student to discuss either a piece of writing or a collection of papers. The main advantage is the personal attention that each student receives in terms of her writing growth. The main problems concern the amount of class time (or out-of-school time) that writing conferences require and the managerial issues that follow from a teacher's dedication of undivided attention to a single student. If a class includes twenty-five students, and if a single writing conference occupies about ten minutes, that's roughly four hours of conferences that a teacher must conduct in order to reach everyone. Writing conferences, then, occupy about a week's worth of instruction. In addition to taking up a great deal of instructional time, they require the teacher to provide some sort of worthwhile activity that the remainder of the class can pursue without being supervised closely.

Writing conferences tend to be conducted in one of two ways. One is a nondirectional approach in which the student does most of the talking and the teacher primarily poses questions. The idea here is for the student to develop agency and ownership with respect to writing and for the teacher to provide a supportive role in the conferences. The other approach is more directive, with the teacher providing an evaluation and recommendations for how the student might improve.

Response to "Final" Products

I put the word *final* in quotation marks because I don't think that a text is ever finished, any more than a person ever is. Rather, a composition—one that has any meaning and authenticity—is tied to a person's growing sense of self. It serves as a temporary, provisional statement of where the person is at the point of composition. It further contributes to the growth process that leads to that sense of self by providing an opportunity to explore and represent ideas and beliefs.

A final draft, then, is final only for purposes of assessment; if it has any meaning, it then serves as a point of reflection and further revision of the ideas—not, in all likelihood, in the text itself but through more private rumination. In this sense, a final draft is also prewriting for the next effort at meaning construction. In the world of school, however, grades matter, and so teachers typically assess final drafts. When doing so, you must think about how to evaluate correctness and how to design a rubric to help you assign grades.

Correctness

Let me start by relating an experience I often had as a younger, more single person attending parties. I'd be doing normal party things—eating, drinking, surveying the field—and would strike up a conversation with a woman who came within range. Inevitably, we'd exchange the "So, what do you?" question. Here's when I always knew that the party was over for me. "I'm a high school English teacher," I'd say.

She'd get a nervous look on her face. "Oh, English was always my worst subject," she'd reply. And then the inevitable: "I'd better not make any mistakes in my grammar," offered with a ruffled chuckle. And within a few minutes, or seconds, she'd spot someone across the room and excuse herself to get as far away from me as possible.

Well, maybe it wasn't my job that chased her away; maybe I should have stuck only to eating. But learning that I was an English teacher was always a deal breaker, no matter how much I protested that I was off duty, or didn't worry that much about grammar, or otherwise tried to distance myself from the vision of the schoolmaster with the menacing red pen. That's the image that English teachers have developed over time. And I think that's unfortunate, not only for my former dating career but for the domain as a whole.

I'm not sure why English teachers are so focused on correcting errors, but that seems to be the case. Mina Shaughnessy (1977) has provided a different conception of errors that I think is more complex and provocative and more sensitive to the growth trajectories of writers. Shaughnessy taught in the New York City community college system during the "open admissions" era when many students had little experience with formal writing. She found that errors were often encouraging signs of growth, rather than discouraging signs of ignorance. This perspective on errors is consistent with a constructivist teaching approach in which learners are viewed developmentally, as works in progress, as is their writing. As such, violations of conventions needn't be flooded with red ink, but should be viewed as efforts by the writer to try something new, a venture that inevitably produces errors somewhere along the line.

The dreaded red pen is problematic in other ways as well. George Hillocks (1986) found that teachers who mark each and every infelicity on a student's paper end up intimidating and terrifying all of the confidence out of young writers. He suggests instead that response to student writers be focused on a few features, preferably those that have been emphasized during instruction. If a conceptual unit features writing narration and the student incorporates dialogue, sequences events appropriately, explores a feeling, and otherwise attempts to tell a story in accordance with the instruction, feedback should focus largely on those qualities. Teachers should offer encouragement, include commentary that is conversational and not just corrective, and not mark each and every error in spelling and mechanics that occurs while the student's focus is elsewhere.

Hillocks further found that when interviewed, teachers *say* that they value a student's ideas over all other considerations, that mechanics are a distant second to content in their treatment of student writing. Yet studies of the feedback provided by these same teachers to their students found that they responded almost exclusively to grammar and usage. That image of the English teacher as member of the grammar police is very difficult to dislodge, even among those teachers who position themselves against the stereotype.

On language, then, I suggest taking a sympathetic, developmental approach to the whole of what students are trying to accomplish through their writing. Responses to student writing should be positive and encouraging so as to help build confidence in what is for many people an onerous task. I'm not saying that you should never draw a student's attention to an inappropriate use of language or punctuation; if writing can't communicate, then it's got problems. Rather, I'm suggesting you consider the overall qualities of writing, especially in relation to your teaching, and respond to student writers accordingly. Think of something that you're awful at and are intimidated by—changing your car's oil, learning to prepare a complicated meal, growing roses, repairing a computer problem, or whatever else ails you—and think about how you'd benefit from being supported as you learned to do it. I doubt if you'd ever want to do it again if all you got was negativity and correction in response.

Rubrics

Grading student work can be a perplexing task. How do you know that all work that receives a B has similar qualities that can be distinguished from all work that receives an A or a C? Making this distinction is especially important when a student or parent questions your grading decisions. How can you answer their challenge in ways that are defensible?

One way is to develop a *rubric* to guide your decisions. A rubric is a scale that specifies how to differentiate between one level of performance and another. In its simplest form, a rubric for a one-hundred-question multiple-choice test might simply say:

90–100 items correct: A

80–89 items correct: B

70–79 items correct: C

60–69 items correct: D

59 or fewer items correct: F

Yet life in a constructivist classroom is not so clear-cut. When grading essays, portfolios, narratives, multimedia projects, drama, and so on, you need to specify how you will distinguish between an A and a B, a B and a C, and so on. But doing all of this takes work. It's much easier to borrow someone else's objective test and answer sheet than to read a pile of essays and evaluate them in fair and respectful ways. You might have guessed by now that what's best for students is not always easiest for teachers, so let's think about how to make distinctions between one grade and another. We'll use the portfolio as an example of how to develop a scoring rubric for an open-ended assignment such as the ones illustrated in Chapter 6.

The following is a series of questions you might ask in thinking about assessment:

- What might students learn from doing this, and how do I know that they've learned it?
- What conventions do students need to follow in order to produce an acceptable form of this genre? These could include issues ranging from the need for a particular form of English (e.g., textbook English) to the need for criteria in an extended definition.
- What level of detail is required to treat the topic sufficiently?
- What degree of cohesion should a student achieve?
- To what degree has the student met each point in the assignment?

The portfolio assignment includes some very clear, unambiguous requirements (e.g., a minimum number of exhibits, an explanation of each, and a synthesis paper). Some students believe that simply producing the minimum requirements should earn them a high grade. In evaluating their portfolios, you need to decide exactly what a student should earn for each level of performance you find in response to the assignment.

The portfolio assignment also includes some requirements that are more open to interpretation than simply meeting minimum requirements. In particular, the essay in which the writer explains how she learned about her own learning process is quite open-ended. You need to address how you will treat these issues when assigning grades to portfolios.

I'll assume that your school follows the traditional A–F grading system. The following is one possible rubric for assessing the portfolio project described in Chapter 4. Note that the assessment points map well onto the assignment's criteria. In turn, you'll need to take responsibility for teaching students how to do the things you'll be grading them on.

A grade of A will be awarded to portfolios that

- are turned in on time
- include the minimum components
- meet minimum expectations for each component (e.g., word minimum)
- clearly explain how each exhibit served as the source of significant learning about oneself, the materials, and/or the student's learning process
- clearly explain in the synthesis paper how the individual exhibits contribute to an overall set of related learning experiences explained in terms of a related set of points

A grade of B will be awarded to portfolios that

- are turned in on time
- include the minimum components
- meet minimum expectations for each component (e.g., word minimum)
- clearly explain how each exhibit served as the source of significant learning about oneself, the materials, and/or the student's learning process
- do not clearly explain in the synthesis paper how the individual exhibits contribute to an overall set of related learning experiences explained in terms of a related set of points

A grade of C will be awarded to portfolios that

- are turned in on time
- include the minimum components
- meet minimum expectations for each component (e.g., word minimum)

- do not clearly explain how each exhibit served as the source of significant learning about oneself, the materials, and/or the student's learning process
- do not clearly explain in the synthesis paper how the individual exhibits contribute to an overall set of related learning experiences explained in terms of a related set of points

A grade of D will be awarded to portfolios that

- are turned in on time
- include the minimum components
- do not meet minimum expectations for the components (e.g., the synthesis paper does not provide a synthesis, the commentaries are less than a page long or do not indicate reflection on learning)
- do not clearly explain how each exhibit served as the source of significant learning about oneself, the materials, and/or the student's learning process
- do not clearly explain in the synthesis paper how the individual exhibits contribute to an overall set of related learning experiences explained in terms of a related set of points

A grade of F will be awarded to portfolios that

- are turned in after the specified due date
- are turned in on time but do not include the minimum components (cover page, eight exhibits, eight commentaries, synthesis paper)
- do not meet minimum expectations for the components (e.g., the synthesis paper does not provide a synthesis, the commentaries are less than a page long or do not indicate reflection on learning)
- do not clearly explain how each exhibit served as the source of significant learning about oneself, the materials, and/or the student's learning process
- do not clearly explain in the synthesis paper how the individual exhibits contribute to an overall set of related learning experiences explained in terms of a related set of points

While not solving all problems, a rubric of this sort will help you evaluate the portfolios in a fairly consistent manner. You will find rubrics especially useful as you experience fatigue from grading: that is, when you've been grading for a while and your attention begins to slip and you need a reference point for making distinctions among performances. You will also find rubrics useful if your grading decisions are challenged by a student, parent, or administrator. If your rubric makes clear distinctions and you can demonstrate how your grading is informed by these distinctions, you will have fewer headaches to contend with.

Not everyone believes that using rubrics is a good idea. Alfie Kohn (2006), for instance, says that "rubrics are, above all, a tool to promote standardization, to turn teachers into grading machines or at least allow them to pretend that what they are doing is exact and objective" (12). He cites Linda Mabry (1999) as saying that

> rubrics "are designed to function as scoring guidelines, but they also serve as arbiters of quality and agents of control" over what is taught and valued (678). Because "agreement among scorers is more easily achieved with regard to such matters as spelling and organization," (676) these are the characteristics that will likely find favor in a rubricized classroom. Mabry cites research showing that "compliance with the rubric tended to yield higher scores but produced 'vacuous' writing" (678). (13)

He further lauds Maja Wilson (2006) for her critique of rubrics:

> In boiling "a messy process down to 4–6 rows of nice, neat, organized little boxes" (2), she argues, assessment is "stripped of the complexity that breathes life into good writing" (23). High scores on a list of criteria for excellence in essay writing do not mean that the essay is any good because quality is more than the sum of its rubricized parts. To think about quality, Wilson contends, "we need to look to the piece of writing itself to suggest its own evaluative criteria" (42)—a truly radical and provocative suggestion. (14)

I certainly share the concerns of Kohn, Mabry, and Wilson about any reductive approach to evaluating student work, even if I think that *rubricized* is too awful a word to use once, much less twice, in the same essay. I disagree, however, with the idea that rubrics necessarily produce thoughtless evaluations for teachers, even if they might for assessors in large-scale evaluations, as Hillocks (2002) has found. I would say, indeed, that the critiques themselves are reductive: they assume that efforts to make evaluations fair and consistent inevitably lead to box checking rather than careful reading. In my view, it all depends on what's in the boxes and how a teacher interprets the task of evaluation.

I believe that a carefully designed rubric can lead to richer reading. I also think that if rubrics become "'arbiters of quality and agents of control' over what is taught and valued," the problem is that the rubric is out of synch with the teaching and the values the rubrics are meant to embody, not that rubrics are inherently off target. A well-crafted rubric that is in tune with the instruction helps a teacher not only read the students' writing sympathetically but also provide a systematic method for reflecting on how well the students have been taught how to produce the assessed qualities.

Yet a rubric can result in fairly rigid approaches to assessment. To return to the construction metaphor, a rubric establishes a strict building code that students' constructions must meet in order to pass inspection. In terms of the question Who's building whose building? the answer is necessarily: The students are building buildings designed according to the teacher's code. It's important, then, to have a rubric that enables students to build within the code while varying their buildings according to their living needs.

It's important to think of the effects of using any particular evaluative tool on student work. At the risk of belaboring the metaphor, a code designed for one kind of building in one part of the country might not work well for buildings designed elsewhere for other purposes. An inspection code written for a restaurant in Milwaukee would not take into account the structural needs for a skyscraper in San Francisco, where the possibility of an earthquake necessitates the use of particularly strong materials used in configurations designed to resist the effects of tremors. The inspection code dictates much about how a building will be constructed.

Similarly, a grading rubric provides both constraints and affordances for how students will construct their texts in school. Just as a building code in San Francisco ensures that buildings will be strong enough to withstand an earthquake, a good rubric may require students to do things that they wouldn't do by choice, yet that are good things for them to know how to do.

Is there only one code available for evaluating the soundness of a student text? No, there are many available, each encouraging the production of a different kind of text. The question then becomes What kind of text are we encouraging students to produce? Does the evaluative instrument—the rubric—limit students more than it enables them? Does the rubric take into account the possibility that a student's idea for a functional text might be judged as insufficient by the teacher's rubric? Does the rubric deny students the opportunity to construct an innovative text by specifying the terms of production?

One final point: The question of which standards to use when evaluating writing raises an important issue about the nature of writing. Is a piece of writing good or bad, without respect to who's reading it? Think about the idea proposed by Martin Nystrand (1986) that the quality of writing is a function of the relationship between writers and readers. In this view, good writing is writing that is in tune with its readers. A highly technical research report might be a splendid piece of work to other researchers, yet might be obscure gobbledygook to the person on the street. The text itself is not good or bad; rather, different readers are more or less in tune with the writing conventions used by the writer.

The use of rubrics typically imposes a single set of conventions and expectations on student writing. Most frequently rubrics represent the conventions preferred by the text's sole reader, the teacher. As a teacher, then, you should consider ways to provide both varied readerships for your students' writing and varied or flexible ways in which to evaluate their work.

These are perplexing questions faced in any school assessment (and, for that matter, in any assessment anywhere). I justify the instructional approach outlined here by saying that yes, the goal of instruction is to produce a particular kind of text in a particular kind of way. I think it's worthwhile to do because the goal is to teach students *generative* ways of reading; that is, procedures for how to do something. Throughout the year, I teach them procedures for reading in other ways as well. My intention is to teach them a repertoire of procedures for using literacy tools, to teach them that they have a tool kit available that they can use in a variety of ways. Each tool provides constraints and affordances, and it's important to understand both when using it.

Finally, evaluation, like death and taxes, is one of the inevitabilities of life in school. You can't teach without giving a grade in most schools. And you need to grade in ways that students (and often their parents) find consistent, equitable, and defensible. A rubric is a way to specify the code you're using to evaluate student work.

If you're uncomfortable writing the code by which you assign students their grades, you could look for alternatives, such as dedicating class time to having students produce the rubrics. While helping with the question of who's building whose building, it would raise a different set of questions, such as Do students' expectations for a soundly constructed text meet expectations by which these texts will be judged elsewhere? Is the process of arriving at these judgments an experience so worthwhile that it outweighs the importance of meeting adult standards for text production? These are serious and difficult questions that you must ask in any reconsideration of how to identify the standards by which student work is formally evaluated.

Undoubtedly, there is much more to say in this debate. I recommend a website suggested to me by many teachers, http://rubistar.4teachers.org/index.php, which provides information and models for designing rubrics. An interesting frame experiment would be to use rubrics in some classes and not others and see how the different methods affect student learning and inform your teaching.

Summary

The issue of response to student writing—or student composition, if you accept the idea that students may create texts that are not written—is broad and complex. I should say that in spite of my dependence on things like rubrics, I have often labored over whether a student's work should get a B– or C+; even with criteria in mind, these decisions can be very vexing. And they make a big difference to students, whose futures often depend on the ways in which teachers tip the scales in high-stakes grading decisions. I've taken classes where my grade average for a marking period was a 79.4, and the teacher gave me the C+. Those sorts of decisions always really honked me off because they seemed so arbitrary and punitive, and if anything made me dislike and distrust the business of schooling even more than ever—and I was not one who really enjoyed my school experiences on the whole. And so I encourage you to give a lot of thought to how you evaluate students, what you evaluate them on, and what the consequences of your evaluations will be for them.

Part III

Designing the Conceptual Unit

8 *Why Conceptual Units?*

A conceptual unit of instruction dedicates a period of time—roughly four to six weeks of fifty-minute classes or two to three weeks of ninety-minute classes—to *sustained attention to a related set of ideas*. These ideas are pursued through a variety of texts, both those read (usually literary) and those produced (usually written). This sustained attention allows students—and, given a provocative topic, the teacher—to consider a related set of issues from a variety of perspectives with increasing understanding.

This consideration ultimately provides opportunities for each student to construct a personal interpretation or perspective, ideally one that takes into account and synthesizes the various ideas explored through the unit texts and discussions. By considering the same topic, the class can work toward a sense of community, where it is expected that students will appreciate and critique the ideas their classmates produce in response to the unit texts. By considering other student texts in conjunction with commercially published ones, the class can work toward a contemporary vision of how a particular topic might be imagined in their own society.

The Parts That Make Up the Whole

A conceptual unit is designed to organize students' learning around a particular emphasis. Literature, nonfiction texts, and related artistic texts provide the stimulus for student inquiry into the unit topic. The texts, it's important to remember, include those produced outside the class (typically in published form) and those produced by students. Students do not simply react to texts and consume previously produced knowledge. Rather, they have an active role in constructing new knowledge through their engagement with the unit concepts. They produce texts of their own that contribute to the class' exploration of the key unit questions and raise new questions.

A conceptual unit is not simply a collection of texts on the same topic. One key characteristic of a conceptual unit, as opposed to one that is simply about a topic, is that it involves students in a conversation that deepens as they progress through the texts, activities, and discussions. To be considered conceptual, the unit must focus on a set of key concepts that students engage with over time. This extended consideration is designed to help students pursue a set of ideas that will help them

- come to better personal understanding of the topic and their related experiences
- gain fluency with tools that will enable them to read and produce new texts in the future
- work within a social context in which they can develop this new knowledge to the best of their potential

A conceptual unit typically includes all or most of the following: a rationale, an inventory, goals, assessment, lessons, activities, discussion, texts, tools, and composing.

Rationale

A rationale is the argument that you make to justify your selection of a unit topic and its contents: its materials, activities, assessments, and so on. I believe that writing out this rationale is the most effective way of articulating reasons for teaching decisions. At the same time, I recognize that doing so takes precious time that busy teachers might decide to invest instead in the lesson plans themselves, in doing bureaucratic paperwork, in reading and thinking about the texts included in the unit, or in taking a break from all this work. Yet all teachers eventually must defend their decisions to their colleagues, their students' parents, their administrators, and other stakeholders. So the better prepared you are to explain your decisions, the less stressful these occasions will be. Having a persuasive rationale is especially important if you teach in a school in which a constructivist approach is not widely employed and you need to justify why you are teaching against the grain.

Inventory

An inventory is a vehicle that helps you learn about your students. Most school textbooks are written for a generic student. However, you will have all kinds of students, most of whom are quite unique and precious to their parents, and perhaps to you. If you view your role as teaching students as well as teaching the subject, then it's a good idea to know who they are, including

- what they're interested in
- what their goals are for being in your class
- what they know about particular topics
- what they've already read
- how they use language and how they write
- what other skills they have that you can build on in the classroom

Knowing this information can help you design appropriate instruction. You won't make the mistake of teaching them things they already do well, or pitching instruction too far beyond what they know, or teaching in ways that have nothing to do with their own purposes. It's possible that you teach in a district that restricts your decision making in these areas. Even so, teachers often develop ways to meet their own goals and their students' goals while also satisfying other people's requirements.

Inventories can be taken in a variety of ways. You can learn a lot about students, for instance, by having them write an introductory letter about themselves—you will not only learn about their interests but also get a sense of their writing fluency. You can develop some kind of questionnaire that asks about their background in education, their interests in school, their interests outside school, their reading experiences and preferences, their attitudes toward writing, and other information you would find useful in planning your teaching. You could provide them with literature of different degrees of difficulty and ask them to respond to it, which would help you to identify appropriate reading material for the class.

You should be prepared for a broad range of performance on these inventories. Knowing this range can help you make good decisions about your teaching, such as whether you need to plan to use different materials within a single class.

Goals

Instructional goals refer to the unit's destination. This destination is the ultimate learning that you anticipate for students as a result of their experiences during the unit. Their ultimate learning comes about through their production of a *culminating text*—that is, something that they create that synthesizes their learning. Note that I refer to this final assessment as a learning opportunity, rather than simply as a test of content mastery. I strongly believe that assessment and learning ought to go together hand in hand; each assessment ought to provide an occasion for new learning as students extend their thinking through producing the unit's culminating texts. Most commonly these texts are some kind of extended writing, such as an essay, a narrative, or a research report. Students, however, should have opportunities to learn through the production of other kinds of texts as well, including those grounded in the arts.

The goals you set imply a path for the instruction to follow. Identifying worthwhile goals, then, is a key facet of planning worthwhile instruction.

Assessment

Goals are tied to the inevitable question of *assessment*. Whether or not you like it, or whether or not you have philosophical objections to grading, you will almost certainly have to issue a grade for each student. Ideally these grades will correspond to students' learning. If they are enabled to produce culminating texts that they find worthwhile, then there is a good likelihood that your assessment will be what some call *authentic*. The unit goals you set should provide students the opportunity to create culminating texts that you can assess in ways that you and your students believe reflect their learning during the unit.

When knowledge is reduced to right and wrong answers, assessment is fairly straightforward and simple. When knowledge is open-ended and constructed, as I advocate in this book, assessment becomes much more problematic. I recommend that you use a *rubric* to help you distinguish between different levels of student performance on the texts they produce.

Lessons

I use the term *lesson* somewhat hesitantly because, for many, it connotes the kind of authoritarian teaching that I have been arguing against. For most, a lesson implies a top-down learning relationship in which the student does what the teacher says. Furthermore, there's a possible connotation of being punished, as in being "taught a lesson"; one of my dictionary's definitions for lesson is "reprimand," and that's not what I'm encouraging here. In an ideal world I'd use a different term, but *lesson* is still a commonly used word in schools, so I use it for simply pragmatic reasons.

A lesson is a shorter unit of instruction within the larger conceptual unit. If, for instance, you are teaching a unit on animals as symbols and have a goal of enabling students to see how symbolic animals can represent human characteristics, you might include a lesson in which students are introduced to the idea that literary animals can symbolize people and their (often negative) tendencies. This lesson might include different parts of the unit that I describe here: *discussion* of *texts* such as a set of fables, an *activity* in which they *compose* a fable of their own using the *tool* of writing, and an *assessment* of their fable.

It's important to remember that, while lessons are identifiable as pieces of the larger unit, they should be integrated and sequenced, rather than discrete. You are, after all, designing *a unit*, which means that the lessons need to be related to one another and to the overall conceptual knowledge that students construct.

Activities

An activity is a hands-on experience, often taking place within a lesson. It is related to the unit concepts and helps to prepare students for reaching the unit goals. It typically involves

- interaction with other people
- the manipulation of ideas and/or objects
- the production of an idea and/or text
- the inductive development of strategies for learning
- an open-ended task

Activities are, not surprisingly, active. Let's say, for instance, that you would like to teach students a lesson on how to make inferences in their reading. One accessible way to introduce this idea is through an activity such as a spy game (see Hillocks 1972). First you tell small groups of students that a spy has been captured. Then you present them with the contents of his pockets: coins from foreign countries, a rabbit's foot, a scrap of paper with code on it, a set of paper clips strung together, a ticket to the opera, and/or any other clues you want to provide. Each group then makes inferences about the spy's personality, qualities, characteristics, and mission. Because there is no real spy, each group may legitimately arrive at different inferences, as long as it can explain them. The groups then discuss their inferences with the class, comparing and critiquing one another's ideas.

Following this activity, the class may move to examining characters from literature to make inferences that will help them construct a response. If they work in small groups on their analysis of the narrator of a poem, they are engaging in another activity, although with a more complex text to analyze. These activities could lead to individual efforts to analyze literature in terms of the inferences they can make about narrators or other characters.

Discussion

By discussion I mean talk in which participants exchange ideas. I distinguish this variety of talk from a *lecture* in which one person provides information or opinions (including literary interpretations) for others to record. Many teachers regard their classes as being discussion oriented even when input from students is quite limited. To count as a discussion, an exchange needs to be

- *open-ended* (that is, not having a specific or correct answer or destination)
- *authentic* (that is, concerned with the purposes and interests of all participants, not just a few)

- *democratic* (that is, equally open to all and involving the greatest possible number of willing participants)

Most classroom discussions take place as whole-class or small-group efforts. Typically, whole-class discussions are led by teachers. In this book I've also outlined an array of alternative arrangements through which students become responsible for leading discussions in either whole-class or small-group settings (see Chapter 3).

In my experience, discussions include people with roughly two different dispositions. One disposition is that of *arguing to win*. Lawyers do this: right or wrong, their goal is to win the argument. Participants who take this stance typically do not view themselves as learners in the discussion; rather, they see themselves as contestants. The other disposition is that of *arguing to learn*. Participants who take this stance typically view discussions as opportunities to think through ideas and learn from the others involved. For them there are not winners and losers. They cannot help but benefit from the discussion, even if they ultimately change their minds about the ideas they express. I'll leave it to you to decide what kind of disposition you'd like to promote in your own classroom.

Texts

A text is any meaning-laden product. You are probably familiar with literature as a text. Texts also include art, dance, film, and other artifacts that have a potential for meaning. In most cases a text is tangible (e.g., a poem, a sculpture, a film), but it can be fleeting: a song, an expression, and so on. Texts include both those that students read (also referred to as *materials*) and those that they produce.

Tools

This book uses a lot of construction metaphors. Tools are important to all builders, including teachers and students. A tool is any instrument through which you act on your environment. For a carpenter, the hammer, saw, and other accoutrements are the tools of the trade.

Students who construct knowledge also use tools. Through the tool of language, they can communicate, explore ideas, and impose order on their worlds. Like other tools, language can have more specific constructive purposes. Students can use language to argue, to tell stories, to classify, to amuse, to deceive. Students can also use nonverbal artistic devices to construct meaning-laden texts. They can draw, for instance, to signify relationships they see in literature. They can communicate through body language. The key to all of these actions is that they must be used in service of the construction of meaning.

Teachers, too, use tools. These include conceptual tools that serve as umbrellas. An educational theory such as constructivism, for instance, may be applied to reading, writing, math, science—to any learning situation where the emphasis is on constructing knowledge rather than receiving it. Teachers also use practical tools. These include any methods that you use to enact your teaching: lesson plans, small-group activities, handouts, and so on. Different tools help achieve different ends. I advocate the development of a big and versatile *tool kit* to help you carry out your teaching and for students to use in their learning.

Composing

I use the term *composing* to describe the act by which people make things that have meaning and/or use for them. In school, these things are what I have previously called *texts*: essays, drawings, dramas, and so on. I believe that the emphasis of teaching and learning ought to be to engage students in acts of composition that produce meaningful texts. These acts of composition involve

- the use of an appropriate tool or set of tools
- an understanding of the conventions and genres within which one is working and an understanding of the effects of breaking these conventions
- an extended process that usually includes planning, drafting, feedback, reflection, and revising
- building on prior knowledge and understanding as a basis for the construction of new ideas and a new text
- new learning that takes place through the process of composing
- regarding both the process of composing and the ultimate text as sources of meaning.

In school, writing is typically considered to be synonymous with composing. As you can see, however, much school writing would not meet the criteria for my definition of a composition (e.g., writing factual short answers on an exam). And other kinds of production (writing a musical score, choreographing an interpretation of a story, designing a house in an architecture class) do meet these criteria. When I refer to composition, then, keep in mind that I am talking about a way of producing texts, rather than a way of producing a particular kind of text.

Seven Types of Unit

There are seven main kinds of organization for conceptual units. There may be others, but these cover most ways to create units from the literature curriculum. Any kind of unit design ought to lead class members (including potentially the teacher) into new understandings. As such, it needs to be complex enough to generate thoughtful consideration about whatever thread ties the unit texts and lessons together. Simply considering a topic does not make a series of lessons a conceptual unit. Rather, that topic needs to help students develop frameworks for thinking about issues so that they can think about new situations (including new texts) through that framework.

Therefore, a unit on friendship ought to do more than have students read stories about friends. It should approach these texts so that students develop frameworks for thinking about new situations that develop in their experiences with friends, observations of friendships, or textual experiences with friendship. One of a teacher's responsibilities in designing a unit, then, is to think about how different sequences of activities and readings will contribute to students' ability to develop these generative frameworks for thinking about the unit concept. The conceptual growth of students during a unit was aptly described by Hillocks, McCabe, and McCambell in *The Dynamics of English Instruction, Grades 7–12*: "One of the most important things that any literature unit can do is to provide a conceptual matrix against which the student can examine each new work he reads. Insights into any given work are partly the result of experience in reading others because concepts grow by comparison and contrast" (1971, 254).

The kinds of unit that I outline are described in terms of the kinds of texts that students read. Keep in mind that I use the terms *text* and *read* broadly to include any production that represents something else, including images on computer screens, film, art, music, architecture, dance, and other forms of representation. I also view *student texts* as critical parts of any conceptual unit. In some ways student compositions are the unit's most important texts, because they distill what students have learned through their engagement with the unit. These texts are important not only for assessment purposes but for all students in the class to learn from, and so a conceptual unit should provide opportunities for students to read and think about what their classmates have produced in relation to the unit concepts.

Theme

By a theme I mean an idea or motif that ties together the texts, activities, and discussions of a unit. A theme often refers to a set of experiences, ideas, concepts, or emotions shared by people within and often across cultures. Themes include presumably universal experiences such as rites of passage, dealing with peer groups, coping with loss, social responsibility, and other topics that are frequently the subject of art and literature.

Such archetypal experiences provide a compelling way to organize an English curriculum, one that is responsive both to recurring patterns in all art forms and to students' authentic interests in learning. Students are engaged in integrated inquiry into topics that parallel their social development or that help to lead their development. Texts and readers should be mutually informative; that is, texts should bring new understandings to their readers, and readers should bring their own histories of experiences to project meanings into the texts. The themes that students study can

- help them consider pivotal experiences in their lives, such as their relationships with their friends or families
- introduce them to issues that they may not yet have considered, such as what it means to be a responsible citizen

By studying thematic units, then, students can potentially see literature and related texts as useful tools and touchstones in their own development as people.

Period

A *period* can also provide the basis for a conceptual unit, particularly when authors from that period write from a cultural perspective that provides them with a common set of themes. The era known as the Victorian period, for instance, encompassed the sixty-three-year reign of Queen Victoria of England. Its literature reveals the sentiments, beliefs, tastes, and accomplishments of the English people of that time. Victorian literature was often staged around the class struggle that followed the Industrial Revolution in Great Britain, creating tensions among the working class, the new industrial middle class, and the old aristocracy. The literature of Dickens typifies the Victorian period, with sympathy extended to the poor, the working class, and their children.

Periods needn't extend quite as long as the Victorian period. American colonial rhetoric, beat literature of the fifties, the Vietnam era (see Johannessen 1992), and other shorter periods can provide the basis for a conceptual unit.

Movement

A *movement* is a belief system that is expressed through a variety of media and is part of a broad philosophical perspective. Romanticism, for instance, had a coherent set of principles. It emphasized the imagination and emotions over intellect and reason, believed in the innate goodness of people in their natural state, had a reverence for nature, held a philosophical idealism, believed in individualism, rejected political authority and social convention, celebrated the human passions, and embraced religious mysticism. A movement such as romanticism, unlike most literary periods, extends across nations and time periods. Romanticism, for instance, had large followings in Germany, France, England, and the United States, although at different times and for different durations.

A movement, because it represents a coherent worldview, can provide the basis for a conceptual unit. Other movements include the enlightenment, naturalism, transcendentalism, neoclassicism, surrealism, realism, poststructuralism, Marxism, and nihilism. Designing a unit around a movement enables the inclusion of historical and philosophical writing as well as art, architecture, and other artifacts that embody the beliefs of the people who subscribe to the movement.

Region

Often, a geographic region can serve as the means for organizing a conceptual unit. Authors and artists from a particular region often share common outlooks, themes, and styles. You may have studied, for instance, southern fiction, Great Lakes authors, or the Harlem Renaissance. In my university instruction my students have designed conceptual units featuring the authors of the state in which we lived (e.g., Oklahoma authors, Georgia authors). At times these units have come under the heading of something like *a sense of place*, in which a sense of place was a function of a region's history, geography, culture, and other distinctive features.

Genre

A *genre* refers to works that share codes: westerns, heroic journeys, detective stories, comedies of manners, and so on. These genres are often produced through a variety of media: short story, drama, novel, film, graphic novel, and so on, which themselves are referred to as genres.

By genre I do *not* mean strictly form-oriented groupings of literature—poetry, drama, the novel, and other structures; these make a diffuse and unproductive means of organizing a curriculum. The short story, for instance, is so various in form and theme that I find it an odd basis for grouping literature for study. Typically, students are asked to recognize such elements as plot, setting, character, rising action, and other features. Yet plot seems to be a hopelessly diverse trait given the myriad ways in which a story can unfold. "The Secret Life of Walter Mitty" jumps between Walter's real and imaginary worlds. "The Short Happy Life of Francis Macomber" feeds bits of the past into the present. "The Bear" takes place in several eras that are not presented sequentially, and it's an awfully long short story that's organized into chapters—how do we explain that? (Answer: We avoid the question.) In other words, the genre of the short story is a questionable organizing principle because reading one short story rarely helps a student to read the next. All that they have in common is that they are (more or less) short and that they are stories.

I use *genre* to refer to texts that employ a predictable, consistent set of codes. Authors of satire, for instance, typically use a set of devices such as exaggeration, voicing opinions different from their own, creating foolish characters, and so on, that are designed to invite particular responses. Jonathan Swift's *Modest Proposal* argues that society can solve both its hunger problem and its persistent condition of having a social underclass by having its comfortable classes eat babies of the poor. Taken literally, this suggestion is horrifying. An astute reader, however, knows how to recognize Swift's use of irony and understand that he is criticizing attitudes toward the poor rather than introducing a culinary solution to a social problem. In this conception, a genre is not confined to a single medium but rather includes multimedia texts that rely on common interpretive codes.

Works by a Single Author

If an author has produced a body of work that is highly compelling or holds a significant place in literary history, then that author's work could provide the basis for a unit of instruction. The work of a single author is amenable to a unit approach because the works tend to rely on a set of themes and techniques that students can follow across texts. The main question you should ask yourself when considering this means of organization is this: With all of the literature ever written at my disposal, and with 180 or so school days available, how do I justify committing 20 of those days to just one writer?

In other words, you need to consider the impact of dedicating 10 percent of your instructional time to one author. You often won't have much choice in the matter when it comes to Shakespeare, who is often required reading at all high school grade levels—including American literature.

Learning a Key Strategy

Literature is a very particular kind of text. You don't read it the same way you read a science report. In a science report, you assume that the speaker is seeking accuracy, precision, and logic. Often, however, the speaker in literature is a highly flawed character whose worldview, diction, and so on are different from those of the author. The author relies on readers to recognize the character's flaws and disagree with the narrative perspective. Huck Finn's narration in *The Adventures of Huckleberry Finn*, for instance, assumes the inferiority of Jim; yet other evidence presented by Twain suggests that Jim is the book's most noble character. Knowing how to read an ironic narration, then, is a key strategy that is useful in becoming an informed reader of literature or other satiric works.

A unit can be organized around strategies for recognizing and interpreting literary codes. By this I do *not* mean memorizing lists of literary terms. I refer instead to knowing how authors use literary techniques. A unit built around this approach would take a technique and have students analyze it in a series of increasingly sophisticated texts. Michael W. Smith (1991), for instance, has written an extended unit on understanding unreliable narrators in which students begin by reading Calvin and Hobbes comics and move from there through more sophisticated literature. Having formal strategies for recognizing and interpreting literary codes can be very useful for students in their subsequent reading.

Benefits of the Unit Approach

Learning design principles based on unit organization was very beneficial to my high school teaching career. While I obsessively thought about my teaching and was constantly tinkering with my plans, I was not plagued by daily uncertainty because I had learned to plan ahead and design conceptual units. I therefore found teaching to be less stressful than did many of my colleagues because I was not always struggling to figure out what to do next. I was also happier with my teaching because my students saw continuity in what we did from day to day and week to week and saw it within the context of questions that mattered to them. In various units, we considered questions such as

- What does it mean to be a success?
- What does one do in the face of peer pressure?
- How does discrimination affect society and its individuals?
- What is a social conscience, and at what point and in what form does one register a protest against a social wrong?
- How does it feel to be an outcast?

I should also add that taking this approach made my classes far more interesting to me, because the answers were different for each class. Instead of explaining the same interpretation to students class after class, year after year, and having them repeat it to me on tests, I had the opportunity to be involved in discussions that were as infinitely varied as the students themselves. My classes were places where I did a lot of learning as I listened to my students construct for themselves an awareness of how they understood and acted within their worlds.

A Drawback of the Unit Approach

One drawback to the unit approach is that it could potentially lead students to pigeonhole the texts they read. Let's say, for instance, that you teach Charles Dickens' *Hard Times*. You could include this text in a unit on Victorian literature, grouping it with other texts from this period to illustrate the conditions and perspectives of that time. You could include it in a unit on satire, teaching it along with other satiric works to help students understand the conventions of the genre. You could include it in a unit on the theme of progress, using Dickens' portrayal to question whether increased industrialism represents social progress.

All of these decisions could potentially enable students to have fruitful experiences with the novel. The drawback is that by emphasizing one aspect of the novel, you might preclude other ways of approaching it. It's important for you to remember, then, that your unit approach will be beneficial in that it will, in a sense, narrow students' vision and help them focus on the unit concepts. But this more narrow vision also has the potential to prevent them from seeing other worthwhile ways to approach the individual texts of the unit. One way to resolve this problem is to enable open-ended opportunities for thinking, such as journals and student-led discussions.

A Rationale for Teaching with Conceptual Units

The study of literature by means of conceptual units may be justified in a number of ways. If you can't defend something, then you shouldn't teach it.

The Need for Integrated Knowledge

Many curriculum theorists argue that effective instruction seeks to help students make connections that cohere around principles. Arthur Applebee, for instance, conceives of curriculum "as a domain for culturally significant conversations" that take place across space and time (1993, 200), suggesting the need to explore a set of questions across a series of related texts. Conceptual units are well suited for integrated learning, enabling students to explore a topic over time through the lenses offered by a variety of texts. Such an approach will avoid the problem of fragmentation that Applebee (1996) sees as characterizing much of the English curriculum. This fragmentation in turn works against students' ability to integrate knowledge and experience the domain coherently.

A well-designed conceptual unit can promote the kind of integration and continuity that Applebee sees as essential to an effective curriculum, one that students actively participate in and help to construct with their own contributions and compositions. Furthermore, Applebee argues for the importance of extending this sense of coherence to the curriculum as a whole. That is, learning for the whole year should contribute to the development of an *overarching concept*. An overarching concept helps to connect class discussions and student productions from unit to unit, giving students an overall sense of direction and continuity for their learning. Whereas most curricula emphasize a series of facts and skills to be mastered, this conception of curriculum focuses on ideas, particularly as students enter and transform the subject of English and grow through the process of their inquiry.

The notions of overarching concepts and human growth also fit well with Csikszentmihalyi and Larson's (1984) views on human happiness. Their study of adolescents focused on identifying the kinds of experiences that put them *in the flow*, a state in which they were so heavily involved in what they were doing that they lost all track of time. It will surprise few to reveal that flow experiences rarely occur during mainstream school classes, particularly during that most common classroom practice: listening to a teacher talk. Ultimately, Csikszentmihalyi and Larson identify happy people—that is, those whose life work most frequently provides for flow experiences—as those who develop overarching themes for their activity.

A literature curriculum that students experience and contribute to, that provides them with a domain for developing themes to guide their life's actions and decisions, can make two key, related contributions to their education. First of all, through transactions with provocative texts, it can provide them with a strong literary education and thus enable them to participate in and contribute to a major tradition in arts and letters. Second of all, it can enable them to experience this tradition in a way that allows them to understand the social conditions, life experiences, and literary conventions that guide the production of literature and other texts—including those that they produce—and help texts serve as vehicles for their growth into happy, productive citizens.

Schemata and Scripts

Another rationale for conceptual units comes from cognitive psychologists' *schema theory*. A schema is a network of knowledge that includes both elements and processes. Having schematic knowledge enables a person to understand situations that are new yet related to ones already known; an effectively designed conceptual unit will help students understand new material that is related to familiar material. This approach to schooling is quite different from the approach in which assessment tests students' recall of what they have already read and discussed (or heard presented by the teacher).

You probably have schemata for many familiar routines in life. Let's say, for instance, that you enter a restaurant. If you have eaten out before, you likely have a general schema for how the evening will proceed. You will be seated at a table, a waiter will come and take your order, you will wait for a period of time, the food will come in a particular order (appetizers, soup or salad, main course), you will eat it, be offered an opportunity to order dessert, be given a check, and then will either pay the waiter or the cashier and leave (leaving a tip of roughly 15 to 20 percent).

Your knowledge of how the experience's script will unfold will help you conduct yourself in appropriate manner. You should not, for instance, juggle flaming torches or play the bagpipes while waiting for your food, unless the restaurant has a very special theme. You will also be alert to particular signals that indicate a variation in the script. At an Ethiopian restaurant, for instance, you will eat your food with your hands instead of with silverware. If the expectations of your script are violated—for instance, if your waiter brings the main course before the soup—you have a way of recognizing the discrepancy and likely a means for resolving it (complaining to the manager, etc.). Your schema for dining out, then, enables you to anticipate the rules of propriety, sequence of events, and elements of the setting so that you can understand, appreciate, and enjoy your meal.

Organizing instruction by conceptual units fits well with schema theory. If prior knowledge helps us anticipate new situations, then studying texts that are conceptually unified makes sense. Often students already have prior knowledge that can help them engage with the unit concepts. Coming-of-age experiences, for instance, appear to be archetypal among young people. Anyone who has had a coming-of-age experience has a script for such events, just as people who have dined in restaurants have scripts for eating out. And, just as people tend to eat in restaurants repeatedly over time and refine their restaurant scripts through exposure to new restaurant experiences, people have many coming-of-age experiences rather than just one. The prior knowledge from personal experience (and likely from prior reading and media viewing) can form the basis for understanding how the theme works in newly encountered literature, film, and art. In a reciprocal process, these newly encountered texts can provide the basis for reflection on the prior experiences.

Furthermore, each text can serve to develop a schema that in turn helps a reader to understand both the experiences that are at the heart of the theme and the textual conventions that authors use to help convey a theme. For instance, a coming-of-age story typically involves a character who exhibits immature behavior at the outset, has a transforming experience, and gains greater wisdom or maturity at the end. This script presumably parallels the kinds of experiences that young readers have as they negotiate adolescence. By organizing literature according to literary themes or genres, teachers can thus help students refine their schemata for both their own unfolding experiences and their knowledge of narrative conventions.

Transactional Learning

Additional support for using conceptual units within an integrated curriculum comes from Louise Rosenblatt's *transactional theory* of response to literature, outlined primarily in two books: *Literature as Exploration* (1996), originally published in 1938, and *The Reader, the Text, the Poem: The Transactional Theory of the Literary Work*, published in 1978. She based her ideas on the educational philosophy of John Dewey (1934), who outlined a transactional theory of human development in *Art as Experience*.

Rosenblatt proposed her theory at a time when university literary theorists were concerned with developing text-centered approaches to literary criticism that minimized the value of a reader's affective response or personal constructions of meaning. Rosenblatt argued instead for a democratic view of reading that gave the ordinary reader as much authority in determining a literary work's meaning as that accorded to a professional literary critic.

Rosenblatt asserts that readers need to attend carefully to the words a writer uses to craft a work of literature. What those words might mean, however, is a matter of personal construction. This construction is based on

- a reader's personal experiences
- the cultural factors that shape both readers and texts
- the social environment of a classroom and its effects on a reader's response
- the psychological makeup of individual readers that provides a particular frame of mind for interpreting events in particular ways

The same text might be read quite differently by two readers in the same class who bring different cultural expectations to the experience, or who have different personal experiences, or whose psychological makeups provide different frameworks for interpreting events.

Let me give an example of an occasion when students interpreted a story in a way that initially struck me as naïve but ultimately made sense when I recognized the reason for their interpretation (see Smagorinsky and Jordahl, 1991). Following several class discussions of stories from Ernest Hemingway's *In Our Time*, a student teacher I was supervising, Ann Jordahl, had the students interpret a final selection from the collection, "The Three Day Blow." In this story a three-day storm maroons Nick Adams and his companion Bill in a cabin, where they drink liquor steadily and talk about their lives.

In their essays, several boys argued independently that the story was a cautionary tale against excessive alcohol use. This interpretation initially gave us concerns about both our teaching and the boys' reading. Both Ann and I had been, after all, college English majors. In graduate school, we had both been required to satisfy the English department's master's degree requirements as well as those of our education program, including the notorious and cutthroat master's exam: four hours of writing on each of two consecutive days, in response to questions requiring the synthesis of our understanding of four previously issued texts (in my case, Dickens' *Hard Times*, Orwell's *Down and Out in Paris and London*, Marx and Engels' *Communist Manifesto*, and Shakespeare's *Timon of Athens*—perhaps the Bard's worst play). Performance on this exam often made the difference between being accepted to or rejected from the University of Chicago's doctoral program in English literature.

Furthermore, the school where we were teaching, Oak Park and River Forest High School (IL), was the *alma mater* of Hemingway himself, a source of great pride within the English department—and as a consequence, a source of considerable knowledge about Hemingway among faculty members. Based on our knowledge of Hemingway, we knew that his life and literature did not suggest a didactic reading of his work when it came to consuming alcohol in earnest.

As we thought about these boys and their response and tried to make sense of it, we realized that all of them were football players. We also remembered that athletes in the school were put through regular and extensive programs on substance abuse, one of which they had recently attended. If we return to Rosenblatt, then, we see that they likely had

- witnessed other teenagers who'd had problems with drugs and alcohol (*personal experiences*)

- been taught to view alcohol consumption as unhealthy and destructive (*cultural orientation to reading*)

- developed a framework for interpreting the behavior of drunkards (*psychological framework*)

When we considered what they brought to the text, it seemed more reasonable that they would interpret a pair of besotted characters as symbols of the ravages of alcohol. The lesson we learned was that what students bring to stories is often quite different from what college literature majors bring to stories. We decided that, when teaching Hemingway in the future, we should provide some background on his life and values to help inform their response to the stories.

Some people might find this to be a heavy-handed intervention that interferes with the students' personal efforts to construct meaning from literature. I've spoken with many educators who feel that teachers should honor all readers' responses to literature, particularly first readings. They believe that it's more important for students to be allowed the latitude to interpret the story on their own terms than for a teacher to introduce information that might affect those interpretations. Rather than trying to settle this issue—about which there is considerable disagreement—I'll leave it to you to think about whether students should have the opportunity to construct whichever understandings they arrive at or whether a teacher should provide what she feels is useful information that could help inform their understandings.

To return to Rosenblatt: However you interpret her transactional theory, its emphasis on what readers bring to texts and in turn construct from them contributes to a rationale for organizing literature according to concepts. If, for instance, themes represent archetypal experiences, then they can serve students well in two ways. First of all, students will bring critical prior knowledge to their reading, giving them authority as knowledgeable readers of literature. If students have had experience with justice, or puritan values, or satire, or whatever topic is covered, then those experiences provide them with knowledge about the topic that deserves acknowledgment and respect in the classroom.

Secondly, their consideration of the concept through literary study ought to provide them with opportunities to reflect on their experience and construct new knowledge. They can thus develop a relationship with literature and classmates that potentially enriches their understanding of themselves, the literature, and one another. This approach does not promote an anything-goes classroom where any interpretation by a student is acceptable. It does, however, honor the ways in which students can find meaning that has a basis in the actual language of the text, whether that meaning matches the teacher's or professional literary critics' readings or not.

The Virtual Library of Conceptual Units

I've created the Virtual Library of Conceptual Units, available at www.coe.uga.edu/~smago/VirtualLibrary/index.html. (There's other good stuff at the website too, so surf around.) These units, developed by students at the University of Georgia, illustrate all of the principles of unit design I outline in this book. Help yourself, both for examples of conceptual units and for good teaching ideas for your classroom. There's also a set of unit outlines. Each outline includes

- a topic (e.g., the American dream, success, new kid on the block)
- materials (e.g., novels, poems, films, songs, and other texts that illuminate the topic)
- key concepts and problems that could conceivably organize the instruction (e.g., for a unit on cultural conflict: In what ways are the cultures different? Is one culture more powerful than the other? If so, in what way? In the author's view, is one culture superior to the other? If so, in what ways? Do you agree with the author's judgment? What is the outcome of the clash? Is the outcome fair? Why or why not? How do characters change as a result of their experience with another culture?)

I refer to units in the Virtual Library in subsequent chapters, so bookmark it and enjoy.

Summary

Planning a yearlong curriculum around an overarching concept, and providing attention to that concept through units of study, provides coherence and continuity for both teachers and students, helping students revisit critical issues in their worlds or important learning strategies as they continue to delve into new texts and ideas. Teaching thus avoids the sort of fragmentation that can discourage students' synthesis of ideas, and promotes integration of learning across texts and experiences that are both diverse and related. Now let's turn our attention to the nuts and bolts of planning units of this sort.

9 *The Basics of Unit Design*

Although this chapter suggests a particular order for the process of beginning your planning of a conceptual unit, it's entirely possible that you will not strictly follow these steps in designing your own unit. In fact, it's likely that you will not plan a unit strictly in stages, but instead will jump around: you will consider good books to teach, think of how they'd fit together into a unit of instruction, think of good reasons to teach them, think of additional texts to include, refine the topic of the unit, and so on. However, it would be confusing if I were to write this book so that it made spontaneous leaps the way your mind will while planning a unit. My intention, then, is to treat each area separately with the understanding that you will employ each in conjunction with others, in whatever sequence works for you.

Identifying Unit Topics

Identifying a unit topic is a complex process that involves the consideration of a variety of factors. In the best of all possible worlds, you—perhaps in conjunction with your students—would pick topics and teach them. However, every decision you make comes within the context of a range of factors that constrain your choices. A number of influences may enter into your deliberation of what topics will work well for you and your students. I present them in no particular order; the relative importance of each will vary from setting to setting.

The Curriculum

Curricular Restrictions

One constraint that most teachers deal with is the confines of the curriculum for the course they are teaching. To give an obvious example: Most U.S. high schools dedicate the senior year to British literature. It would be hard to justify teaching a unit on the Harlem Renaissance in a British literature class, although teaching Shakespeare in American literature is often required. Understanding

the confines of a curriculum, then, is an important step in determining what
is and is not available to teach to particular groups of students.

If you teach out of an anthology, you are likely in safe territory with regard to the topics and texts you and your students read because the anthology has been approved at so many levels. If you teach beyond the anthology, things can get more interesting because individual works of literature
can include themes or actions that may be controversial in some communities. To cite one annual source of contention: J. D. Salinger's *Catcher in the
Rye* is often taught in schools because of its engaging portrayal of teen angst.
Holden Caulfield's narration is, however, quite profane, causing the book
to be banned by some boards of education and contested by parents even
when a board does approve the novel.

Curricular Overarching Concept

Another concern in planning units is the overarching concept that unifies
the curriculum over the whole course. You should ask, to paraphrase Applebee (1996): What larger conversation should students be engaged in that
in turn suggests good topics to build units around? I'll suggest a few possibilities. An American literature curriculum might ask, for instance, *What
does it mean to be an American?* The question, of course, assumes that America
refers to the United States and not any of the nations to its north or south,
a premise that some might question; for the present, we'll simply accept the
premise and leave the debate for another time. Students might explore this
question through a variety of units, possibly including the following:

- *protest literature*, beginning with the colonial rhetoric that helped
  launch the American Revolution and inscribe American values
  in the Constitution, and also including key protest literature from
  other eras such as the various women's and civil rights movements

- *the Puritan ethic*, which would seek to understand what this ethic is
  and how it has endured throughout American history and helped
  to shape the American character

- *success*, in which students would consider what a successful person
  is in the United States and whether one person's notion of success
  works for others or whether the same actions would be considered
  successful in different situations

- *frontier literature*, including literature that gives the pioneers'
  perspective on western expansion and literature that provides the
  aboriginal people's view

- *the works of Mark Twain*, whose characters (particularly Huckleberry
  Finn) are often thought to be quintessentially American

- *cultural conflict*, which would help illuminate the issues involved
  when (1) a country is inhabited by natives whose society is
  threatened by the arrival of explorers from radically different

cultures; (2) the ensuing nation is designed to embrace immigrants who bring new ways that can conflict with established customs; (3) commerce, politics, and other factors inevitably bring the nation into contact with other countries; and so on

- *gender roles*, which might look at how those roles have changed over time and examine how a conception of gender plays a role in fulfilling the American dream
- *the authors and artists of [your state]*, which would help students see how their own state fits in with broader themes and perspectives of American society, and help acquaint them with significant authors and artists from their own part of the country

These are not the only unit topics available within this overarching concept, but rather one set of possibilities. I imagine that a teacher would provide variety from year to year, or possibly even for different classes within the same year. If, for instance, you are assigned five classes of American literature, you might contemplate the benefits of dividing your assignment into two preparations so that you don't get burned out or bored from teaching the same thing five times in one day.

Students

When asked, "What do you teach?" some teachers answer, "Students." Rather than viewing themselves as subject-area specialists, they see themselves first as teachers of the people who are in their care. Taking this approach will make you different from some people in the teaching profession. There are those who feel that they teach a subject rather than students. When you believe that you are teaching the subject, you release yourself from much responsibility to make sure that your students are learning. You also can ignore the particular characteristics and needs of your students, since it's their job to learn the subject. What matters is that you know your subject well and present it effectively.

Where you fall on the continuum of teaching students or the subject is a personal matter. If you find this book useful, you probably think that it's important to teach both. In thinking about which units to teach, reflecting on who your students are can help you make good choices. Following are some considerations that ought to enter into your thinking.

Culture and Community

As a teacher you are caught amid many tensions. One that you no doubt feel every day is the tension between viewing everyone as being equal or the same and viewing everyone as unique and different. Teaching students of different races is a good example. On the one hand, you will be encouraged to be color blind—that is, to try to view your students as being the same, regardless of race. On the other hand, you will be encouraged to understand cultural differences that require you to acknowledge and respect the perspectives and behaviors of students whose cultural upbringing has been different from yours.

Understanding cultural differences can be both illuminating and dangerous. Let me give an example provided by my friend and colleague Carol Lee, an African American educator from Chicago. Carol has spoken about the widely believed notion that African Americans come from an oral culture. This belief is grounded in the historical fact that slaves were typically prohibited from learning to read and write, which forced them to develop oral communication to a highly refined degree. And there's strong evidence to support this belief and to use it to interpret modern circumstances.

Carol has argued persuasively, however, that this belief has had a negative impact in schools. Often, white teachers believe that because African American students come from an oral culture, they should not be expected to read and write with the same fluency as white students. As a result, the effort to understand culture results in a very limiting set of expectations that underestimates the potential of African American students.

Therefore, understanding culture, while important, can also be dangerous if the understanding results in limiting stereotypes. And, of course, race is only one aspect of culture. Ethnicity is a factor, as well as regional factors, religion, gender, and countless others. Knowing each can help you understand your students but may also cause you to operate according to limiting stereotypes.

Developmental Level

Although your students' age or grade level is not an absolute indicator of what they should study, it does provide some broad guidelines for what is appropriate to teach. Of course, in a class at one grade level you will have students of differing ages, levels of maturity, levels of knowledge, and so on. This variation makes it hard to say that something is an especially ripe topic for students at a particular grade. On the other hand, there are probably some things that are more appropriate to teach particular groups than others.

Let's say, for instance, that you are teaching seventh-grade students in a typical suburban community. Your students will primarily be twelve or thirteen years old. Would you teach them a unit on transcendentalism? Probably not. The language would be too forbidding, the concepts too abstract. Ideally, you would choose a topic that was appropriate for their adolescent interests and provided literary codes suitable for their reading experiences.

Developmental psychologists have described some tendencies that could help us make decisions about what is developmentally appropriate. Over the course of adolescence, children move in thought, feeling, and action in the following ways:

- from simple to complex
- from concrete to abstract

- from personal orientation to impersonal or multipersonal orientation
- from spontaneous activity to thought with less activity
- from conception of objects themselves to conception of their properties
- from literal to symbolic
- from absolute to relative

In general, then, they develop an ability to step back and see the big picture. As they grow older, students are able to grapple with problems of greater abstraction and are increasingly able to stand back and view themselves as participants in a larger society. Thus, topics for young adolescents might be centered on the immediate social worlds of young protagonists: peer pressure, friendship, new kid on the block, and so on. Toward the end of high school, they might consider topics that place the individual in relation to broader society, with the topics requiring the contemplation of more abstract terms: success, justice, progress, changing times, and the like. (Each unit topic that I refer to in this book—these included—is detailed in the Unit Outlines linked from the Virtual Library of Conceptual Units.)

In thinking about students' developmental levels, teachers should consider Vygotsky's (1978, 1987) belief that *teaching leads development*. In other words, if you think that students are at a particular level, don't teach *to* that level. Rather, lead them to a higher level of development—think of it as a sort of cognitive carrot and stick. Instead of designing a static curriculum targeted at students' presumed levels, teachers who follow this principle are attentive to where students are and where instruction might take them.

Interests

Another factor in deciding on unit topics is students' interests. In suggesting this emphasis, I am not saying that you ought to pander to students' more trivial pursuits. Instead, I'm saying that if one of our goals is to make school learning something that students view with anticipation, then we should consider what they find interesting when evaluating possible topics of inquiry.

Simply finding out student interests and building a curriculum around them is not sufficient. One reason is that some student interests would not make for appropriate English class topics. I recall teaching high school sophomore boys who were quite interested in the misogynist humor of the raunchy stand-up comic Andrew Dice Clay. I had to provide a stern lecture on respect when they incorporated this interest into a project that they performed before the class to the obvious discomfort of many girls. While I was generally open-minded about how students could interpret things and express themselves, there were some kinds of expression that were not available in my classroom.

In general, however, knowing students' interests can be useful when these interests coincide with topics related to unit concepts. There are many ways to get to know what students are interested in. One is to listen to them talk. Another is to see what kinds of icons they wear on their clothing (or draw on their desks). You can also invite more formal accounts of their interests, such as by having students write you an introduction to themselves, or having them write a user's manual for themselves, or having their parents, guardians, or other significant adults write you a letter about them.

Needs

I see needs as being different from interests. Interests refer to those things that, when all is relatively well, students want to learn about. Needs refer to deeper psychological issues. Some of these are developmental and shared by just about everyone passing through a certain point in life, while others are created by particular circumstances.

Common needs result from certain kinds of predictable experiences. I've already referred to the coming-of-age experience as an archetypal passage that can provide the basis for a good, developmentally appropriate unit of instruction. Others might include units on conflict with authority, the trickster, peer pressure, the outcast, rites of passage, and any other social rite or character type that most students are likely to be dealing with in their lives.

Needs that are created by particular circumstances might be tied to archetypal experiences, but they have a more local impact because of events affecting the community. Let's say that a community is experiencing a rise in gang involvement among its youth. It might be appropriate to teach a unit that deals with gangs, cliques, and peer pressure. Or perhaps there are increasing instances of bullying and violence in school. Studying a topic such as discrimination or alienation and discussing the literature in terms of events in school might help students think through the causes and effects of such behavior.

Unless you are trained as a psychologist or counselor, you should be very careful about how you deal with students' needs and equally careful about how you solicit and respond to their thoughts and feelings on sensitive topics. You also need to be prepared to allow students to resist efforts to have them reveal their feelings. I strongly believe that literature and writing can serve as vehicles for people to reflect on and understand better the experiences of their lives. I believe just as strongly that teachers have no right to require personal revelations from students who don't want to share them. Keeping to oneself is a right that all students have, and that should be respected, no matter how much a teacher believes in the power of spoken and written reflection.

At the same time, you have an obligation to ensure a healthy environment for your students. If you think that a student's withdrawal has its roots in depression, drug use, suicidal thoughts, or other threat to his well-being, then you should share your concern with a counselor or school psychologist who can intervene in knowledgeable and appropriate ways.

Teacher

Teachers ought to consider their own interests and needs when deciding what topics to teach. They should reflect on the value of their judgment in knowing what students might benefit from studying, even if the students haven't identified it as an interest. To meet your own needs, think about your interests and your knowledge.

Interests

Just as classes should be of interest to students, they should also be intriguing to their teachers. Students know when teachers are going through the motions. Many student evaluations of teachers that I've read over the years have stressed the importance of teachers being enthusiastic and passionate about their work. Nothing kills enthusiasm like teaching topics and books that you don't like.

The corollary of this axiom is that you should not teach something just *because* you find it interesting. Millions of students have been punished because teachers persistently teach their favorite books, year after year, no matter what students think. Consider your interests, yes, but consider them in the context of other factors. Perhaps it's a good idea to think of it this way: Part of your pleasure from teaching a book comes from the response it gets from students. If your favorite literature is painful for students, then consider their suffering to be a part of your overall experience.

Knowledge

A second factor for teachers to think about is their own knowledge. What do you know about? Teaching within your area of expertise can make you an excellent resource for students in their learning.

On the other hand, some teachers decide to teach a topic or work *as a way to learn about it*. Some have even suggested that it's a good idea to teach a book every so often that you haven't read before, so as to share the students' experience of reading without knowing the outcome. This approach is quite different from the standard image of the English teacher, who knows in advance where all of the foreshadowing and rising action and alliteration are and is eager to point it out and require students to identify it on a quiz.

Reading a book for the first time with students, however, is a good way to stay in tune with their experiences with literature and to model a different conception of what it means to know something. It shows the teacher in the role of reading tentatively and provisionally, as readers do the first time around, instead of in the role of knowing the book as a concrete whole, as most teachers are accustomed to doing.

Selecting Materials

If you view teaching as primarily concerned with the content of your discipline, then the traditions of your discipline will provide you with a canon of literary works that students should read. While the traditional canon can provide excellent reading for secondary school students, it should be one of several factors in settling on the materials for your unit. The issue of broadening the canon raises an old conundrum for teachers of literature. The problem concerns the long-standing tension between the idea that certain works are required reading of all educated people and the idea that the canon meets the needs of professional literary critics more than it does the needs of the general reading public—adolescents in particular.

Teachers are caught in this tension. For the most part they have earned degrees in English and so have taken part in traditional literary study as a kind of formal scholarship. Most of their students, however, will not view literature as a field of scholarship and will instead read for pleasure, escape, fulfillment, knowledge, personal connection, or other personal reasons. In fact, I taught high school English from 1976 to 1990 to more than two thousand students, and to my knowledge, a total of zero of them went on to become English teachers. How teachers manage the tension between their own love of classic literature and their students' preference for other kinds of reading will influence the choices they make about the content of the literature curriculum.

In selecting materials, you should take into account the following concerns.

Tracking

Many schools group students according to their perceived ability or level of performance. A typical school will have two or three tracks. Over the years, in various schools, I have come across a variety of names for tracks: Advanced Placement, aegis, high ability, honors, advanced college prep, college bound, college prep, high average, average, regular, low average, vocational, essential, remedial, developmental, basic, and color codes that students quickly translate to some level of ability or performance. My all-time favorite name comes from a class for students who had failed a subject the previous year. Students retaking the class in summer school enrolled in a course called Encore!

Tracking, while the target of much criticism in universities, is nearly ubiquitous in schools throughout the United States. Tracking is popular for several reasons. It sorts students into groups based on some combination of perceived achievement, competence, and performance. Having relatively homogeneous groups of students makes life easier for many teachers because they can move at one pace, use a uniform set of texts, and otherwise cater instruction to the needs of particular groups of learners. Many parents also like tracking, especially those of students in the higher tracks.

In my very first year of teaching, I taught in an untracked school and confess that I had a very difficult time providing instruction that kept all students consistently engaged and challenged. I hope that if I'd continued teaching in untracked schools I'd have found ways to serve the whole range of students better. During that first year, however, I frequently found myself frustrated that I was moving too fast for some and too slowly for others and serving too few students well.

My purpose here is not to say which system, tracking or untracking, is better. Each is problematic in its own way—in a sense, it's a matter of choosing which problems you'd rather live with. I've taught in both kinds of system and know that resolving the problems of one approach only creates new problems. I've also taught in both high schools and universities and know that the logic that prevails in one is not always persuasive when argued within the other.

Rather, my purpose is to alert you to the fact that the presence or absence of tracking should influence your decisions about teaching. If your school is untracked, you need to be prepared to meet the needs of the whole range of students in your school, all in a single group, suggesting the need for differentiated materials within single classes. If your school uses tracking, then your decisions about materials should be responsive to the reading abilities and interests of your students, and you should be alert to the ways in which race- and class-based discrimination can account for the different populations you find in different tracks.

Literary Value

Educators have often disagreed about the extent to which certain types of texts are sufficiently scholarly to serve as educational materials. The very existence of a literary canon and of a Great Books program suggests that at least some people would differentiate between literature of high quality and literature of lesser value. Indeed, *Sound and Sense*, a poetry volume found in many English department bookrooms, provides examples of high- and low-quality poems and explains why they are so according to principles of New Criticism. The question of what makes something literary is one that all teachers should consider. Furthermore, it is one that students should contemplate. Having students establish criteria for identifying works of literary merit can be a central aim of a literature curriculum.

This book is not designed to answer the question of what distinguishes literature that is great from literature that is not. Rather, it is designed to get you to think about how and why you make decisions. In considering literary value, then, you might ask:

- To what extent should I rely on the wisdom of literary critics in identifying works of literary merit? That is, is relying on the traditional canon sufficient?

- Are the criteria for excellence the same for adolescents and for adults? For mainstream adolescents and college English majors? For students in high and low tracks? For members of one cultural group and members of another? If they are different, whose criteria should prevail in decisions about what to read for school?

- When choosing a text for a particular thematic unit, will any text that fits the theme do, or are some better selections than others? If some are better selections, are they universally better or better relative to different groups of readers?

- What is important in having a satisfying experience with reading? How can one distinguish the traits that result in such satisfying experiences? Are these traits the same for all people? If they are different, how do teachers and students make decisions about which texts are appropriate for reading in school?

Variety of Textual Forms

Another consideration should be the range of textual forms available to illuminate the themes of the literature. Unless your unit topic is restricted to an author who specializes in a particular medium (e.g., Emily Dickinson's exclusive use of poetry), or that focuses on reading particular types of literature (e.g., the detective novel), you should look at what is available in short story, novel, poetry, drama, film, music, fable, sacred story, myth, essay, art, architecture, dance, and any other artistic form.

Appropriateness

By appropriateness, I refer to the extent to which texts meet the rules of propriety that govern life in your school and community. I'll give an example of why this factor is important. A teacher I know grew up in a small, conservative, rural community in the 1970s. When in high school, he was caught reading Eldridge Cleaver's *Soul on Ice*, a book of essays recounting Cleaver's experiences as a Black Panther, civil rights activist, and, at one point, rapist. Upon being found with this book in his possession, he was suspended from school. The next year, he moved to a community in a metropolitan area with a more diverse population and liberal mind-set. He was surprised to see *Soul on Ice* on the required reading list for his senior year.

My point here is that you need to differentiate between what you think is a good text and what people in your community will find objectionable. The texts you personally find riveting may include sex, violence, profanity, and ideologies that may create problems between you and your students' parents. I think, for instance, that the John Woo gangster film *Hard Boiled* is an extraordinary achievement. There's no sex and relatively little profanity, but roughly 230 people die violent, visceral, often slow-motion deaths. The lead character Tequila is played by Chow Yun-Fat. Tequila is indeed a Ruthless Supercop, which is a more accurate translation of the film's Chinese name. Throughout the film he seeks to bring to justice the arms smugglers who kill his partner in the film's famous opening scene, set in a Hong Kong teahouse and filled with mayhem and fluttering birds. It's a legendary action film that could fit well within a number of themes or other organizing principles—friendship, justice, social responsibility, loyalty, irony, success, and others. It is widely regarded as a best-of-genre film, having been included in the Criterion film collection, which produces technically superb editions of "the greatest films from around the world" that stand as "the defining moments of cinema" (www.criterionco.com/asp/about.asp). Yet I wouldn't show it in school because the violence, no matter how artfully filmed, is just too much.

Variety of Authorship

Studies of high school literature curricula (see Applebee 1993) have shown that most books taught in American public high schools have been written by what are known as either DWMs (dead white males) or PSMs (pale stale males). There's a good economic reason that literature anthologies feature works by the deceased: dead men collect no royalties. The preponderance of white males troubles many, however. In the traditional literary canon, both white culture and masculine outlooks provide the worldview presented through literature. This worldview then becomes the norm through which other views are considered to be in deficit. Women and nonwhites are less likely to see themselves and their worlds reflected in the curriculum and therefore feel less a part of the educational enterprise. Of course there are exceptions to these rules, but these points are frequently made in objections to the content of the traditional canon.

With this condition in mind, I'd suggest looking for variety in authorship, particularly when that variety provides for different points of view. When selecting materials, make an effort to include both canonical works and works from underrepresented traditions and cultures. You may find that items from your broadened list will not always be available, but if you teach so that students have options for their reading, you may find that students who want different kinds of experiences will find the books or other texts on their own. Who knows, you may even learn that some students spent Friday night watching *Hard Boiled* for your English class.

Summary

Developing unit topics and choosing materials are the beginning stages of designing a unit. Of course, it's unlikely that I've eliminated all surprises; schools, while designed to be repetitive and predictable, always defy the odds and provide their inhabitants with new situations all the time. Undoubtedly, something will come up that I haven't anticipated. Yet this review should help acquaint you with much of what you need to know to get your unit design off the ground.

10 *Your Unit Rationale*

In Chapter 8 I wrote a rationale for a constructivist, unit-based approach to teaching. A rationale is a persuasive essay in which you explain why, of all the things on earth you could possibly teach, you've decided to teach this. In selecting your unit topic, you've already gone through an informal process of providing a rationale for your unit. You've thought about the community you teach in and how its characteristics might suggest topics. You've thought about the students' developmental needs and the topics that might help meet them. You've given a lot of thought to the concepts that the unit texts will involve. You've also considered the merits of possible texts to include and what students might learn from them. However, there are other reasons that might help you justify your unit topic.

Think of your rationale as serving rhetorical needs. One useful way to think of the rationale is this: If someone were to challenge your teaching, how would you defend it? Teachers are under attack from various quarters. The media are always criticizing schools for one reason or another. Irate parents frequently come to school to voice their displeasure with this or that. University professors typically blame secondary school teachers for any shortcomings of college students. Taxpayers often claim that schools are overfunded, even though teachers are paid disproportionately low for their level of education. Students frequently complain about instruction being irrelevant or tedious.

Even among the faculty, teachers are known to snipe at one another's methods and decisions for various reasons. If any combination of these people asked you to defend your teaching, what would you say? "It's in the curriculum" and "It's always been done this way" and "You're illiterate if you haven't read *At Swim-Two Birds*" are not very satisfying or persuasive answers. Your rationale is your ticket to teaching in ways that you believe in. It's important, then, to write a good one.

Another person you need to persuade is yourself. If you don't teach with conviction, students will be the first to know. It's important, therefore, for you to think through your teaching decisions as carefully as possible so that students can see that you are acting in principled ways.

Your rationale may focus on one of the following justifications or include attention to several. For each type of justification, I have listed units from the Virtual Library of Conceptual Units that employ it.

Psychology or Human Development

Many units can be justified because they respond to the psychological needs of students. Literature often deals with common human experiences about the pressures, changes, dilemmas, aspirations, conflicts, and so on that make growing up (and being grown up) such a challenge. Adolescent literature in particular often features youthful protagonists dealing with the kinds of problems that students are likely experiencing, both those that have endured across the ages and those that are more current. The field of developmental psychology has provided abundant descriptions of the stages that most people go through during their maturation and can help provide a rationale for a number of units that deal with youth culture and the challenges of growing through it.

In the Virtual Library of Conceptual Units, see examples of this type of rationale in the following:

Adu, Glenn, Johnson, and Moore: "R-E-S-P-E-C-T: Finding Out What It Means to Me"

Aveni, Barbakow, Ingram, and Stewart: "Testing the Boundaries: A Unit on Censorship in America"

Brown, Hummel, Mann, Taylor, and Wright: "Freedom and Identity"

Davis: "Family"

Evans: "The Dynamics of Family"

Feldman, Lynn, and Winter: "A Sense of Self"

Ficco: "Negotiating Boundaries: Making It Through Adolescence Alive"

Headrick: "Life Paths and Destinations: Toward Meaningful Textual Transactions for a 12th Grade British Literature Class"

McDaniel: "Individual Liberty"

Cultural Significance

Some units are worth teaching because they are culturally significant. In other words, the material within them is worth engaging with because their themes are central to an understanding of a particular culture, whether national, local, or distant. Here are a few examples of culturally significant topics from each of these three categories.

National

Some topics are related to themes that are central to national concerns. Puritan literature, for instance, can be justified because the Puritans were among the first Europeans to establish a stable society on this continent and operated according to values that are still pervasive in modern American society. Note, for instance, the ways in which Americans are scandalized by the private lives of their public figures; now compare this reaction with the ways in which Italians respond to similar behaviors.

Local

Learning about a local culture can help establish a sense of pride and identity between students and their communities. A unit on a sense of place or local authors (e.g., the writers of Ohio; prairie literature) can allow a teacher to feature local writers and help students engage with themes that have historically been central to their region and culture.

Distant

School should do more than help students know their own cultures; it should also help acquaint them with others. These cultures needn't be situated across the globe; they can be "distant" even while in close proximity. It might be useful, for instance, to have students read a body of literature by members of a race other than their own in order to learn about how life is viewed and experienced differently, even within the same general setting. While in high school, I read books by African American writers (e.g., Richard Wright's *Native Son*, Claude Brown's *Manchild in the Promised Land*) that were culturally distant from me and opened my eyes to worlds that, while remote from my own experiences, were important for me to understand in order to be a good citizen in a pluralistic society.

In the Virtual Library of Conceptual Units, see

Bogdanich and Butler: "Passing to the American Dream"

Wright, Rosenberg, Hellman, and Furney: "Beyond Tacos and Piñatas: A Unit on Hispanic Literature"

Literary Significance

Another way to justify a unit topic is to argue that it has literary significance that makes it essential to any kind of cultural literacy. The works of Shakespeare, for instance, have been performed for nearly four centuries across the world's stages. Therefore, you might mount a convincing argument that studying Shakespeare is central to understanding the themes of Western culture and the metaphors that are invoked to explain it.

You could also argue that particular periods or regions have produced literature that has historical and cultural significance. The Harlem Renaissance, for instance, served to establish African American writers as a significant group in American letters, the first minority group to achieve this stature in the United States. Southern fiction helped to establish the identity of the antebellum South (primarily from a white perspective) and illustrate its tensions in rebuilding its economy and culture in the twentieth century. Constructing these arguments would require some research into the genre and likely the reading of some cultural or literary criticism that establishes its significance.

In the Virtual Library of Conceptual Units, see

Berry, Donovan, and Hummel: "Romeo and Juliet"

Ehret: "Teaching Cultural and Historical Literacy Through Satire"

Ficco: "Negotiating Boundaries: Making It Through Adolescence Alive"

Headrick: "Life Paths and Destinations: Toward Meaningful Textual Transactions for a 12th Grade British Literature Class"

Mann: "Mary Shelley's *Frankenstein* and the Responsibility of the Creator to His Creation"

Civic Awareness

Some units of study help students to understand their roles as citizens in their communities, states, and nation. In units on such topics such as justice, social responsibility, self-reliance, and protest literature, students consider the role of the individual in society. In justifying such units, you might consider the importance of developing a citizenry that knows its history, laws, customs, rights, and responsibilities and uses that knowledge to act responsibly for a more equitable, democratic, and dynamic society. In preparing a rationale for such units, you might argue that throughout American history, citizens have taken action to achieve what they feel is just, and that these actions have been driven by different social goals, different types of conscience, and different understandings of law.

Examples abound: native people who resisted the European explorers, patriots who defied the British, abolitionists who defied the slave owners, slaves who escaped via the Underground Railroad, war protesters of various degrees of legality and violence, civil rights demonstrators, women fighting for the right to vote, women fighting for workplace equity . . . the list goes on and on. A unit focusing on one of these topics can find its justification in the historical background that students can learn through the unit texts and in the code of civic ethics they will develop through their engagement with the problems they read about.

In the Virtual Library of Conceptual Units, see

Aveni, Barbakow, Ingram, and Stewart: "Testing the Boundaries: A Unit on Censorship in America"

Buxton and Kramer: "Educational Issues as a Medium Through Which We Educate"

Davis: "Family"

Dyer: "Science Fiction: Critiquing the Present, Exploring the Future"

Ehret: "Teaching Cultural and Historical Literacy Through Satire"

McDaniel: "Individual Liberty"

Focus on a Current Social Problem

Some units of study find justification in their effort to help adolescents understand and make choices about problems they face in their lives. A unit on peer pressure, for instance, would be justified in a community where teen smoking, drinking, drugs, and other behaviors were a threat to the security and health of teens. A unit on problem resolution could be justified in a community in which students were increasingly violent toward one another (see, e.g., Gevinson 2005; Gevinson, Hammond, and Thompson 2006). In a community that has experienced a devastating loss, a unit on coping with loss might help students find the tools they need to work toward an understanding of their tragedy.

In the Virtual Library of Conceptual Units, see

Dyer: "Science Fiction: Critiquing the Present, Exploring the Future"

Estey: "I Will Speak Up! For Myself, for My Friends, and for What I Believe In!"

Evans: "The Dynamics of Family"

Ficco: "Negotiating Boundaries: Making It Through Adolescence Alive"

Frilot and Tubiak: "The Exploration of Self Within Society"

Headrick: "Life Paths and Destinations: Toward Meaningful Textual Transactions for a 12th Grade British Literature Class"

Lancaster and Warren: "Mental Illness"

Preparation for Future Needs

Teaching is a future-oriented career. Most of what teachers do in the classroom is in preparation for what they think students need next. Teaching students what they will likely need later on is therefore a good justification for a unit.

College

One reason that teachers often give for teaching something is that it will help students succeed in college. I never found this reason to be terribly compelling. Among other things, it doesn't help those who don't go to college. It's also based on the idea that if you know something before you go to college and are required to learn it there, then you're ahead of the game because you've already learned it. This assumption defines knowledge a little too narrowly for my taste.

Nonetheless, it's conceivable that you could justify teaching some things on the basis that students will need them later in college, particularly if what students get is tools rather than simply facts. For instance, a unit on satire could focus on teaching students how to recognize and interpret satires so that when they read *Gulliver's Travels* in college, they will recognize the literary techniques used by Swift and understand the ways in which he is criticizing society.

Social Needs

Teachers might also teach a topic because they feel that they will be preparing students to help construct a better society in the future. Teachers might note, for instance, that people in general do not act with care and tolerance for those who are different or less fortunate from the way they are. Anticipating the need for a more compassionate society, you might decide to teach a unit on the outcast or the effects of discrimination.

In the Virtual Library of Conceptual Units, see

Cooney: "Technology and Progress"

Dodd, Garrard, and Welshhans: "Humanity and Voice in Literature: Building Bridges Among the Past, Present, and Future"

Relevance

Many teachers justify their instruction by arguing that it is relevant to students' interests and personal situations. This relevance often comes in terms of a correspondence between students' current life situations and the actions of characters in the texts they experience. Many readers find that they empathize with, learn from, see hope through, or otherwise relate to characters' dilemmas and predicaments. Presumably, students take a greater interest in characters like themselves than they do in characters and settings that fall well outside their range of experience. The quality of relevance often justifies the use of young adult literature in school classrooms, even while these texts may be considered lowbrow by educators who value the literary canon.

In the Virtual Library of Conceptual Units, see

Berry, Donovan, and Hummel: "Romeo and Juliet"

Brown, Hummel, Mann, Taylor, and Wright: "Freedom and Identity"

Dyer: "Science Fiction: Critiquing the Present, Exploring the Future"

Kee: "Researching the World"

Robinson: "Greed"

Alignment with Standards

Aligning instruction with various standards documents may serve as a sound justification for teaching decisions. The National Council of Teachers of English and International Reading Association collaborated on a set of standards in the mid-1990s to describe the literacy expectations for students. The National Board for Professional Teaching Standards has provided standards by which to evaluate teachers. Many states and districts provide core curricula that outline in considerable detail the particular skills and knowledge that students should develop in school. A rationale based on the instruction's alignment with standards may persuade colleagues and administrators that instruction is appropriate and in accordance with such centralized expectations for teaching and learning.

In the Virtual Library of Conceptual Units, see

Culjan: "A Different Dimension: Fantasy, Folktales, Myths and Legends"

Estey: "I Will Speak Up! For Myself, for My Friends, and for What I Believe In!"

Writing a Rationale

A rationale is a type of argument, a genre that typically includes a number of key elements. Your rationale should be based on a consideration of a related set of questions:

- What concepts are central to the topic of this unit?

- Why am I teaching this unit and its concepts?

- What *type(s) of justification* am I primarily relying on to support my rationale (e.g., psychology or human development, cultural significance, etc.)?

- Within each justification, what are the main *claims* I can make about its relevance to the unit I'm proposing (e.g., studying protest literature is important because it helps students understand the role of conscience in social action)?

- For each claim, what kinds of *evidence* can I provide that would be persuasive to others, and how can I include a *warrant* that explains the ways in which the evidence I present supports my claim?

- What *counterarguments* against my rationale can I anticipate, and how can I provide a *rebuttal* for them?

- How can I provide a rationale for each of the texts that my students will read in conjunction with the unit focus?

With these criteria in mind, you have the framework to construct a rationale for your own proposed unit. While there is no single procedure for writing a rationale, there are some kinds of planning you might want to try. Keep in mind that ultimately you will be producing a persuasive piece of writing, so however you proceed, you should think in terms of coordinating a set of related claims that support a general thesis, each supported by some kind of evidence. You should also keep a potential audience in mind for this argument. If you decide to teach a controversial book, whom must you convince that it's acceptable? The answer to this question might depend on where you teach. If you teach in a mixed-race community and wish to assign Steinbeck's *Of Mice and Men*, which includes language offensive to many African Americans yet which is often admired by middle-class white teachers, how will you pitch your rationale? Considering your audience, and the sorts of claims and points needed in order to persuade these readers or listeners, will work to your advantage in providing a sound, convincing justification for your curricular choices.

Summary

You must be ready to justify your teaching decisions, especially when they fall outside the range typical in your school. Inevitably, you will have your teaching contested by someone, or many someones. The better prepared you are to defend your instruction, the more likely it will be that you can teach in ways that you find important and satisfying. Because the teaching profession can often be frustrating, it's important to have as much control and authority over your teaching practices as possible in order to feel that you are having the effect on students' lives that you hope for. Providing a convincing rationale for your choices is one way to become both a contented teacher and perhaps ultimately a curriculum leader in your school and district.

11 *Outlining a Unit*

In this chapter I take one unit of instruction from the sophomore curriculum and identify a set of goals that students could work toward. I've designed the third unit of the year, on discrimination, to illustrate how I might think as I plan a conceptual unit. My teaching of the unit should keep whole-course goals in mind. For the whole semester, for instance, students will be keeping a portfolio. I need to include regular attention to what might go into the portfolio: what the purpose is, what might make a good exhibit, how to reflect on an exhibit's contribution to the student's learning. Because many students will never have kept a portfolio before, I need to devote some explicit instructional time to how to select and reflect on an exhibit.

These are the responsibilities that I have to my students. I can also assume some learning responsibilities of my own. For instance, as a teacher I could produce some portion of these texts along with my students. They might be interested, for instance, in knowing of some of my own experiences with discrimination, perhaps represented through a multimedia production. I might keep my own portfolio about what I learn about teaching from my experiences during the year.

In addition, I should always *teach reflectively*. In other words, through my evaluation of students, I should always be evaluating my teaching. If students are not learning, how can I change the environment or the structure or content of the lessons? Do some groups of students perform better in my class than others and, if so, why? Do I find myself less patient with some students than others and, if so, can I identify a reason and consequences for my response to them? How do students treat one another in my class, and are there changes I can make to promote better relationships?

In turn, the students have the responsibility to take advantage of the opportunity I will provide. If my instruction is designed in thoughtful ways, they ought to use these tools and activities to grow to the greatest extent possible in their quest toward the unit goals. Through our production of these texts, the class can become a construction zone where there is an ethic of productivity within a respectful environment. Though I'll rarely have 100 percent success in achieving such a classroom, I can set up my class to encourage most students toward that end.

Whole-Course Considerations

I began by identifying a small set of overarching concepts for the sophomore curriculum as a whole, providing a brief rationale for each.

- *Negotiating Thresholds* (theme): I have previously described the appropriateness of this theme for the sophomore course. In brief, sophomores tend to adopt a group orientation and can benefit from considering ways of negotiating the contact they have with other groups. These groups include social groups within their peer culture, the groupings provided by different age and grade levels within their school, and the general distinction between the adolescent and adult worlds that they are in transit between.

- *Self-Determination* (stance): I want my students to develop the stance that they are capable of learning on their own. My role, then, is to teach them how to learn. If we succeed, then they will find the course useful after they leave it; they will not view me simply as a fact dispenser whose utility ends the day of the last exam. Facts, of course, will be central to the knowledge they learn in my class. But the facts will not be an end in themselves. Rather, they will serve as tools for students to use as they construct knowledge. Students will learn how to find facts on their own, how to distinguish a fact from a fraud, how to use facts to construct new paradigmatic and narrative knowledge. In other words, they will learn how facts function. Doing so will be part of our overall effort to help them understand and realize their potential for learning independently and knowing what they need to know.

- *Dramatic Images* (strategy): My experiences as a teacher have taught me the importance of having students generate images that help them visualize literature. Students can render their understanding of literature through art, drama, dance, and other artistic and theatrical forms. I have found through my research that doing so not only provides a way to represent their understanding but can contribute to the understandings that they reach.

Earlier I identified a series of culminating texts that students could produce for final exams in relation to these overarching concepts. Now I will narrow my scope to a single unit within this whole course and identify goals for that unit.

Conceptual Unit on Discrimination

The year begins with a unit on coming of age, which provides an opportunity to explore the kinds of transitions that students make in moving from ninth grade to tenth. (See Smagorinsky 2002 for a detailed account of how to plan such a unit.) Often the summer has placed them in situations that have enabled significant transformations of the sort explored in coming-of-age literature. By beginning with the coming-of-age unit, I have an opportunity to include attention to the writing of narratives, through which the students may recount, reconstruct, and reflect on critical personal experiences in relation to the unit theme. From there, we move to an open-ended writing workshop in which students work for several weeks to develop writing of their choice.

Given that, at least in publications (e.g., Atwell 1998), students often choose personal narratives for their workshop writing, the unit on discrimination provides a good opportunity to move to paradigmatic writing. The primary writing that they do in this unit, then, is an extended definition of discrimination. Because discrimination is subject to so many permutations, I provide an element of choice by allowing each student to pick a particular kind of discrimination to define: racial discrimination, reverse discrimination, discrimination based on age, gender discrimination, discrimination based on physical or mental conditions, or whatever other topic interests him.

I also include a multimedia production in this unit. In the coming-of-age unit, I start by having students write narratives and then get into small groups to dramatize a narrative based on their writing. In this way, prior to reading, the students have exposure to a series of stories that are concerned with coming-of-age experiences. The opening unit thus includes a formal kind of writing of the sort often found on high-stakes writing assessments as well as a more kinesthetic means of relating a story that contributes to students' ability to generate images for their reading. The discrimination unit also has a balance between formal writing and multimedia composing.

In the coming-of-age unit I use Cindy O'Donnell-Allen's method of teaching students to maintain double-column reading logs (see Chapter 2). We return to these logs as well in the discrimination unit. This time, however, I don't need to teach them how to produce the logs; I can simply assign them. We thus have both formal and informal writing in this unit.

Finally, in this unit I teach students how to generate questions in relation to a text and to lead their own discussions. The main feature that all four of the culminating texts share is that they are open-ended and require students to construct knowledge for themselves through the available tools.

Materials

For the unit's major work, I've selected a canonical text, Richard Wright's autobiography, *Black Boy*, a staple of many sophomore curricula. I also want other types of texts represented. For this unit, because discrimination has historically been the subject of many kinds of expression, I include songs, poetry, and short stories. I might also use the Google Image search engine to find statues, paintings, political cartoons, and other works of art featuring discrimination.

The materials I've selected are as follows. In making these selections I've tried to seek a balance of men and women, old and new, U.S. and international, and this race and that, and I've made other efforts to include multiple perspectives on this complex topic. I recognize that any given school might have limitations in terms of what's available to teach, so these choices may need revision in particular settings. Also note that my own taste in music is undoubtedly dated to the adolescent mind and that you might search for more contemporary selections than my ancient affections can provide.

Songs

The Weavers: "Sixteen Tons"

Vanessa Williams: "Colors of the Wind"

Dave Matthews Band: "Cry Freedom"

Bob Marley and the Wailers: "War"

Johnny Clegg and Savuka: "Inevitable Consequence of Progress"

Randy Newman: "Short People"

The Crüxshadows: "Leave Me Alone"

Neil Young: "Southern Man"

Creedence Clearwater Revival: "Fortunate Son"

Poems

Maya Angelou: "On the Pulse of Morning"

Peter Blue Cloud: "The Old Man's Lazy"

Elizabeth Brewster: "Jamie"

Short Stories

Maria Campbell: "Play with Me"

Leslie Marmon Silko: "Tony's Story"

Kurt Vonnegut: "Harrison Bergeron"

Shirley Jackson: "After You, My Dear Alphonse"

José Antonio Burciaga: "Romantic Nightmare"

Ray Bradbury: "All Summer in a Day"

Autobiography

Richard Wright: *Black Boy*

Unit Goals

For the major unit goals, I selected assessments that evaluate a range of ways of knowing. I also included assessments of two types:

- *In-Process Texts and Activities*—that is, those that students do as part of their learning *during* the unit. These texts and activities are designed to be exploratory and formative, with attention primarily to what students learn. The final look of their product is of less concern.

- *Culminating Texts and Activities*—that is, those that students do toward the *end* of the unit. These texts and activities should be more concerned with expectations for form, although they should also serve as opportunities for new learning.

The *in-process* texts and activities ought to contribute to students' ability to produce satisfying *culminating* texts and activities. There are dozens of worthwhile goals you could set for any unit of instruction. To help focus the students' attention on objectives they can realize in rich and productive ways, I suggest identifying a small set of goals to serve as the major assessments for the unit. These goals should be consistent with the overarching concepts of the course as a whole. When you plan other units within the curriculum, you should vary the goals and assessments to account for students' multiple ways of knowing.

For the discrimination unit, I want to provide for a range of ways of knowing that fit within the three overarching concepts identified previously. In other words, I want students to begin to understand how to negotiate thresholds, to develop a stance that they will determine much about their own learning, and to learn procedures for generating images to represent literary relationships and actions. Let's take a look at one possible set of goals for this unit.

In-Process Texts and Activities

Self-determination is among the year's overarching concepts. I hope that during the course of the year, students will develop the stance that they are in control of their learning. I want them to believe that they know what they want to learn and know how to learn it.

But hoping isn't enough. I need to make sure that I teach them ways of learning that contribute to that kind of confidence and authority. Teaching for self-determination, therefore, requires that I help students learn procedures for setting goals and posing questions that they would like to answer.

If they have had a typical education, they are probably inexperienced at posing their own questions about their schoolwork; they have spent most of their school life answering questions asked by teachers.

Because of their inexperience at asking questions, I want to give them opportunities that have two features:

- The students may take risks and make mistakes without being punished by a bad grade.
- They have the opportunity to work collaboratively and receive feedback while learning as part of an instructional scaffold.

Two goals that could potentially provide these opportunities are keeping a *response log* and leading *student-generated discussions.*

Double-column reading logs.

Keep a reading log in response to the literature we are studying during this unit. To keep your log, do the following:

- Divide each page with a vertical line down the center.
- On the left side of each page, record significant passages from the literature you read.
- On the right side, across from each passage, include at least one question of each type for each work of literature studied:
  - ‣ Ask *open-ended questions* that would help you understand the passage better.
  - ‣ Give your personal *response* to the passage (i.e., any thoughts you have in connection with it).
  - ‣ Give your personal *evaluation* of the passage.
  - ‣ Think through a possible *interpretation* of the passage.

    Three rules:

1. Remember that your journal does not need to follow the conventions of textbook English. Rather, the purpose is to think about the literature without worrying about the form your thoughts take.

2. Turn in your response log every two weeks. I will read your log and respond to your comments. If you make an entry that you do not want me to read, place an *X* at the top of the page and I'll skip it. Really.

3. Keep in mind that *I am required to share any thoughts or suggestions of violence, suicide, substance abuse, family abuse, or other harmful behavior with the school counselors.*

Student-led discussions.

To discuss Richard Wright's *Black Boy*, the class will organize into five small groups, with each group being responsible for leading a discussion of four chapters of the novel. Each group will be responsible for conducting a class discussion on its chapters for one full class period. To lead your class, you may adopt any format you wish: regular English class, nonviolent talk show format, town hall meeting, courtroom, or other mode of your choice. Your discussion should meet all of the following requirements:

- Each group member should take a roughly equal part in leading the discussion.

- You should make an effort to include each other class member in your discussion.

- The questions you pose should not ask for factual information from the story, unless those facts serve to help explore open-ended questions (i.e., those without a single correct answer).

- The questions you pose should include at least one of each of the following categories:

    inferences about characters or events within the text (e.g., How does joining a gang affect Richard's life?)

    generalizations from the text to society at large (e.g., In what ways is Richard's story from the first half of the twentieth century relevant to today's society?)

    the *effects of literary form or technique* (e.g., Do you think that Richard's presentation of his experiences is realistic?)

    the *purpose of a particular event* in terms of the text's meaning (e.g., How does Richard's life in the orphanage shape his perspective on life in the United States?)

    evaluations of the literature (e.g., What parts of the story do you like best and least? Why?)

    emotions that students have in response to the story (e.g., How did you feel when Richard burned down his grandparents' house?)

    personal connections to the story (e.g., What connections do you feel with Richard during his employment at the optical company?)

- During the discussion, you should also work at getting students to elaborate on their initial comments.

Culminating Texts and Activities

The in-process assessments are designed to teach students strategies for learning both stance and procedures for personal inquiry. They focus on the process of inquiry more than on the precision of the final product. For culminating texts and activities, your focus includes attention to the final form of the effort and how it meets particular conventions. This attention to form does not eliminate attention to process, but rather stresses the idea that certain kinds of texts have particular features that readers expect to find. These formal features serve as codes to help readers invoke the appropriate reading conventions. The more faithfully a writer works within these conventions, the more likely it will be for readers to be in tune with the writer's intentions (Nystrand 1986).

A simple example: A reading log does not call for correct answers or conventional English because the emphasis is on using writing as a tool for thinking, rather than on producing an impeccable product. A reader who expects standard conventions might consider students to be bad writers when they are in fact using the logs as intended. It behooves a writer to know which conventions to call on in producing particular kinds of writing. Culminating texts should be responsive to the need for appropriate conventional form.

Following is a set of assignments for culminating texts that meet all of these goals for the unit.

Extended definition of a particular kind of discrimination.

> Throughout the unit we have considered the effects of discrimination, on both the person who discriminates and the person who is being discriminated against. We have looked at questions of discrimination in a variety of situations, using examples from current events, from your personal experiences and observations, and from literature. In some cases, there has been disagreement on what counts as discrimination.
>
> Your task is to write an essay in which you provide an extended definition of discrimination of a particular kind, such as gender discrimination in the workplace, racial discrimination in housing, religious discrimination in school, age discrimination in hiring, or any other sort that interests you.
>
> To do so, provide the following:
>
> - a general introduction in which you provide an overview for your definition
> - a set of *criteria* or rules that state clearly what discrimination is and is not
> - for each criterion, an *example* from literature, current events, or your personal experiences that illustrates the rule at work; at least half of your examples must come from the literature studied in class
> - for each criterion, a *counterexample* from literature, current events, or your personal experiences that appears to meet the conditions of the rule yet that lacks some essential ingredient; at least half of your counterexamples must come from the literature studied in class

- for each example and counterexample, a *warrant* that clearly explains why the rule is or is not being met
- for your whole argument, a *counterargument* expressing the viewpoint of someone who might disagree with you
- for the counterargument, a *rebuttal* in which you defend your position
- conventional grammar, spelling, punctuation, and usage throughout your essay
- evidence of having written at least one rough draft that has been submitted for peer evaluation

Multimedia project.

You have read a number of literary works that concern the theme of discrimination. To show what you have learned through your engagement with this literature, create an interpretive text in any form of your choice: collage, painting, poetry, music, drama, sculpture, performance art, or other textual form. You are also welcome to combine forms to produce your text. When designing your text, keep the following in mind:

- The project should in some way depict your understanding of experiences with discrimination.
- It should make some kind of reference to at least one work of literature studied during the unit.
- You may produce your text individually or in a group of any size up to three.
- You will have one class period in which to work on your text and must do all additional work outside class.
- You must prepare a three- to five-minute presentation of your text to the class in which you explain its significance and what it illustrates about your understanding of discriminatory experiences and/or literature.

Summary

We now have a simple outline of the unit goals. I'll flesh out each as I put them into practice during the unit design. A few reminders: For each of these assignments you'll need a rubric for assessment; for each responsibility you assign to students, you must simultaneously assign yourself the task of teaching them how to meet the responsibility; and the whole range of assignments should allow diverse students access to success in learning about the topic and performing well on the assessments.

12 *Setting Up the Construction Zone*

The next step is to plan classes so that students can work productively toward the unit goals. I continue using the construction metaphor I have used throughout the book, characterizing the classroom with Newman, Griffin, and Cole's (1989) term *construction zone*. In this construction zone, teachers help students build and reflect on texts that they find useful and important.

If the unit goals are thoughtfully set so that they help students engage with the unit concepts, they should enable students to work toward the production of texts that are meaningful in two ways:

- The *process* of planning and constructing texts will enable students to synthesize prior knowledge and build new knowledge. Both the teacher and other students are available to coconstruct or provide help during this process. This process of composition is usually exploratory, with new ideas discovered as the work of construction unfolds.

- The *product* will be a text that the student can reflect on for continued learning. The text also serves to communicate the student's understandings to others and enable her to reflect on the unit problems in new ways. *Product* does not describe only the finished text. It also refers to the text at any point during the composing process, when its builder(s) can step back, consider its form, and either revise or build on it. And remember that a text is never really finished, even though it may achieve an assessable form for school purposes. If the text matters to the student, then it will undergo continual revision, if not tangibly then psychologically, as the student continues to think through the ideas that generated the text.

Students will build these texts through the use of *tools*. These tools can include language (primarily speaking and writing) and its particular uses (e.g., exploratory talk, analytic essays, reading logs, and so on). The workshop classroom also allows for a broader *tool kit* for text construction. This kit might include music, the movement in dance and drama, various tools for producing art, computers and all of their capabilities, and other instruments that students might find useful in producing texts.

Classroom members' use of these tools will come within an environment overseen by you, the teacher. In your leadership role you will help students learn how to use tools effectively, draw on necessary resources, act as productive crew members, and understand the nature and purpose of the texts they are constructing. At times you might be a facilitator, at times you might provide clear and explicit information, at times you might turn over leadership responsibilities to students. At times you might work along with students, constructing texts according to the same guidelines they are following. You might also produce texts from research that you are conducting on the relation between your teaching and their learning, on the kinds of human relationships that follow from your teaching in your classroom, or on students' lives outside the classroom so that you better understand how to build on their knowledge and strengths.

You will use your good judgment about which role is most appropriate for which circumstances and needs. You will make all of these judgments with an awareness of the overall context in which you are teaching, including your department, your school, your community, and your state. You should be a good citizen of all of these social groups, keeping in mind that one responsibility of citizenship is to work for change when systems don't serve their constituents well.

Teaching Language

The humanities department of the community college where I teach has a long-standing policy regarding our demand for sentence-structure correctness in all the composition courses that we provide. That policy holds students accountable for total control over the rules that govern sentence structure. Any student paragraph or essay that contains one sentence error (comma splice, fused sentence, or fragment) cannot receive a grade higher than a C; two such errors result in a D; and three or more result in an automatic F. This is a demanding approach, but all our department members favor it, and all adjuncts must adhere to it. Our theory is that the sentence unit is the foundation upon which the paragraph and, subsequently, the entire essay are built, and we all acknowledge the consequences of a weak foundation.

—Professor Walter H. Johnson,
"The Sentence-Structure Dilemma"

The definition of insanity is doing the same thing over and over and expecting different results.

—Attributed to Rita Mae Brown, Albert Einstein, Benjamin Franklin, Rudyard Kipling, a Chinese proverb, and others

As I have argued, language is a tool through which students may express themselves, construct meaning, communicate, and accomplish other ends. In Professor Johnson's view—and in the view of many others—this tool has great limitations when used in the classroom. Professor Johnson would prefer that written speech be produced according to a single set of conventions. He also believes that the sentence is the essential unit of communication, one that works only in its most pristine form. As you can imagine, I disagree with Professor Johnson's view of how teachers should respond to students' written work. I see language as much more malleable and flexible and do not believe that rigid rules do much except discourage people from wanting to write in school.

The teaching of grammar, broadly defined, is a pretty gnarly responsibility for English teachers. A lot of people just hate grammar instruction. I googled "hate grammar," for instance, and got more than 4.5 million hits. Then I googled "hate Osama bin Laden" and got about 4.3 million. So you have some idea of how popular this grammar thing is. You should familiarize yourself with some important debates surrounding the teaching of grammar so that when setting up your classroom as a construction zone, you will be prepared for students to use language in many and varied ways to build meaningful texts in relation to your curriculum.

Textbook English and Problems with Teaching It

The teaching of grammar apart from speaking and writing is among the most widely employed, yet least effective, practices in the English teacher's repertoire. Educational researchers disagree on much, but have reached an astounding consensus for more than 100 years: isolated grammar instruction—no matter whether transformational, descriptive, prescriptive, traditional, or voodoo—does not move students' speech or writing toward the norm established in textbooks (see Weaver 1996 and Hillocks 1986 for comprehensive reviews of this research). Hillocks found that of all methods of teaching writing that appeared in educational research during the twenty-year span of his review, grammar instruction was the only one that was ineffective for writers (see Graham and Perrin in press, who've found that isolated grammar instruction actually has a *negative* effect on the quality of student writing). Among the explanations for this result is that grammar instruction occupies a whale of instructional time that would better be spent on just about any other method of teaching writing.

The National Council of Teachers of English is in agreement on this issue. In *Position Statement on Grammar Exercises to Teach Speaking and Writing* (1985), the council states that isolated grammar and usage exercises are "a deterrent to the improvement of students' speaking and writing." It further urges "the discontinuance of testing practices that encourage the teaching of grammar rather than English language arts instruction." It appears, then, that there is remarkable agreement that isolated grammar instruction is at best futile and at worst harmful—at least among researchers and opinion leaders in NCTE. This universally baneful view leaves many of us scratching our heads and wondering why it remains such a ubiquitous classroom practice.

The Persistence of Traditional Grammar Instruction

No one has yet provided a satisfactory answer to the question of why grammar instruction persists in spite of such overwhelming evidence and such widespread opinion that it has so little value. Extrapolating from research conducted by Johnson et al. (2003) on the persistence of the five-paragraph theme in the face of near-universal condemnation among composition theorists, I can suggest some possible reasons for grammar's stability in the English curriculum:

1. Based on their own experiences as students, teachers have internalized the idea that grammar instruction is essential to students' learning about how to speak and write properly.

2. Many state, district, and school curricula specify grammar instruction, down to how to cross *t*'s and dot *i*'s, leaving teachers with little alternative but to teach it, even if it might not actually be possible to cover the English language as specified in all of its glorious detail. Natalie Gibson reports that at her first teaching job, the school had its "own curriculum in addition to the state's [Quality Core Curriculum]. It combines QCC objectives and standardized test objectives. I was supposed to teach the reading *and* language art curriculum in one daily 50-minute class period. It was an insane amount of material to cover. I have learned since . . . that it would actually take something like 25 years to teach [the state's] curriculum!" (in Smagorinsky et al. 2004, 242).

3. Teacher education programs emphasize the teaching of literature much more than the teaching of writing and language, leaving early-career teachers with few alternatives to the grammar-and-composition textbook for writing instruction.

4. Teachers teach within poor work conditions (too many students, too little planning time, and so on) that limit their ability to contest the curriculum or develop alternatives to the textbook approach to

teaching grammar. With few alternatives and work conditions that press them into service monitoring the cafeteria and doing paperwork rather than doing professional reading, most teachers, who find the first year of teaching so overwhelming in so many ways (see McCann, Johannessen, and Ricca 2005), reach for the most convenient and widely employed tool available: the grammar-and-composition textbook.

5. Institutional pressures such as testing mandates force teachers to emphasize grammar. The continual assault of the battery of standardized tests assesses students' knowledge of the minutiae of grammar knowledge, requiring teachers to teach the superficial correction skills so abhorred by just about everyone except policy makers and test designers and Professor Johnson and his intellectual kin.

Further, there is widespread disagreement on the purposes of language instruction. On a typical faculty, you might find teachers who align themselves with the positions of each of the following commentators, as well as others who have opined on the topic in many and varied ways:

- Safire (1984), who argues that all speakers and writers should employ a pristine version of the English language such as the one that he speaks (see also Professor Johnson)

- Delpit (1995), who maintains that while language variation is inevitable, students must learn the codes of power that give them access to the benefits of the economy

- Smitherman (2006), who finds the notion of standard English to be discriminatory

- Noguchi (1991), who believes that errors carry different degrees of status for their users, and that the trick to language instruction is to eliminate errors that well-educated readers find most egregious (e.g., subject-verb disagreement)

- Shaughnessy (1977), who believes that deviations from textbook English are developmental and indicate that writers are taking risks

- Hymes (1974), who argues that all language use is situational and that the key for speakers is to develop communicative competence

The lack of consensus on what should constitute language instruction, along with the absence of teaching methods that effectively teach the English language no matter how construed, leaves the grammar textbook as the default means of addressing the language strand of the English curriculum.

Why Grammar Instruction Is So Tricky

It is perhaps commonsensical, at least to some notions of sense, to think that by teaching grammar, we will change the ways in which students speak and write. However, teaching grammar can be more difficult than it seems, for several reasons.

There Are Many Sets of Rules

One assumption behind grammar instruction is that people agree on what correct grammar is and so can distinguish right from wrong in students' usage. Yet in spite of claims that there is a well-defined standard for the English language, what is right according to one set of rules is wrong according to another. Let's take one recurring within-sentence structure, the list consisting of three or more items. According to the Harvard comma rule, a writer inserts a comma following the penultimate item (e.g., the good, the bad, and the ugly). The *Publication Manual of the American Psychological Association* (American Psychological Association 2001) prescribes the use of the Harvard comma rule. Yet the Modern Language Association does not; writers using MLA eschew the comma that precedes the final item in the set.

And so comma use is primarily a matter of choice of which set of rules to follow, rather than which usage is correct. The same goes for beginning sentences with coordinating conjunctions, forbidden in grammar books but employed in the previous sentence by yours truly. My point is simply that while emphasizing absolute correctness—"total control over the rules that govern sentence structure," in the view of Professor Johnson—grammarians are not working with a medium where such a standard exists (Hunt 2006; Schuster 2006).

Students Rarely Hear Textbook English Actually Spoken

Students are surrounded by people who speak English. Few people, however, actually speak the textbook version stressed in English classes. When was the last time you heard the average person use the subjunctive mood properly? "If it wasn't for that . . ." is uttered for more frequently than "If it weren't for that . . ." no matter what your grammar book says. Most people use *between* (used for two items) when *among* (used for three or more) is appropriate. Young people hear ungrammatical structures daily from musicians, athletes, movie stars, disk jockeys, newscasters, and others whom they admire and emulate. Even high-level politicians—including those who demand elaborate accountability systems to make sure that children are being taught their grammar—are known to butcher a phrase now and then.

The point is simply that it's difficult for a young person to accept a construction as incorrect when it's commonly used by everyone around him. In 1971 *National Lampoon* writer Michael O'Donoghue wrote a satirical piece called "How to Write Good." Given that *good* has replaced *well* as the adverb of choice for such constructions, I wonder how many people would, at this point, get the joke. When students hear phrasing of this sort more often than they hear what the textbook says is proper, it's no surprise that they end up conforming to the everyday speech of their surroundings rather than the quaint and curious rules that their textbooks and teachers say are correct.

"Errors" Can Be Signs of Growth

Mina Shaughnessy (1977) was among the first to take a developmental approach to her students' use of language. Instead of punishing her students for making errors—for example, automatically failing them for making three errors, regardless of the paper's content—she viewed errors in a more hopeful light. People make errors, she reasoned, when trying something new, and they will rarely try something new if they will be penalized for their errors. She hoped to accomplish two goals simultaneously: to encourage her students to experiment with new sentence structures and syntaxes and to educate them about textbook English *over time*. She saw errors, then, as potentially positive indications of students' willingness to grow as writers and did not mark down papers initially for deviations from the norm that ultimately would be expected of them.

What's Important Is Knowing How to Speak for Different Listeners

Many people question the idea that a standard version of English even exists, arguing instead that there are many dialects of English, of which textbook English is but one. What counts as proper is a function of who is speaking and who is listening, and what matters most is knowing the codes that provide the basis for what others find appropriate. When knowledge of these codes affects a speaker's upward mobility—for example, when knowing what is proper helps to advance one's economic potential—then learning a dialect such as textbook English is probably a good idea.

Delpit (1995) relies on this premise to argue that speakers of varieties such as African American English benefit from expanding their repertoires to include the syntax, vocabulary, and other aspects of diction that are current in the work environments in which they seek employment. Similarly, a European American pursuing a career as a hip-hop artist would benefit from learning and practicing those dimensions of language use that constitute African American English—syntax, tropes, vocabulary, and so on— along with the posture, attire, tone, attitudes, and other traits that work in relation with the expectations of the hip-hop community.

All Errors Are Not Created Equal (Though They Might Be Created Equally)

Each of the following sentences contains at least one error:

Your continuous complaining is getting on my nerves.

The warts on my nose is getting bigger.

Let's assume that you are the rare person who can distinguish between (not among) *continuous* and *continual* and knows that in order for a person to complain continuously, she (not they) would complain without pause—including while asleep. Then let's assume that you can identify a plural subject and single object of the adjectival (not adjectivial) prepositional phrase, and know that the verb should agree with the subject of the clause and not the nearest noun. (Note, too, that I have violated a comma rule by using a comma to separate the compound verbs in the previous sentence; a comma would be appropriate only with three or more verbs—at least according to the Harvard comma rule.)

Which of these two errors bothers you more? If you're like most people who can identify the errors, the subject-verb disagreement is more (not most) bothersome to you. Errors that really get people's dander up are known as "status" errors (Connors and Lunsford 1988; Hairston 1981). And so, subject-verb agreement errors offend language purists much more than do dangling prepositions and thus should get greater instructional attention. (And we should note that whether something should be classified as a dangling preposition or as an adverbial particle—and thus is either unacceptable or acceptable—is not entirely clear or agreed upon. How, for instance, would you classify *upon* in the previous sentence?) If you agree that departures from the textbook norm are not all of equal severity, then it follows that teachers, rather than view grammar instruction as a field that must be covered in its entirety, should concentrate on educating students about a relatively small number of usage rules, the mastery of which will give them greater status when communicating with those to whom the English language has a pure form.

Methods of Teaching Grammar

Thus far I have outlined why the teaching of grammar is such a controversial topic and bewildering school subject for many students and teachers. As a longtime high school English teacher, I know that critiquing the state of affairs is not sufficient. Within these limitations and competing interests, I need to find ways to teach students about language usage that they will find relevant to their communication needs.

There are several reasons language study is justified, even while it has largely proven to be futile and often counterproductive to its own goals. First, as readers of student writing, teachers want to be able to understand what students are trying to say. Papers written with rambling syntax do not communicate ideas effectively, and in other, more high-stakes settings in which writing is expected, writing produced with deviations from the textbook norm will reduce our students' prospects for advancement. Second, in spite of the problems I have outlined, test designers continue to include large sections on language use that have great consequences for students (when the tests reflect on them) and schools and teachers (when the tests reflect on them). And so attention to language usage has an important, if problematic, place in the English curriculum.

Principles Guiding Grammar Instruction

Based on my understanding of the issues I have outlined and my experience as a teacher, I endorse the following general guidelines for teaching students about language in the English curriculum:

- Don't teach grammar in isolation. Grammar instruction is most relevant when related clearly to students' writing and reading. While there may be occasions when you correct students' spoken grammar, reserve most of your corrective work for students' writing. Correcting students' speech is more likely to silence and humiliate them than it is to change their language usage toward the norm you have in mind.

- Treat grammar as an enabling *tool* rather than as a subject to be learned or a way to measure students' deficits relative to textbook English. Long ago, Pooley (1954) identified four points as germane to the tool approach:

  1. Postpone grammar instruction to the point where it can really become useful to the student. Too much grammar is commonly taught too early.

  2. Teach a few concepts at a time, slowly and thoroughly.

  3. Emphasize those elements of grammar which lead to improved sentence structure.

  4. Teach correctness in specific situations, and use grammar as the explanation of, rather than the means toward, greater correctness. (143; quoted in Reid 2006b, 13)

     Just for fun, I'll note that in item 3 above, Pooley uses *which* when a grammar textbook would say he should have used *that*—unless he was British, in which case it was probably OK. Was this error a problem for you in digesting his views?

- Attention to language is most useful in limited doses. Rather than spend entire class periods or several days or weeks or months covering the gerund, provide language instruction in relatively brief lessons (see Anderson 2006). Perhaps these lessons might be daily oral language segments that are clearly tied to students' experiences with their reading or writing, although not everything I've seen in the name of DOL is consistent with this principle.

- Grammar instruction should be selective and targeted to language issues that may (1) raise questions with some about the speaker's or writer's status, such as subject-verb agreement, unintentional sentence fragments, and comma splices, or (2) result in confusion, such as dangling modifiers and pronoun-antecedent ambiguity. I also see a role for correcting pet-peeve errors in usage, such as using nominative forms in objective structures (e.g., "Miss Education taught the pronoun lesson to she and I.").

- While some grammar instruction is inevitably corrective, it should also be generative. That is, knowledge of how to correct errors is essential for editing writing. But knowledge of how to generate various syntactic structures (e.g., through sentence combining or generative imitation) helps students produce more varied and sophisticated writing.

- Focusing on labels of grammatical components is useful largely for testing students on such knowledge, and even then not so effective. I recommend focusing on attending to linguistic structures without getting carried away by the terminology, but also being aware that this terminology might matter when outside assessors lurk.

- When responding to student writing, focus on a few recurring problems rather than flooding papers with red ink, which can overwhelm writers because there is too much diffuse information for them to process effectively. I understand the temptation to draw students' attention to each error. But if the goal is to improve students' usage, then your best bet is to fix a few things at a time, rather than to try to effect wholesale change all at once.

- Speaking of red pens, think about marking papers with some other color. There's no law that I'm aware of that specifies red ink for grading student papers, and the color has a lot of bad associations for many students. Amazingly, the cover of one grammar-and-composition book shows a student's face placed in the center of wall-to-wall, perfectly aligned red pens. I wonder what motivated the book's designers to cover a book about writing with the symbol that represents many students' most negative experiences with writing, especially those students most in need of help.

Some Good Sources for Teaching Ideas

A number of publications, many by practicing teachers, have treated the teaching of grammar in comprehensive ways—see, for instance, Anderson (2005), Ehrenworth and Vinton (2005), Haussamen et al. (2003), Killgallon and Killgallon (2006), Kolln (1998), Noden (1999), Parsons (2004), Schuster (2003), Shaughnessy (1977), Smith and Wilhelm (2007), Topping and Hoffman (2006), Weaver (1996), Wheeler (1999), and Wheeler and Swords (2006). Instead of attempting to outline approaches to teaching grammar here, I'll simply refer you to these books, along with two special theme issues of *English Journal* (Christenbury 1996; Reid 2006a) for a host of ideas on teaching grammar in useful and often enjoyable ways.

Contexts of Teaching

You do not teach in a vacuum. Rather, you teach within a set of confines or constraints. These parameters can be useful in that they provide a set of guidelines for appropriate decision making. They can also, of course, restrict your choices. Whether you like them or not, however, they exist and provide the context for your teaching. It's important, then, to understand where you teach, whom you teach, and those with whom you teach.

The School and Community Contexts

Your teaching should be responsive to your students and their needs. I don't claim that you can simply take the unit I outline in this book or the units in the Virtual Library of Conceptual Units and teach them anywhere without modification. In writing this book for a broad audience, I am handicapped by the problem that a unit well suited for one context might be less useful in another. I will therefore provide a context for the unit, based on schools where I've taught as well as schools I've observed. The school's profile is typical of many schools across the country. The unit is very similar to units I've taught in schools like these.

Our hypothetical school is a comprehensive public senior high school of two thousand students. It lies in the metropolitan area of an urban center and includes students from across the economic spectrum. It has a three-track system, with the tracks labeled honors, regular, and basic; for upper grades there are more specialized tracks such as Advanced Placement and vocational. The sophomore curriculum I've designed will be for students in the regular track.

Racially, students are 50 percent European American, 20 percent African American, 10 percent Asian American, 10 percent Hispanic American, 5 percent Native American, and 5 percent mixed race. Slightly under half of the students come from homes that include both biological parents. Eighty percent of the senior class will have a part-time job at some point during their senior year. Sixty percent of each freshman class will graduate within four years. Of the remaining 40 percent, 15 percent will move to another district, 10 percent will drop out, 1 percent will be expelled for disciplinary reasons, and 14 percent will graduate following additional coursework. In a typical graduating class, 40 percent of seniors go to a four-year college, with half of them eventually receiving degrees. Of the remaining 60 percent, 20 percent go to a two-year college, 20 percent go to a trade school, and 20 percent enter the workforce, including the military.

The town is characterized by the lack of consensus typically found in diverse communities. In a typical year, the town newspaper will report frequently on

- disputes about property taxes that fund education, with many citizens writing letters to the editor questioning whether the schools provide enough quality to merit tax increases

- concern about school discipline, with many citizens believing that declining behavioral standards are affecting the overall quality of education

- disagreements about the role of religion in school, with some believing that Christian morality should be explicitly taught and some opposing any mention of Christianity (e.g., Christmas holiday, Easter, etc.)

- different notions of educational standards by various community members

- conflicting views on how the town's cultural diversity should be reflected in the curriculum

- questions about whether and how to diversify the faculty and administration to reflect the community's racial makeup

- the belief by minority parents that their children are singled out by school disciplinarians for punishment

- the belief by white parents that minority students get special treatment from teachers and administrators because they are afraid of being called racists, even though the school's assistant principal in charge of discipline is an African American

- concerns among parents about the community's teenagers' safety, sexual activity, violence, and substance abuse, fueled by a belief that there has been a decline in students' character that should be addressed through the school curriculum

- beliefs that students' character is the province of the home and should not be tampered with by teachers and their values

- complaints that the school is too focused on athletics and not focused enough on academics

- despair over the declining athletic facilities and petitions to drop the art and music programs in order to finance upgrades to the football stadium and weight-training room

- other areas of disagreement among the school's diverse constituents

In other words, the community is typical in many ways of twenty-first-century schools: The school is the crucible for many of society's broader concerns. In that it is the one arena that the community's parents all have in common, it has become the primary theatre in which broader conflicts about values and social posturing are played out. It would be difficult even to find a consensus on the faculty over what the mission of the school is, much less to develop agreement among the citizenry about whether the school is a place for socialization to middle-class norms or a site for diverse people to learn one another's social practices; an academic center where students learn their nation's cultural heritage or a nurturing arena in which adults foster the personal growth of young people; an institution that produces graduates who all have similar preparation and prospects or a platform that launches each student in a unique direction; an establishment through which students learn to respect and affiliate with the national purpose or an arena where skepticism and subversion are healthy attributes; or any number of other possible purposes that meet their opposite in public debates about education. In such a setting, teachers need to be alert to the possible response to any of their decisions and prepared to defend their actions when inevitably questioned about them.

Time Considerations

My school has fifty-minute class periods, a common amount of time for school organization. The school year as a whole is divided into two semesters, each of which is partitioned into nine-week quarters. Grades are due at the end of each quarter, with final grades due at the end of semesters. At the halfway point of each quarter, the euphemistically named progress reports (aka failure notices) must be sent home for any student who is in danger of receiving a D grade or lower for the grading period or whose grades reveal a decline in performance.

These grading periods and the time length of individual classes help define the limits of your units. If you decide to teach eight units for the year, you should plan on roughly four to five weeks per unit, keeping in mind that you always lose days to pep rallies, school assemblies, field trips, snow days, preparing students for standardized tests, administering the standardized tests themselves, and other interruptions. The best-laid plans are inevitably thwarted, and you need to continually revise your plans to suit new conditions. But regardless of what happens, you will need to provide closure to your unit of instruction as the grading period comes to an end so that the students' report card grades will reflect their performance on the unit's culminating texts. The main consequence of this deadline is that your instructional planning is never ideal, but designed and modified to function within the parameters of your school's schedule.

Setting Up Shop: Getting Started with Students

Teachers and students often view the return to school in the same bittersweet way: sad to see summer and its pace come to an end but glad to be back in school with their friends. Mostly, the first day of school is a time of getting reacquainted, of getting back into the routine of school. Students will come to class ready to see old friends and socialize. When students think of returning to school, they don't think, "What will I learn about writing and literature this year?" They think, "Who's in my class?" and "Who's my teacher (mean, nice, hard, strict, easy, etc.)?"—usually in that order. These concerns are foremost on their minds when they come into class on the first day.

One way to get started is to take an *inventory* of students' interests and performance levels. Throughout the first few weeks of school, you should look for opportunities for students to tell you about themselves. You could do this in a number of ways:

1. *Personal Experience Writing*: If you do not plan to solicit personal experience writing as part of a unit itself, you might ask students to provide you with a piece of writing in which they tell of some significant event from their recent past—not the classic "what I did last summer" exercise, but something that encourages students to write about something that will help you get to know them and their interests better. Through this writing you could learn about the students and what they find significant and also get a sense of their development as writers. Both pieces of information should influence how you teach. It's possible to build this writing into the first conceptual unit of the year by including narrative writing as a way to explore the unit theme.

2. *Owner's Manual*: You could also learn about your students by having them provide you with an owner's manual for themselves. You might need to review what this should include:

   • a description of the product and its intended use

   • instructions on how to assemble it (optional)

   • a diagram of what it looks like in action

   • instructions on how to operate and maintain it

   • how to know when it's not working properly

   • what steps to take to fix it

   Students usually have fun writing about themselves in this way, and you can learn about their personalities, interests, and writing.

3. *Parent/Guardian Introduction*: Another way to learn about students is by having a parent, guardian, or other significant adult provide a letter of introduction. You might contrive a situation: the student is new to a setting, and this person is writing the letter that will provide entrée. You should always be careful about requiring parental involvement, considering the possibility that some students come from troubled homes.

4. *Survey*: You could also prepare a survey in which you ask students to tell you things about themselves. For example:

Please answer each question as honestly as possible. Your answers will help me to get to know you as a person and also help me to know how to teach this class well. If you do not enjoy doing the thing I'm asking about (e.g., reading) and haven't done any over the summer, just say so—there's no penalty for being honest.

1. What kind of reading did you do over the summer? Please tell:
   - the *type* of reading (newspaper, magazine, novel, Internet, etc.)
   - the *amount* you read (five pages a day, two pages a week, none, etc.)
   - the *names* of things you read (*Rolling Stone* magazine, *Flowers in the Attic*, etc.)

2. Who is your favorite author? What have you read by this author? Why do you consider this author to be your favorite?

3. What kinds of things do you particularly dislike to read? Why do you find them so awful?

4. What's your favorite thing about school?

5. What's your least favorite thing about school?

6. What kind of writing did you do over the summer? Please tell:
   - the *type* of writing (letters to friends, email, instant messaging, text messaging, a novel, etc.)
   - the *amount* you wrote (five pages a day, two pages a week, none, etc.)

7. What purposes do you use writing for outside school?

8. If you could change one thing about the writing you do in school, what would it be?

9. If you could change one thing about the reading you do in school, what would it be?

10. What would you like to learn about the most in this class?

11. If you could give me one piece of advice about how to teach this class, what would it be?

12. If you could change the way school is run, what changes would you make?

13. What are your favorite things to do outside school?

14. Do you think that your favorite things from outside school should be part of what you do for grades in school? Please explain.

15. Do your grades in school accurately reflect how smart you are? Please explain.

From a survey of this type, you can get a sense of what students' experiences with literature and writing are, what their attitudes toward school are, and how you might look for opportunities to build on their interests for more effective teaching and learning.

5. *Response to Literature*: Finally, you could do a kind of diagnostic inventory to see how students make sense of their reading. You could have them read a short work of literature and have them write a response in which they explain how they make sense of it. Their responses could come in the form of either a short essay, an imaginative piece they produce, or short answers to a series of questions you ask about the reading.

From whatever combination of inventories you use, you should get a sense of where the students stand academically and where their interests lie. This knowledge can help you choose appropriate texts to read and develop a suitable set of expectations. For the purposes of this book, where I am working with a hypothetical set of students, we'll assume that my classes include a diverse set of students. They typify the racial composition and economic range of the school as a whole. From their writing I can see a wide span of fluency, from students with a strong voice and facility with language to those who find writing to be painfully difficult. Some students read widely on their own; others rarely read at all. Some have computers in their homes; others lack even typewriters. My instruction, then, needs to account for a wide range of students so that all can benefit in some way.

Summary

The construction zone metaphor characterizes how you might set up your classroom and anticipate your teaching needs. Doing so involves knowing not only your students but the community in which you teach so as to anticipate the various situations in which you might find yourself as the year unfolds. You can never anticipate everything that will happen. Good preparation, however, can ward off too many unexpected surprises of the sort that can complicate your teaching in ways that you'd rather avoid.

13 *Introductory Activities*

By now you have identified your unit goals in the form of a set of assessments. Through these assessments, your students will both

- demonstrate learning that you can assess and
- learn new things for themselves through the process of producing their texts.

Both you and your students now know what you are building toward. It's possible that things will happen along the way to cause these plans to change somewhat, but for the most part you have a set of goals to guide your planning of the unit.

How, then, to begin? I suggest providing a particular kind of instructional scaffold, called an *introductory* or *gateway* activity. An introductory activity is designed to help students develop the kind of schematic knowledge they need to understand the unit's key concepts and problems. It thus provides them with a blueprint for the knowledge they will construct during the unit.

In designing your unit, you should ask, What knowledge will students need in order to work successfully toward the unit goals? I will review some possible ways through which you can introduce students to concepts that will likely be central to the literature they study. As you will see, all provide some opportunity for reconstruction by students. All of the types of introductory activities I describe are designed to have students wrestle with problems similar to those faced by characters in literature. The activities either directly or indirectly ask students to draw on their own experiences in similar kinds of situations to think about either the structure of experience (e.g., the script for a coming-of-age experience) or the substance (e.g., evaluating characters' decisions in problematic situations). By thinking through these questions prior to reading, students will be able to use the blueprint for experience, and the script for action based on this blueprint,

173

to help them understand the characters' actions in the texts they read (see Smagorinsky, McCann, and Kern 1987).

The assumption behind this approach is that students typically have some kind of experience that they can draw on to assist them with new learning. Unfortunately, students often view their personal knowledge as irrelevant to understanding schoolwork and flounder in areas where they could flourish. The introductory activities I describe in this chapter are designed to help students recognize and use their knowledge to make connections with the literature they read, and to help provide them with material for the texts they produce.

It's important to know that many texts require knowledge that students are not likely to have. There are times when they simply need factual information of some kind to help them understand something in their reading. During my earliest years of teaching, I assigned students Robert Frost's "Silken Tent," a poem about a large Arabian tent that, as the sun rose higher in the sky, relied on its central mast for support rather than the guys that supported it early in the day. From my days as a Boy Scout, I knew that guys are ropes that support tents externally, going from pegs in the ground to loops at the top of the tent wall.

A group of girls, however—evidently with no camping experience—interpreted the guys as boys and thought that they were a metaphor for the ways in which a girl relies on boyfriends during adolescence and on herself as she matures. Why these fellows were hanging from a tent was not so clear. In any case, the girls' interpretation was based on their personal construction of the terms of the poem. Not a bad interpretation, though probably not what Frost had in mind. This anecdote illustrates the problem that key knowledge in literature often lies outside students' experiences and requires some explicit teaching. While in general I don't feel that lecturing accomplishes what teachers think it does, I do see occasions where it's useful for students to be provided with relevant facts as aids to their reading.

The activities in this chapter fall under four categories: personal experience writing, opinionnaire or survey, scenario or case study, and writing about related problems. Each of the four types of activity is linked to one of the units in the sophomore curriculum. It is beneficial to vary the kinds of introductory activities that you use so that your teaching doesn't become too predictable. I offer these four types of introductions as possibilities, rather than as the only ways in which you could introduce a unit. I hope that you think about the metaphor of the cognitive map and generate your own approaches to designing introductory activities.

One thing to keep in mind is that the learning process should be recursive. By that I mean that these introductory activities are designed to help students draw on their prior personal knowledge to help them understand issues that come up in literature. In turn, the students' engagement with the literature should help them come to a better understanding of their personal knowledge and experiences. You can help students make these connections in your instructional design by having them return to the introductory activity after their engagement with the literature. For instance, I suggest that when students write about relevant personal experiences prior to reading, they return to these narratives later in the unit and develop them into more formal pieces of writing. Doing so has the added benefit of providing the class with a range of student-generated texts to help illuminate the central concepts of the theme.

Writing About Personal Experiences

Students can write informally—perhaps in journals or reading logs—about experiences that are similar to those of the characters they will study. The act of writing can promote reflection about important experiences that will help students relate to the problems confronted by the characters in the literature. In having students produce appropriate personal experience writing, you need to think about the key concepts and problems in the literature and design a writing prompt to help students think about experiences they've had that would help them understand these concepts and problems.

For my hypothetical sophomore curriculum, half of the units are thematic. The key literary theme should provide you with the topic for your prompt. Other kinds of units can also allow for personal experience writing as an introduction, particularly if they involve a theme. The unit on Julius Caesar, for instance, includes a set of related themes that students likely have experience with: betrayal, ambition, and so on.

For the sophomore curriculum I've designed, it would make a great deal of sense to begin the year with an introductory activity in which students write about a personal experience they've had in which they came of age. Doing so would meet a number of curricular ends:

- It would make their first writing of the year in the narrative genre, which many argue is more familiar and accessible, and more developmentally appropriate, for sophomore students than writing in the paradigmatic mode. Students' initial writing, then, would be something they have an opportunity to feel successful about.

- It would introduce students to the key problems and concepts of the unit.

- It would give them explicit knowledge of the script of coming-of-age literature.

- It could serve as the basis of a classroom drama.

- It could provide the first draft for the unit goal of writing a personal narrative.

- It could provide the class with a host of texts that illuminate the unit theme.

One option with personal experience writing is to have students interview a significant person in their lives, perhaps a parent or guardian, and then prepare a narrative of that other person's experience.

You do need to be careful about requirements to involve parents, however. When I discussed this idea with a group of teachers a few years ago, one of them said that if a teacher gave her this assignment, she'd take a zero rather than do it, because of years of abuse she'd experienced at home. One thing I've learned from years of teaching is that you can't always assume that students come from stable homes or that they've grown up the way you have. It's a good idea, then, to build in options rather than require parental input, perhaps allowing students to substitute a significant adult for a parent if they wish.

The prompt for the students' personal experience writing should ask them to describe the situation in ways that will prepare them for their subsequent reading and writing. The prompt should be specific enough to get students to think about the full range of problems involved, yet not so detailed as to override the spontaneity of their writing. One possible prompt would cue the students as follows:

> Write about a personal experience you've had in which you had a coming-of-age experience—that is, one that caused you to grow up in some way. Make sure to explain
>
> - the immature behavior that you exhibited prior to the experience
> - a transforming experience through which you gained significant new knowledge and maturity
> - the mature behavior that you exhibited following the experience
>
> You are not required to explain these events in this particular order, although you may if you wish. Keep in mind that other students will read about the experience you write about.

This last statement is necessary any time you ask students to share their writing. You shouldn't require students to share what they've written if you haven't advised them of this step ahead of time. Students should always have the option of not sharing if they feel uncomfortable reporting their experiences to others.

This prompt is less detailed than the prompt for the culminating text that they produce for their unit goal. The idea is to get them writing freely about the experience, to use writing as a tool for helping them to think about how experiences can contribute to maturity. Note too that the prompt includes a brief, accessible definition of *coming-of-age experience* to help set the stage for the rest of the unit.

It's important to have some kind of follow-up to an introductory activity of this type so that students compare their responses with those of other students, and so that the whole class has an opportunity to benefit from one another's reflections. Here are some possible ways to follow up personal writing:

- Have students get in small groups, read one another's narratives, and characterize the kinds of experiences that result in significant change. Then, have each group report to the whole class, with the teacher orchestrating the contributions into a discussion on significant experiences and the kinds of changes they can promote.

- Have students get in small groups, read one another's narratives, and choose one or several to use as the basis for short plays to be performed before the class. Following these plays, have the class discuss the kinds of scripts developed by each group for coming-of-age stories. These scripts could serve as the basis for the analyses of stories during discussions and ultimately for an analytic essay students write on an unfamiliar story based on the coming-of-age theme.

- Have students get in small groups and describe the characteristics of a good coming-of-age narrative. Have each group report to the whole class, with the teacher orchestrating a discussion on the traits of good narratives of this type. Have students revise their narratives based on the qualities identified during this discussion as a second draft of the narrative they will produce as a culminating text.

Opinionnaire or Survey

An opinionnaire or survey is a set of controversial statements designed to get students thinking about issues they will later encounter in the literature. At times the statements might come directly from the literature itself. For instance, I once developed an opinionnaire for an American literature unit on protest literature, and one statement on the list was paraphrased from one of the texts we would read, Thoreau's "Civil Disobedience": "The best government is the one that governs the least." If the literature provides no such provocative statements, then you will need to develop them yourself based on the issues that students will eventually think through while reading.

For the sophomore unit on discrimination, you could use an opinionnaire as a way to get students to think about issues prior to reading. One possible set of statements follows:

Each of the following statements expresses an opinion. Rate each statement from 1 (strongly disagree) to 5 (strongly agree).

1. Any set of beliefs is OK, as long as you believe in them sincerely.

2. I tend to go along with whatever my friends are for, even if I disagree with them.

3. People should always try to understand and tolerate other people, no matter how different they are.

4. If you move to a new country, you should adapt to its culture as quickly as possible so that you fit in.

5. I try not to notice people's physical characteristics. That way, I treat everyone the same.

6. A person's religion is never a factor in the kind of relationship I develop with him or her.

7. I never judge people on the basis of their appearance.

8. If you know where people live, you can tell a lot about them.

9. It's harmless to tell jokes about people in which they appear stupid because of their race, hair color, nationality, and so on; people who take offense should be able to recognize that it's all for the sake of humor.

10. Laws are designed to make society fair for all of its citizens.

The key to writing an effective opinionnaire is to write statements that will invite disagreement among students. This disagreement should lead to discussions of issues central to the problems that will arise in the literature. All of the above statements are designed to help students think through what they already know about discrimination and to refine their ideas in light of contrasting opinions expressed by classmates.

You can use opinionnaires in a variety of ways:

- Pass them out and go over the items in order, having a discussion of each.

- Have students complete the opinionnaire individually, then have them discuss their responses in small groups, then follow this with a whole-class discussion.

- Have students answer the opinionnaire questions in small groups, then follow up with a whole-class discussion.

The advantage of the second and third approaches is that they enable all students to participate in the discussion. In a whole-class discussion on a topic that invites strong opinions, some less assertive students have few opportunities to speak. By adding the small-group stage, you will allow for greater participation, particularly among students who feel inhibited by the whole-class setting or who benefit from engaging in exploratory talk.

Scenario or Case Study

Scenarios and case studies describe problematic examples of people who find themselves in thorny situations that parallel the circumstances of the literary characters. Scenarios tend to be brief and intended for small-group discussion followed by a whole-class comparison of the small-group decisions. Case studies tend to be more detailed and complex and used for more extensive study, such as when small groups lead the whole class in an analysis of a single case.

The basic structure and design process of the two are similar, however. Once again, you should write the scenarios or case studies at the intersection of what the literature provides and what the students have experienced. In the sophomore-year unit on conflict with authority, you could design an introductory activity based on a set of scenarios requiring students to evaluate how such problems are negotiated. The following activity could serve this purpose:

> Each of the following scenarios involves an individual coming in conflict with an authority figure. In a small group of four students, read each one carefully. Then, as a group, rank the characters according to how much you admire them, putting 1 by the scenario in which you admire the character's behavior the most, 2 by the scenario in which you admire the character the second most, and so on. You must rank all five of the scenarios—no ties.
>
> 1. Justin Time was on his high school football team. He didn't start but was a reserve linebacker who often played when the team went into special defenses. After a tough loss, the coach mistakenly thought he heard Justin laugh at something as the team was walking back to the locker room. Enraged that a player was not taking defeat seriously enough, the coach ordered Justin to crawl across the parking lot on his elbows in front of the whole team and a few hundred spectators, while the coach yelled at him at the top of his lungs the entire time. Justin thought that a good team player always does what the coach says, so although he initially denied that he had been the one who'd laughed, he ended up following his coach's orders without arguing.
>
> 2. Sybil Rights was a bright young woman, although her grades didn't always reflect it because she didn't always do what her teachers wanted her to do. One time her history teacher gave the class an assignment in which they were to outline the entire chapter from the textbook that dealt with the American government's decision to drop

the atomic bomb on Japan. Although every other student in the class did the assignment, Sybil refused, saying that it was just busywork and that she would not do assignments that she thought were a waste of her time. She decided that she could spend her time better by actually learning something about this incident, so she wrote an essay on the morality of the bombing that she intended to enter in the school's annual essay competition. She ended up getting a zero on the assignment, which lowered her grade for the marking period from a B to a C.

3. Ryan Carraway was a young American soldier stationed in Europe in World War II. His troop was one of many battling the enemy in a hilly region of the war theatre. They had the enemy outnumbered, but the enemy was well positioned at the top of a hill and the Americans couldn't seem to gain any ground in spite of their superior numbers. Finally, an order came down from the commanding officer that Ryan's troop should charge the hill. It occurred to him that his troop was being sacrificed to create a diversion so that other troops could rush up and make a sneak attack from the flanks while the enemy was fighting off his troop. Ryan thought that this was a stupid plan that was doomed to failure and that his life was going to be sacrificed needlessly. Yet, he followed his orders, charged the hill, and, like everyone else in his troop, was killed. Sure enough, the master plan failed. After Ryan's troop was wiped out, the flank attack was foiled and the enemy still held the hill.

4. Freida Hostages had a job working at the local hardware store after school. Usually, she did whatever was necessary, such as unpack boxes, work the cash register, or put price tags on merchandise. She almost always had something to keep her busy. One day, however, a heavy rainfall kept business down. At one point there were no customers in the store and she had taken care of all the little jobs, so she was standing around doing nothing. Her boss hated to pay her for nothing and so told her to scrub the linoleum floor of the store with an abrasive cleaner, a job that Freida reckoned hadn't been done in years. She thought that this task was utterly ridiculous and a waste of her time, but she didn't want to risk losing her job, so she got a bucket, a brush, and some cleanser and went to work.

5. Frazier Nerves stayed out too late with his girlfriend one night, and his parents reacted by grounding him, confining him to his room every night for a month. He thought that this was excessively harsh but knew that arguing would only make matters worse. Still, he had a great desire to see his girlfriend; not only was he madly in love with her, but he also knew of other boys who found her attractive and he thought that if they were not to date for a month he might lose her to someone else. Desperate to maintain his relationship with her but fearful of parental

repercussions, he started sneaking out through his window every night after his parents had gone to bed for a late-evening rendezvous with his girlfriend. He made it through the month without getting caught and with his relationship still intact.

An alternative to writing the scenarios yourself is to take a set of stories from the news. A typical year provides an abundance of current events related to many thematic units of literature. For conflict with authority, you might use stories about athletes coming in conflict with their coaches, workers challenging their bosses, citizens resisting the votes of their Congress representatives, students in adversarial relationships with teachers and administrators, and so on. The main thing to keep in mind is that the stories should illustrate a variety of kinds of conflicts and resolutions (or nonresolutions) so that students think about the problem in complex ways.

Regardless of how you identify the scenarios or cases, you could have students rank the characters' actions from most admirable to least admirable. They could rank them individually, then discuss their rankings in small groups, and then compare their responses in an all-class discussion. The discussions should encourage students to examine closely their attitudes toward authority figures and consider carefully the kinds of dilemmas the literary characters will face.

Writing About Related Problems

My friend, Tom McCann, has spent a great deal of time thinking of ways to teach students how to write arguments. One of his ideas works well as an introductory activity. The format for the activity is based on advice columns such as Dear Abby. The idea is to think of situations that come up in literature and then present students with a letter to an advice columnist that describes a similar kind of situation. Their job is then to write to the person, offering a solution to the problem.

In the sophomore curriculum, the unit on gangs, cliques, and peer pressure would be well suited for an introductory activity of this type. Let's say that the class will read S. E. Hinton's *The Outsiders* as the unit's major work of literature. You could prepare a letter to the Answerline columnist that anticipates the dilemmas raised in the novel and have students write a letter back arguing in favor of a particular solution. The prompt for their writing could look like this:

Pretend that you are a famous newspaper columnist who gives advice to people who write letters to you. Often their problems concern crucial moments in their lives that they need advice about. What kind of guidance would you give to the following person? Make sure that when you write your response you are supportive of the person's problems and give a thoughtful answer. Make sure too that whatever your advice is, you give several reasons that the person should follow it. Also make sure that you explain why your recommended course of action is better than others that the person might follow.

Dear Answerline,

I have a problem that I need your advice about. I have to go to you because I can't tell my parents. They'd just yell at me and ground me if they thought I was in any kind of trouble. Please help me figure out what to do.

The problem actually starts with my best friend. We're both part of a group that always hangs around together. We always stick together, right or wrong. If one of us gets in a fight, the rest are there to help out. If one of us is in trouble, the others are always there. Every time I've ever had a problem, my friends were there to make things right. I could never let any of them down, especially my best friend, Chris, who's always been there for me.

But now I'm worried that things have gone too far. There's another group in our school that we've always had trouble with. They think they're better than we are and always put us down. Usually we just yell things back at them, or sometimes get in a fight, and it's over till the next time. But last week they set fire to Chris' car. Now everybody wants revenge. And Chris has got a gun and wants to use it.

I don't know what to do. If I say I think it has gone too far, they'll call me chicken. If I say I don't want to go along with them, they'll think I'm disloyal. If I call the police, my best friends might get arrested. If I warn the other group, my friends may get hurt. If I lose my friends, I won't have anybody left.

What should I do?

Sincerely,
Fearful in Fredericksburg

The students' job is to write to Fearful, offering a solution to the problem. After all students are done, you could follow the same sequence that I outlined in the other introductory activities: Have students compare their answers in small groups, then have a whole-class discussion in search of a solution.

This introduction, like the personal experience narrative introducing the coming-of-age unit, could additionally serve to prepare students for more formal writing later in the unit. In a unit using this kind of introduction, you could have a goal of producing an argument about problem resolution related to an independently read work of literature. The Answerline letter, then, could introduce students both to the literature and to argumentative writing. Subsequent instruction could focus on making, supporting, and warranting claims and rebutting alternative solutions.

Summary

Introductory activities should prepare students for issues that come up in literature. They often draw on prior knowledge that students can connect with new knowledge. As noted previously, some kinds of reading might require an introduction that helps acquaint students with unfamiliar realms of knowledge. I imagine that if you teach literature from diverse cultures and nations, you will need to help students understand different issues, relationships, literary styles, and other aspects of the texts that may be quite different from what they know through exposure to Western literary traditions. The questions you should ask are these: What does one need to know in order to read this text with the appropriate expectations? How can I help students access the knowledge that will prepare them for this reading? You should also be aware that many people in the field would prefer that readers go ahead with their readings without such preparation. They argue that students' initial constructions are part of their process of meaning making and should not be tainted by the teacher's sense of what's important to know.

It's worth noting that in order to be successful with this approach to teaching, you might need to consider another kind of prior knowledge, about how to do school. As noted elsewhere in this book, students are going to be enculturated to authoritative, transmission-oriented approaches to schooling. In the constructivist classroom, they will be expected to act quite differently by relating their personal knowledge and experiences to their school learning, by asking questions instead of answering them, by constructing knowledge instead of receiving it. Thus, you will likely have to spend some time helping students relearn how to be a student. In other words, they will need prior knowledge about how to do school properly in your class. The unit introductory activity can be an important step in helping them to learn a different way of being a student.

14 *Down and Dirty: Daily Planning*

This chapter is written as though I am thinking aloud while planning a unit. I plan each class very specifically, right down to an anticipated amount of time I will spend on each activity. Some might find such microlevel planning to be a bit too heavily scripted. The purpose, however, is not to write a script, but to try to anticipate how classes will go from day to day.

One word on lessons before we continue: It's important to design good individual lessons that are related to the unit goals. It's also important for the lessons to be interrelated and to build cogently toward the unit goals. If we think in terms of our construction metaphor, let's say you are making a shirt, and you design and construct excellent individual components: a sleeve, a collar, another sleeve, front and back pieces, and so on. While they might be fine pieces individually, if they are not coordinated to suit a particular reason for wearing a shirt—to stay warm in winter, to match a pair of shoes, to evoke a feeling or mood, to meet the expectations of an occasion—then the shirt might both lack overall coherence and serve its purpose poorly. Lessons within a unit, too, must both stand individually to meet a unit's goals and work together coherently to serve the unit as a whole.

For the sake of convenience, I start teaching the unit on a Monday, although life does not always allow for such neat scheduling. I want to move straight into the introductory activity. I could introduce the unit on discrimination in a variety of ways. I could do an Internet search, for instance, and locate a number of short newspaper articles on controversial incidents of discrimination. I could then create a scenario activity out of them, perhaps simply asking students to rate each incident as involving discrimination or not. By doing so, they would begin the process of working on criteria for their extended definitions of a particular kind of discrimination.

I think, however, I'll try something new and different. Let's say that our school has a set of computer labs and that my state core curriculum emphasizes technology. I can dovetail several possibilities into a single activity by beginning the unit with collaborative webquests that investigate discrimination. I might even take this activity one step further and combine the introductory activity and webquest with a jigsaw activity. This activity could also serve as a vehicle through which students will identify the specific topics on which they'll write their extended definitions of discrimination. You may see on pages 186–222 what it might look like in terms of a daily lesson plan.

Week 1

Day 1 (Monday)

3 minutes: Attendance, housekeeping.

5 minutes: Walk to the computer lab and get seated and settled (of course, I've reserved the lab ahead of time).

10 minutes: Provide hard copy of the following prompt and review the assignment with the students:

> For the next month or so, we are going to be reading and thinking about what it means for one person to discriminate against another, or for one group of people to discriminate against another. To begin our consideration of discrimination, we will go to the computer lab and do *collaborative webquests*. The procedures are as follows:
>
> 1. Each of you will get in a group of no more than five students and pick a particular kind of discrimination: against old people, against young people, against foreigners, against people of a particular race, against women, against men, against gays and lesbians, against people of particular religions, against left-handed people, against conscientious objectors to war, against war veterans, against short people, against tall people, against people with mental health issues, or whatever other kind of discrimination that your group agrees to investigate on the Internet. The only limitation is that no two groups may research the same topic.
>
> 2. To create your webquest, there are several good instruments available on the Internet. One way to locate them is simply to type "webquest" into a search engine and you will find links to sites such as http://webquest.org. These sites will guide you through the process of conducting your webquest and provide you with all of the tools you'll need to produce it, including examples of webquests. Ultimately, you may submit your webquest to be displayed at http://webquest.org.
>
> 3. Your task is to search the Web for information about your topic and use the links you find to construct your collaborative webquest.

32 minutes: Students work on their webquests until the bell. Teacher circulates to make sure that students are on task and working according to the webquest requirements.

Day 2 (Tuesday)

The class meets in the computer lab.

3 minutes: Attendance, housekeeping.

47 minutes: Students complete their webquests and, if they wish, post them to a website.

> Through these first two days, each student should have become an expert in a particular kind of discrimination. The webquest activity thus serves as the first stage of the jigsaw activity in which students participate in small-group discussions on one aspect of a text or problem. On Day 3 the class will move to the second stage of the jigsaw, in which each group member will go to a separate group—each consisting of one member from each webquest group—and report on and discuss the five different forms of discrimination investigated thus far.

Day 3 (Wednesday)

3 minutes: Attendance, housekeeping.

5 minutes: Explain the jigsaw procedures as follows:

> Each webquest group will now disperse into new groups according to the following procedures:
>
> 1. In each group of five, assign each student a number from 1 to 5.
> 2. Those assigned 1, assemble in one corner; those assigned 2, assemble in the next corner going clockwise; those assigned 3, assemble in the next corner going clockwise; those assigned 4, assemble in the next corner going clockwise; those assigned 5, assemble in the center.
> 3. Each group now includes one person from each webquest group. Your task is for each student to lead a discussion of roughly seven minutes on what you learned from your webquest.

40 minutes: The groups discuss the webquests according to these instructions, with the teacher circulating to help students stay on task.

2 minutes: Return the desks to their original positions; exeunt.

> Note that for the first three days of the unit, the teacher has done little talking aside from setting up activities and monitoring them. The students, meanwhile, have been involved in the open-ended task of investigating some sort of discrimination, which undoubtedly has provided space for exploratory talk about both the technology employed and the concepts they have researched. They have also been working through possible criteria for their extended definition of discrimination of some kind as they've read about real events in which discrimination was alleged. Further, each class member has now been designated as an expert in an area of specialization. In a number of ways, then, the unit

has opened with teacher and student roles that are dramatically different from those that typify most school instruction.

Now, some sort of whole-class follow-up is appropriate, in which the teacher orchestrates the ideas and contributions of the students based on both stages of the jigsaw activity.

Day 4 (Thursday)

3 minutes: Attendance, housekeeping.

47 minutes: The teacher orchestrates a discussion based on the two phases of the jigsaw activity. He queries each group on the following questions:

1. What is, and what is not, discrimination of the type you investigated during your webquest?

2. On what basis did you decide that a particular action is an act of discrimination?

3. How can you formulate a rule (aka criterion) that helps you distinguish discrimination from nondiscrimination?

4. Provide an example of something that is discrimination according to your criterion and something that almost meets the criterion but is not discriminatory.

5. Explain why the example meets the criterion and why the contrasting example does not meet the criterion.

This discussion is appropriate for a variety of reasons. First, it maintains the open-ended approach established through the webquest and jigsaw activities. Second, it provides an opportunity for the whole class to follow the reasoning of each group. Third, it begins the process of writing extended definitions by having the students develop criteria, examples that illustrate the criteria, contrasting examples that do not meet the criteria, and warrants that explain the examples and contrasting examples in terms of the criteria. By going through this process, students should be reasonably well prepared to begin their reading of literature that focuses on discrimination.

It's possible that this discussion will extend into the next day; predicting the length of such a discussion can be difficult, and it may vary from class to class. For now, I'll plan one class session for the discussion, with the understanding that it might take two.

Day 5 (Friday)

3 minutes: Attendance, housekeeping.

Fridays can be hard days to teach, for obvious reasons. It's possible that this Friday will extend the previous day's discussion. If we've wrapped up the discussion, I think I'll give everyone a break and play a vocabulary game. When I taught high school English, I tried many approaches to teaching vocabulary. At first, I identified words from the forthcoming reading, had the students look them up, and then tested them on the whole list. I particularly remember doing this with the word *pusillanimous*, which appeared in some of the colonial rhetoric we were reading for American literature. I was dismayed to find that the students had a lot of trouble both on the test and in their reading with my vocabulary word selections.

I tried a number of different ways of doing vocabulary, few of them resulting in students learning new words. I thought I had a great system when I had groups of students act out word definitions (e.g., a purse snatcher reprimanded with "Stop, miscreant!"). They enjoyed doing the skits, and their memory of the words was quite good, but the activity was not generative; that is, the students didn't learn any strategies for learning new words beyond the one that was the subject of the performance.

I finally settled on a set of games modeled after TV game shows: *Jeopardy, $25,000 Pyramid, Password, Family Feud,* and *Balderdash.* The games were all based on some sort of strategy for understanding the meaning of unfamiliar words, in particular using context clues and using knowledge of roots and affixes. These games were quite popular with my students and achieved their purpose: I found students not only figuring out word meanings but, because they enjoyed the wordplay, also inventing new ones. I especially remember a boy who included the fine word *ichthyophagous* in an essay to describe himself eating a fish that he'd caught.

So today, time permitting, we'll play a vocabulary game. Instead of occupying space here with a description of the games, I'll refer you to the website where they are posted: www.coe.uga.edu/~smago/ Vocabulary_Games/ExpansionsIndex.htm. Each game is described in detail, and all of the materials I have used are provided.

Week 2

Week 2 provides an opportunity to develop the students' nascent understanding of discrimination. Instead of jumping right into the literature, I'll continue to work at scaffolding the students' understanding of the concept with something both familiar and enjoyable: music. A lot of popular music across the decades has dealt with issues of discrimination, so I'll work with a selection of tunes that I'm familiar with that will help the students explore the topic. Fortunately, a lot of young people are exposed to "classic rock" of the sort I tend to listen to, so the songs might have some appeal to them. I'll also encourage them to bring in their own music, which I'll be less familiar with.

Day 6 (Monday)

3 minutes: Attendance, housekeeping.

45 minutes: Provide copies of song lyrics and recordings of the songs listed below or other songs that feature various types of discrimination (with school-appropriate lyrics, of course). Have each group select one song either from the list or from their own collections, with each group picking a different song. Their task is to create a storyboard for a music video for the song. Doing so will require them to pay careful attention to the lyrics, particularly the images concerned with discrimination. Their task is as follows:

> In small groups of three to five students, select one song from the following menu or a song of your choice (with, of course, school-appropriate lyrics) that deals with discrimination, and create a storyboard for a music video about the song.
>
> The Weavers: "Sixteen Tons"
>
> Vanessa Williams: "Colors of the Wind"
>
> Dave Matthews Band: "Cry Freedom"
>
> Bob Marley and the Wailers: "War"
>
> Johnny Clegg and Savuka: "Inevitable Consequence of Progress"
>
> Randy Newman: "Short People"
>
> The Crüxshadows: "Leave Me Alone"
>
> Neil Young: "Southern Man"
>
> Creedence Clearwater Revival: "Fortunate Son"
>
> A storyboard is a set of drawings that outlines the major events in a sequence of action, such as the major scenes in a music video. As of this writing, you can find an example of a storyboard at www.danhausertrek.com/AnimatedSeries/Storyboard.gif.

To prepare your storyboard, you should consider the following questions about the song:

- What or who is being discriminated against by whom?
- How is the discrimination carried out?
- What images might tell the song's story?

- What is the role of color, lighting, and other effects in telling the story?

- What images best portray the song's story of discrimination?

Your storyboard should consist of five to ten panels that you will first draft on paper and then either copy onto an overhead transparency or convert to computer images to show the class as you play the song. Distribute the song's lyrics to accompany your presentation.

2 minutes: Return the desks to their original positions; exeunt.

Day 7 (Tuesday)

Depending on how far the storyboarding has progressed, Day 7 will either continue with the storyboarding or begin with the presentations. I'm guessing that the storyboarding will take a little more time, especially if the kids get involved with computer software, so I'll plan to complete the storyboards. If the students finish, we can always start the presentations ahead of schedule. The plan, then, might look like this:

3 minutes: Attendance, housekeeping.

45 minutes: Complete the storyboard activity.

2 minutes: Return the desks to their original positions; exeunt.

Day 8 (Wednesday)

3 minutes: Attendance, housekeeping.

47 minutes: Students play their songs and present their storyboards. Each of the groups in the audience should prepare at least one question for each of the presenting groups. We might not get to all of the questions, but groups should be prepared to ask them.

Day 9 (Thursday)

We move at this point from songs to poems. For the purposes of this unit, I've done some Internet searching and located a set of poems that fit well with the unit on discrimination:
Maya Angelou: "On the Pulse of Morning"
Peter Blue Cloud: "The Old Man's Lazy"
Elizabeth Brewster: "Jamie"
You may be more limited by your textbook, or you might be able to find different poems that you feel work better for how your unit is

going. My selection of this set of poems is illustrative rather than pre-scriptive.

The students by this time have had experience with looking at texts for issues of discrimination. I want to continue with that effort. Since the students are keeping reading logs, we'll dovetail the poetry reading with the reading log assignment to generate an analysis of the poems. The day's activities, then, might look as follows:

3 minutes: Attendance, housekeeping.

20 minutes: Pass out a copy of the first poem, Peter Blue Cloud's "The Old Man's Lazy."

Provide the following prompt for students:
Use your double-column reading log to generate a set of responses and questions to the poem. We will use your responses and questions as the basis for a discussion about the poem.

This task helps to establish a routine for the class: using the reading logs as the source of discussion questions and responses. Again, the idea is to trust students' ability to take control of their own learning by putting the onus and direction for response to literature in their hands.

25 minutes: Small-group follow-up: Students work in small groups of their choice to use their reading log responses as the basis for an exploration of what the poem reveals about discrimination.

2 minutes: Return the desks to their original positions; exeunt.

Day 10 (Friday)

Here I want to help establish the routine sequence of thinking individu-ally, sharing ideas in small groups, and then moving to a whole-class dis-cussion that builds on and synthesizes the various small-group ideas.

3 minutes: Attendance, housekeeping.

47 minutes: Whole-class discussion based on the previous day's individual and small-group work. There are many different ways in which to conduct this discussion. One is simply to ask for students to come forward with their ideas and hope that a free-flowing jam session follows. With some groups of students, this sort of discussion may indeed emerge from the previous day's exchanges. If students are more reticent, a methodical approach might be necessary, such as calling on each group individually to report on its discus-sion and have the remainder of the class pose questions to the group after-

ward. Each of my five small groups would then have about nine minutes to report on its response log and small-group ideas.

It's possible that some time will be left at the end of the class. Teachers have used this time in a variety of ways. The students' favorite is always free time, which is great for them but not necessarily great for teachers. One way I used to manage this time was to play the spelling game, "Ghost." The object of the game is for students to successively add letters to a word, without being the person whose letter puts the finishing touches on a real word of three letters or more. Proper nouns do not count as words in this game. To start, the first player says a letter, say *b*. The next player then thinks of a word that starts with this letter, perhaps *bat*, and adds a letter, in this case *a*, to the string. The next player thinks of a word that starts with those two letters and adds a third letter that continues spelling a real word without completing the spelling of a word. For instance, if the third person thinks *bath* and adds a *t*, she has spelled *bat* and is out.

At this point, the next player begins with a new letter and word. If a player believes that the previous contestant is bluffing—say, if the sequence is *b-a-x*—the person may challenge the contestant. If the challenged student does not have a word in mind, he is out and the challenger begins a new word; if the challenged student does have a word, then the challenger is out and the next student begins a new word. The competition proceeds until only one person is left. This game is fun for most students and occupies short periods of time that otherwise might become chaotic.

Week 3

The beginning of the third week might call for some evaluation of how well the unit has gone. If students have been slow to grasp the issues, I might want to backtrack a little and include some more work with accessible materials. Let's assume, though, that the kids are moving along well in terms of their consideration of issues of discrimination. In this week, we'll read some short stories that explore questions of discrimination. I want to continue with the activity-based approach in order to continue to provide varied structures for thinking about the unit concepts.

One reason I want to vary the classroom organization is to escape the rut that students often find themselves in when teachers do more or less the same thing every day. Varied structures keep students on their toes and add a sense of intrigue to the class in terms of how they'll approach the topic each day they enter the class. Another reason to vary the ways in which students approach the texts is to provide the broadest possible access to success for the widest range of students imaginable. Critics have found schools to be most congenial to middle-class white students (whether boys or girls, it depends on whom you ask). By making activity and collaboration central to most classes, you will allow for more students to find ways to connect to the unit concepts. And so we'll continue to approach each text in a different way, while maintaining our focus on the same unit theme.

Day 11 (Monday)

Today we'll move to a short story from the list of materials. Because the students will be largely in charge of their own discussions, I can be flexible in terms of which story I select; I could even provide a menu of choices from which students may pick, although the ensuing whole-class discussion might lack the coherence that would follow from having all students read a common text.

I want to read a couple of short stories that approach discrimination from different angles and discuss them in different ways. From the menu of short stories I've identified, let's go with Leslie Marmon Silko's "Tony's Story" and José Antonio Burciaga's "Romantic Nightmare." Two discussion techniques that might work well are the found poem and the body biography.

Another issue to consider is how to manage the reading. Different schools treat homework differently. In some, there's an expectation that students will do several hours of homework each night; in others, administrators and teachers limit homework because many students' circumstances don't allow for dedicated study time after school. How you treat this question is no doubt a function of where you teach. In my hypothetical school, I'll allow for both in-class and out-of-class reading. For instance, instead of playing ghost during the last moments of Friday's class, I could have the students begin reading "Tony's Story" with the expectation that they'll complete the assignment over the weekend and be ready at the get-go of Monday's class to discuss it. However, in my hypothetical class, I have students who are more likely to sleep on a bed of nails than do homework over the weekend, so we'll start fresh on Monday without the burden of weekend homework.

Here's how the beginning of Week 3, then, might work with these texts and formats in mind:

3 minutes: Attendance, housekeeping,

47 minutes: Teacher begins by making three reading assignments, with students having Monday's class to work on as many as they can complete:

Leslie Marmon Silko: "Tony's Story"

José Antonio Burciaga: "Romantic Nightmare"

Richard Wright: *Black Boy*

Students then have the remainder of the class to read, with the understanding that they will discuss the two short stories on Tuesday and Wednesday of this week. They will have several weeks to complete their reading of *Black Boy*, which will constitute their homework for the bulk of the unit.

Day 12 (Tuesday)

3 minutes: Attendance, housekeeping.

25 minutes: Working in small groups, students produce a found poem based on "Tony's Story," in response to the following prompt:

In small groups of three to five students, produce a *found poem* based on "Tony's Story," by Leslie Marmon Silko. A found poem is a "poem" that consists of significant words and phrases found in a source text such as Silko's short story. Your task is to discuss the story in your group with the goal of identifying the story's most important words and phrases, which you then put into the form of a poem. All words in your found poem should come directly from the Silko story. You will write your found poem on an overhead transparency and share it with the other groups in the class. Your presentation of the found poem may suggest additional meanings by the colors you choose and the ways in which you position the text. In other words, your poem needn't look like a regular poem consisting of a series of black-print words on a white background; it may also include shapes, images, and other ways through which you convey the meaning of the text.

22 minutes: The students present their found poems to the group, with the opportunity to field questions following their readings.

Day 13 (Wednesday)

3 minutes: Attendance, housekeeping.

45 minutes: Students construct body biographies in response to José Antonio Burciaga's "Romantic Nightmare," using the following prompt. (There are body biography models on the Internet that are available through search engines, which you might download and provide to students.)

In small groups of three to five students, select one character to represent and interpret through a *body biography*. A body biography is a visual and written portrait illustrating several aspects of the character's life within the story.

You have many possibilities for filling up your overhead transparency. I have listed several, but please feel free to come up with your own creations. As always, the choices you make should be based on the text, for you will be verbally explaining (and thus, in a sense, defending) them at a showing of your work. Above all, your choices should be creative, analytical, and based on the story.

After completing this portrait, you will participate in a showing in which you will present your masterpiece to the class. This showing should accomplish these objectives. It should

- review significant events, choices, and changes involving your character

- communicate to us the full essence of your character by emphasizing the traits that make him who he is

- promote discussion of your character

Body Biography Requirements

Although I expect your biography to contain additional dimensions, your portrait *must* contain the following:

- a review of significant happenings in the story

- visual symbols

- an original text

- the three most important lines from the story

Body Biography Suggestions

1. *Placement*: Carefully choose the placement of your text and artwork. For example, the area where your character's heart would be might be appropriate for illustrating the important relationships within her life.

2. *Spine*: Actors often discuss a character's spine. This is his objective within the story. What is the most important goal for your character? What drives his thoughts and actions? This is his spine. How can you illustrate it?

3. *Virtues and Vices*: What are your character's most admirable qualities? Her worst? How can you make us visualize them?

4. *Color*: Colors are often symbolic. What color(s) do you most associate with your character? Why? How can you effectively work these colors into your presentation?

5. *Symbols*: What objects can you associate with your character that illustrate his essence? Are there objects mentioned within the story itself that you could use? If not, choose objects that especially seem to correspond with the character.

6. *Formula Poems*: These are fast, but effective, recipes for producing a text because they are designed to reveal a lot about a character.

7. *Mirror, Mirror . . .* : Consider both how your character appears to others on the surface and what you know about the character's inner self. Do these images clash or correspond? What does this tell you about the character?

8. *Changes*: How has your character changed within the story? Trace these changes within your text and/or artwork.

(This assignment was created by Cindy O'Donnell-Allen.)

2 minutes: Return the desks to their original positions; exeunt.

Day 14 (Thursday)

3 minutes: Attendance, housekeeping.

25 minutes: Students present their body biographies to the class on an overhead projector, with time following each presentation to field questions and comments from the teacher and other students.

22 minutes: If there is no further discussion of the short story or the issue of discrimination, students may read ahead in *Black Boy*.

Day 15 (Friday)

My next task is to teach the students how to write an extended-definition essay. I think I'll start this instruction on a Monday rather than a Friday, because the weekend's hiatus is likely to erode whatever understanding of the activity students gain today. So Friday may be devoted to one of two things: in-class reading of *Black Boy* or a vocabulary game from the activities listed at www.coe.uga.edu/~smago/Vocabulary_Games/ExpansionsIndex.htm. This decision will be a judgment call, depending on how I see the unit going thus far. My plan for Friday, then, might be:

3 minutes: Attendance, housekeeping.

47 minutes: Either in-class reading of *Black Boy* or vocabulary game based on *Family Feud*.

The unit is now about half over. One feature I'd like to stress is that the approach I'm taking requires more work outside class in terms of planning and less work in class because the students are engaged in activity. To me, however, the planning is challenging and enjoyable, so it's not such work after all; as Confucius once said, "Choose a job you love, and you will never have to work a day in your life."

And the infinite variety of work that students produce when they're given open-ended opportunities makes my classroom life more interesting and educative for me; I see things in literature that I might not have noticed because my students are enabled to bring their myriad resources and experiences into their interpretive process. To me, that's far more challenging and interesting for both them and me than my repeating the same official interpretation over and over, class after class, year after year, even though it might not be the best interpretation for young readers and requires so little of them cognitively, not to mention that it asks so little of me as a professional.

Week 4

In the fourth week I'll begin scaffolding students' writing of extended-definition essays. This effort will require systematic scaffolding for paradigmatic thinking, which will work in conjunction with the narrative and alternative ways of responding to literature to help give students a well-rounded understanding of the unit concept.

We won't jump right into defining discrimination. Rather, we'll produce two essays. The first will be on a topic of great familiarity to the students so that they can learn the procedures without the additional burden of learning new content. After this initial experience, the students will define a kind of discrimination of their choice, perhaps the type on which they did their webquest. Although everyone will write extended-definition essays, both the specific topics and the definitions produced will be open to seemingly infinite variation. The essay instruction, then, while uniform, will enable students to work in the constructivist spirit of the general teaching approach.

As a teacher, my first job is to think of a topic for definition that the students will find accessible and interesting. As often is the case, my mind turns to music. I have met few people who do not like music of any kind, and I've especially met few teenagers who are not downright passionate about some kind of music. Every culture of which I'm aware has music as a central means of enjoyment, ritual, spirituality, or other dimension of existence. And so the idea of defining what makes excellent or "totally excellent" music of some kind appears to be a good way to scaffold students' thinking about how to write an extended definition, which they will later apply to an area of discrimination.

Further, by having students define excellence in a particular kind of music, I am also supporting students' ability to work on one of the course's final exam projects, an extended definition of quality literature. The instruction, then, meets a number of my goals for the unit and course as a whole.

Day 16 (Monday)

3 minutes: Attendance, housekeeping.

45 minutes: Before giving the students the actual assignment, I want to immerse them in the task itself. I'll start by presenting them with a slew of possibilities for kinds of music to think about, using the following handout:

What Is Good Music?

Just about everyone likes music. But not everyone likes the same kind of music. And even within a musical genre, there's disagreement about which performers are good, which are bad, and which are ugly. Our task in this activity is to work in small groups of three to five students to select a particular kind of music and decide what music within this genre is good and what is not so good. It's OK for more than one group to choose the same kind of music.

Following is a list of musical genres. Pick one from this list or another genre that I may have overlooked. After making your selection, begin working out a set of rules or criteria for what makes music within this genre of high quality. To do so, think of examples from real musicians you are familiar with.

This process will be similar to the one with which we started the unit, in which we developed some rules or criteria for defining particular kinds of discrimination that you researched through your webquests.

Here are some musical genres to consider. Remember that you are not confined to this list.

acid rock	disco	opera
African American congregational gospel	gangsta rap	polka
	goth	progressive rock
	gothic rock	psychedelic rock
alternative rock	Gregorian chant	punk
American folk	grunge	punk rock
arena rock	hard rock	rai
atonal jazz	heavy metal	redneck rap
bagpipe	indie rock	reggae
bebop jazz	jazz piano trio	rhythm and blues
big band jazz	J-pop	rock musical

bluegrass	J-rock	rock opera
Broadway musical	jubilee gospel	rockabilly
calypso	klezmer	salsa
Celtic	K-pop	samba
chamber orchestra	K-rock	ska
Chicago electric	mambo	smooth jazz
blues	marching band	soft rock
Christian rap	mariachi	soul
classic rock	Mongolian throat	stoner rock
classical guitar	singing	string quartet
classical symphonic	Motown	swing
cool jazz	Native American	techno
country and	flute	tejada
western	neogrunge	Tibetan chant
C-pop	new age	Zulu isigubudu
C-rock	New Orleans jazz	Zulu maskanda
delta blues	new wave	Zulu mbaqanga

2 minutes: Return the desks to their original positions; exeunt.

Day 17 (Tuesday)

On the second day of the extended-definition instruction, I'll help students take their initial ideas and provide a structure for them to work within. Fortunately, I've designed an activity based on my experience as a member of a jury in a Chicago street gang murder trial (see Smagorinsky 1994) in which I've provided extended definitions for three kinds of killing: murder, voluntary manslaughter, and self-defense. (The courtroom activity, which also appears in Smagorinsky 2002, is pretty darned swell.) I've extracted the definitions from that activity and used them here. The day's lesson, then, might look like this:

3 minutes: Attendance, housekeeping.

25 minutes: Pass out and review the following handout:

In the small groups you established yesterday, you will produce an extended definition of high-quality music of a particular genre. An extended definition includes four primary traits:

- *criteria*, or rules that state a standard that something must meet for inclusion in the category

- *examples* that illustrate each criterion

- *contrasting examples* that provide an illustration of something that superficially appears to meet the criterion but falls short in some critical way

- *warrants* that explain how the examples illustrate the criteria and how the contrasting examples fall short

The following provides examples of actual court definitions for three types of killing, distributed by the circuit court in Cook County, Illinois: murder, voluntary manslaughter, and self-defense. In a real court, the jurors are provided only with the description of each charge. For this activity, you'll receive additional information to help clarify the definition: an example of a situation that meets the criterion, a contrasting example that seems to meet the criterion but lacks some essential ingredient, and a warrant that explains why each example and contrasting example does or does not illustrate the criterion.

Murder

The charge for taking someone's life is murder if one of the following criteria is met.

Criterion 1: A person intends either to kill or to injure another person critically or knows that the act he or she intends to commit could cause death.

Example: Joe hates Bob and fires a gun at Bob's head from a distance of two feet with the intention of killing him. *Warrant*: The act is murder because it is intentional with the knowledge it could cause death.

Contrasting Example: Joe believes his gun is not loaded. He playfully points it at Bob and pulls the trigger. The gun, however, is loaded, and the bullet kills Bob. *Warrant*: The act is unintentional and therefore not murder.

Criterion 2: A person knows that the act he or she commits creates a strong probability of death or serious injury.

Example: Bob secretly puts arsenic in Joe's coffee, knowing that the poison will probably kill him. *Warrant*: Because the act is intentional and Bob is aware of the consequences, it satisfies the criterion.

Contrasting Example: Bob puts sugar in Joe's coffee, not knowing that Joe has a lethal allergy to sugar. *Warrant*: Bob is unaware of the consequences of his act, and therefore, his action is not murder.

Criterion 3: A person attempting a forcible felony such as kidnapping, hijacking, arson, armed robbery, or rape kills a person in the process.

Example: Joe, in robbing a bank with a loaded gun, shoots and kills a guard, who had shot first at Joe. *Warrant*: The act takes place during a felony and therefore is murder, even though the guard shot first.

Contrasting Example: Joe observes Bob shoplifting clothing from Joe's store and begins to chase him. When Joe catches him, Bob pushes him down, causing Joe to strike his head on the ground and die from a severe concussion. *Warrant*: Although Bob has killed Joe while Bob was committing a crime, the crime is not a felony, and so the act that caused the death is not murder.

Voluntary Manslaughter

Taking someone's life is voluntary manslaughter if one of the following criteria is met.

Criterion 1: A person acts with sudden and intense passion after being seriously provoked by the person killed.

Example: While Joe is driving, he's being followed and harassed by Bob, who is using his car to bump and swerve into Joe's car. Bob, angry because Joe has married his ex-wife Sally, forces Joe's car off the road and into a deep ditch. They both get out of their cars and argue heatedly. Bob makes lewd and obscene remarks about Sally's extramarital behavior and about Joe's mother's extramarital behavior. Joe punches Bob, killing him. *Warrant*: The combination of the threatening actions with the car and the insults to his wife and mother have provoked Joe to a sudden and intense passion, so the act is voluntary manslaughter.

Contrasting Example: Bob's car bumps into Joe's car at an intersection. They get out of their cars and argue about whose fault it is. When Bob accuses Joe of being an irresponsible driver, Joe strikes and kills Bob with a tire iron. *Warrant*: The initial situation was not severe enough to be called "seriously provoked," so this is not voluntary manslaughter.

Criterion 2: A person acts with a sudden and intense passion after being seriously provoked and tries to kill the person provoking him or her but accidentally kills someone else.

Example: Joe breaks into Bob's house and begins to shatter Bob's collection of priceless Ming vases and tries to set the drapes on fire. Bob's mother tells him to stop, but he continues and then threatens her with bodily harm, calls her obscene names, and spits in her face. This enrages Bob, who pulls a gun and shoots at Joe. He misses and the bullet accidentally kills the butler. *Warrant*: Because the combination of destruction of precious property and the disrespect and threats to his mother had provoked Bob to a sudden and intense passion, the act is termed voluntary manslaughter.

Contrasting Example: Joe ridicules Bob's haircut. This enrages Bob, who pulls a gun, shoots at Joe, and misses. The bullet accidentally kills an innocent bystander. *Warrant*: This is not voluntary manslaughter because the insult is about a minor issue, and therefore Bob has not been seriously provoked.

Criterion 3: A person incorrectly but honestly believes that if he or she does not kill the other person, his or her own life will be endangered.

Example: Joe shoots and kills Bob, who had been threatening him with a gun. Joe finds later that Bob's gun was not loaded. *Warrant*: Because he honestly believed his life was in danger, Joe has committed voluntary manslaughter.

Contrasting Example: Bob owns a store. Joe enters, looking very suspicious and seeming to have a gun in his coat pocket. Bob, thinking that Joe might rob and kill him, pulls out a gun and kills Joe. *Warrant*: Because the threat is not certain, this is not voluntary manslaughter.

Self-Defense

Taking someone's life is done in self-defense if one of the following criteria is met.

Criterion 1: A person reasonably believes that he or she is in imminent danger of death or great bodily harm and has exhausted every reasonable means to escape the danger other than by using deadly force.

Example: Sally is threatened with rape in a deserted part of a city. She first screams for help. The attacker tackles her and begins to pull off her clothing. She tries unsuccessfully to defend herself with physical resistance. She finally shoots and kills her attacker when she has no other means of defending herself. *Warrant*: Because she has tried several means of escape and is still greatly threatened, this act is one of self-defense.

Contrasting Example: While Sally is walking in a dangerous part of town, Joe asks her for the time. She walks faster and he follows. When he taps her on her shoulder, she turns and shoots him fatally. *Warrant*: Because Sally has tried only one means of escape and because Joe's intentions are uncertain, this act is not considered one of self-defense.

Criterion 2: If two people are involved in physical confrontation and one person withdraws from physical contact with the other person and indicates clearly to the other person that he or she wishes to withdraw and stop the use of force, but the other person refuses and continues to use force, any action by the person wishing to withdraw is an act of self-defense.

Example: During a heated argument over a $100,000 gambling debt that Joe owes to Bob, and subsequent knife fight, Joe offers to stop fighting, but Bob refuses and again attacks. Joe then stabs Bob to death. *Warrant*: Because Joe has done everything possible to end the conflict, his act of stabbing is one of self-defense.

Contrasting Example: During a heated argument and knife fight over a $100,000 gambling debt, Joe backs off to catch his breath. Bob then attacks and Joe stabs him to death. *Warrant*: Joe did not pause to end the conflict but only to rest, so Joe's act is not done in self-defense.

20 minutes: The students begin to formulate their extended definitions of quality music of a particular type, using this template. One main difference they should understand is that the legal definitions on the handout require a person to meet only one of the criteria in order to be included in the category. In an extended definition of quality music or quality literature, it's likely that the text in question would need to meet all of the criteria.

2 minutes: Return the desks to their original positions; exeunt.

Day 18 (Wednesday)

3 minutes: Attendance, housekeeping.

45 minutes: Students continue working in small groups on their extended definitions of a particular kind of music.

2 minutes: Return the desks to their original positions; exeunt.

Day 19 (Thursday)

I'll assume that things wrapped up nicely and neatly on Wednesday and that we can move into the feedback stage today. Here's an opportunity for students to give one another feedback on their efforts from the previous three days.

3 minutes: Attendance, housekeeping.

25 minutes: Students provide one another with peer feedback on the first draft of their extended definitions of a particular kind of music. I'll provide them with the following prompt:

> Exchange your criteria, examples, contrasting examples, and warrants for your extended definition of a particular kind of music with another group (or set up a three-way exchange). Read the definition carefully and provide feedback in response to the following questions. Your feedback should be written in the margins of the paper you are evaluating; you may also discuss your evaluation with the group whose paper you critique.
>
> 1. Is each criterion clearly worded so that you understand what is and is not included in the definition?
>
> 2. Is each criterion illustrated by an example that is clearly explained and convincingly tied to the criterion by means of a warrant?
>
> 3. Is each criterion illustrated by a contrasting example that is clearly explained and convincingly tied to the criterion by means of a warrant?

20 minutes: Students receive their feedback and begin to revise their extended definition. In addition, they should write a brief introduction and conclusion. To do so, they should respond to the following prompt:

> Use the feedback from your fellow students to revise your criteria, examples, contrasting examples, and warrants.
>
> Finally, provide a brief introductory paragraph in which you explain what type of music you are defining and which qualities you expect to find in such music. These qualities should correspond to your criteria.
>
> After explaining the criteria and supporting illustrations, provide a concluding paragraph in which you summarize your beliefs about this kind of music and what makes for a high-quality performance of it.

2 minutes: Return the desks to their original positions; exeunt.

Day 20 (Friday)

> I anticipate that the students will need more time to complete a revision that they can turn in for a grade. Today's class, then, will provide some time to complete their group essays before presenting them to the class. If my forecast for time allotment is off, I can always fall back on a vocabulary game for today. But in all likelihood, the students will need time to sharpen their work before turning it in.

Because I'll grade this extended definition, I need to develop a rubric that will help the students anticipate my grading decisions and help me be consistent as I work my way through their essays. I'm a busy guy, just like you, and will save a step if I can. So I checked with the RubiStar website to see if there was a rubric already developed that I could borrow and adapt. Good news: The site has several examples in its bank of rubrics developed by teachers. But not so good news: none matches very well what I'm interested in evaluating in my students' writing. So I borrowed some of the evaluation categories I found in the online rubrics and worked from scratch on others in order to develop a rubric suited to my instruction. I might plan the class, then, as follows:

3 minutes: Attendance, housekeeping.

15 minutes: Pass out and review the following rubric for evaluating extended definitions.

30 minutes: Students work on their revisions, using the rubric and peer feedback as guides.

2 minutes: Students submit the extended definitions; return the desks to their original positions; exeunt.

EXTENDED DEFINITION

CATEGORY	A	B	C	D	F
Introductory paragraph	The writer clearly identifies the topic of the paper and summarizes the criteria in the definition.	The writer identifies the topic and summarizes the criteria, but one or the other lacks clarity.	The writer identifies the topic and summarizes the criteria, but both explanations are sketchy and/or worded unclearly.	The writer includes an opening paragraph but does not clearly explain the topic or the criteria.	There is no introduction.
Criteria	Each criterion is worded so that the reader clearly understands what is and is not included in the definition.	Most, but not all, of the criteria are worded so that the reader clearly understands what is and is not included in the definition.	Some, but not all, of the criteria are worded so that the reader clearly understands what is and is not included in the definition.	The writer makes an effort at writing criteria, but the wording makes it difficult to understand what is included in the definition and what is not.	There are few or no criteria.
Examples	Each example is explained in sufficient detail so that the reader clearly sees how it supports the criterion.	Most, but not all, examples are explained in sufficient detail so that the reader clearly sees how they support the criteria.	Some, but not all, examples are explained in sufficient detail so that the reader clearly sees how they support the criteria.	The writer provides examples, but it's not clear how they are related to the criteria.	There are few or no examples.
Contrasting examples	Each contrasting example is explained in sufficient detail so that the reader clearly sees how it supports the criterion.	Most, but not all, contrasting examples are explained in sufficient detail so that the reader clearly sees how they support the criteria.	Some, but not all, contrasting examples are explained in sufficient detail so that the reader clearly sees how they support the criteria.	The writer provides contrasting examples, but it's not clear how they are related to the criteria.	There are few or no examples.

Extended Definition *(continued)*

CATEGORY	A	B	C	D	F
Warrants	The writer clearly explains how each example and contrasting example illustrates the criterion to which it is related.	The writer explains how most examples and contrasting examples illustrate the criteria to which they are related.	The writer explains how some examples and contrasting examples illustrate the criteria to which they are related.	The writer makes an effort to relate the examples and contrasting examples to the criteria, but this relation is not clear to the reader.	There are few or no warrants.
Conclusion	The conclusion both summarizes the definition and extends it to provide a new insight based on the thinking that has gone into the definition.	The conclusion summarizes the definition but does little to extend it to provide a new insight based on the thinking that has gone into the definition.	The conclusion summarizes the definition but does not extend it to provide a new insight based on the thinking that has gone into the definition.	The conclusion does not clearly summarize or extend the definition.	There is no conclusion.
Form	The writer's introduction, each criterion, and conclusion are separated into different paragraphs.	The writer's introduction, each criterion, and conclusion are separated into different paragraphs.	The writer's introduction, each criterion, and conclusion are separated into different paragraphs.	The writing is all in one paragraph, or the paragraph divisions appear arbitrary.	The writing is all in one paragraph, or the paragraph divisions appear arbitrary.
Mechanics, Spelling, Grammar, Usage	For the most part, the writing is clear and free of problems.	For the most part, the writing is clear and free of problems.	The writing includes some problems that impede the reader's effort to understand what the writer is saying.	The writing includes many problems that impede the reader's effort to understand what the writer is saying.	The writing includes many problems that impede the reader's effort to understand what the writer is saying.

Week 5

The class has done a lot of work thus far in terms of considering issues of discrimination and learning how to write extended definitions. One thing that might raise concerns is that all of our attention to learning processes has resulted in relatively little reading. Rather than having reading assignments every day and lots of quizzes, study guides, and worksheets on them, we are spending more time thinking about how to read and how to write in relation to reading. We thus have the old breadth versus depth conflict. Obviously, my bias is toward doing more with less—that is, having fewer assignments but thinking about them in greater detail. Taking this approach might put me at odds with some of my colleagues or with the district testing schedule. But I believe strongly that valuing depth of analysis over breadth of coverage both engages students more with the curriculum and produces more long-lasting memories and understanding of what we do cover.

In the fifth week, we will turn our attention to the unit's main text, Richard Wright's autobiography, *Black Boy*. My goal is to have small groups of students lead their own discussions on the novel. Because they are inexperienced in leading discussions, I'll have to teach them how to pose different kinds of questions, following which they'll lead the class' consideration of the story.

Day 21 (Monday)

3 minutes: Attendance, housekeeping.

10 minutes: Pass out and review responsibilities for student-led discussions:

To discuss Richard Wright's *Black Boy*, the class will organize into five small groups, with each group being responsible for leading a discussion of four chapters of the novel. Each group will be responsible for conducting a class discussion on its chapters for one full class period. To lead your class, you may adopt any format you wish: regular English class, nonviolent talk show format, town hall meeting, courtroom, or other mode of your choice. Your discussion should involve all of the following:

- Each group member should take a roughly equal part in leading the discussion.
- You should make an effort to include each other class member in your discussion.

- The questions you pose should not ask for factual information from the story, unless those facts serve to help explore open-ended questions (i.e., those without a single correct answer).

- The questions you pose should include at least one of each of the following categories:

inferences about characters or events within the text (e.g., How does joining a gang affect Richard's life?)

generalizations from the text to society at large (e.g., In what ways is Wright's story from the first half of the twentieth century relevant to today's society?)

the *effects of literary form or technique* (e.g., Do you think that Richard's presentation of his experiences is realistic?)

the *purpose of a particular event* in terms of the text's meaning (e.g., How does Richard's life in the orphanage shape his perspective on life in the United States?)

evaluations of the literature (e.g., What parts of the story do you like best and least? Why?)

emotions that students have in response to the story (e.g., How did you feel when Richard burned down his grandparents' house?)

personal connections to the story (e.g., What connections do you feel with Richard during his employment at the optical company?)

- During the discussion, you should also work at getting students to elaborate on their initial comments.

5 minutes: Explain that they'll need to organize into five groups of roughly even size. Have students pick their groups and organize into them.

2 minutes: Explain that you will give them practice in generating the seven types of questions they should ask, using a story from the ones they have studied to this point (e.g., "Tony's Story"). The procedure will be for you to define each type of question and give an example and for each group then to come up with a similar type of example from the same story.

15 minutes: Define what an inference is (to make an educated guess about something that's not literally stated). Provide an illustration of an inferential question about "Tony's Story" (e.g., What is the difference between Tony's and Leon's feelings toward the power of the arrowhead necklace?) and explain clearly why it requires an inference. Have each group generate an inferential question about the story, and invite groups to share theirs with the class. Clarify how each question generated by students meets the expectations for this question type.

13 minutes: Define what a generalization to larger society is (to state what the story is saying about life in general). Provide an illustration of an inferential question about "Tony's Story" (e.g., Why are Native American men who come back from the army "troublemakers on the reservation"? How does Leon believe that war veterans should be treated?) and explain clearly why it requires a generalization. Have each group develop a generalization question about the story and invite groups to share theirs with the class. Clarify how each question generated by students meets the expectations for this question type.

2 minutes: Return the desks to their original positions; exeunt.

Day 22 (Tuesday)

3 minutes: Attendance, housekeeping.

9 minutes: Define what literary form and technique are (e.g., irony, figurative language, etc.). Provide an illustration of a question about technique for "Tony's Story" (e.g., What does Tony's dream symbolize?) and explain clearly why the question requires an understanding of technique or form. Have each group generate a question about the story's form or technique and invite groups to share theirs with the class. Clarify how each question created by students meets the expectations for this question type.

9 minutes: Define what a significant event is (an event that causes substantive changes in the lives of the characters). Provide an illustration of a question about significant events for "Tony's Story" (e.g., What role reversal do Tony and Leon engage in? How do you explain it?) and explain clearly why this question is centered on the significance of an event. Have each group generate a question about the story's significant events and invite groups to share theirs with the class. Clarify how each question created by students meets the expectations for this question type.

9 minutes: Define what an evaluation is (to judge the quality of the literary work or parts thereof). Provide an illustration of an evaluative question about "Tony's Story" (e.g., Did you feel that the three main characters were realistically portrayed? Would your answer change if you knew that the story is based on a real event?) and explain clearly why it requires an evaluation. Have each group generate an evaluative question about the story and invite groups to share theirs with the class. Clarify how each question created by students meets the expectations for this question type.

9 minutes: Define what an emotional response to a story is (how the story made them feel). Provide an illustration of an emotional question about "Tony's Story" (e.g., How did your feelings about the three main characters change during the course of the story?) and explain clearly why it involves

an emotional response. Have each group generate a different emotional question about the story and invite groups to share theirs with the class. Clarify how each question created by students meets the expectations for this question type.

9 minutes: Define what a personal connection to a story is (a link between the reader's personal experiences and those of literary characters). Provide an illustration of a question requiring a personal connection for "Tony's Story" (e.g., What would you have done if you'd been in Tony's or Leon's situation in the final section of the story?) and explain clearly why it requires a personal connection. Have each group generate a personal connection question about the story and invite groups to share theirs with the class. Clarify how each question created by students meets the expectations for this question type.

2 minutes: Return the desks to their original positions; exeunt.

Day 23 (Wednesday)

3 minutes: Attendance, housekeeping.

25 minutes: Have different groups take responsibility for different sections of *Black Boy*. You could do this through voluntary assignment or through a lottery of some sort. It's possible that students who do not want to read the whole book will lobby heavily for early chapters. A lottery system would take the pressure off you about which groups lead which discussions and add incentive for all students to complete the book.

Once the discussion-leading responsibilities are distributed, remind students that the format of the discussion is up to them. Successfully led student discussions have come in all manner of formats. Encourage them to have fun with the assignment, though not at the expense of their discussion-leading responsibilities, and not out of proportion with the seriousness of the issues raised in the book. They should plan to lead their discussion for a full class period and so should make sure that their planning, while including a minimum set of questions from the types prescribed, also poses other questions for students to discuss. They might look to their reading logs to see what other kinds of questions they could pose for their discussions.

You might distribute your grading rubric prior to the small-group preparations. The following is one way to differentiate the grades for student performances:

Rubric for Grading Student-Led Discussions

A discussion receiving an A will be characterized by the following:

- Each group member takes a roughly equal part in leading the discussion.

- The discussion includes at least 75 percent of other students in the class.

- The questions posed ask for factual information only when those facts serve to help explore open-ended questions (i.e., those without a single correct answer).

- The questions include at least one from each of the following categories:

  - inferences about characters or events within the text

  - generalizations from the text to society at large

  - the effects of literary form or technique

  - the purpose of a particular event in terms of the text's meaning

  - evaluations of the literature

  - emotions that students had in response to the story

  - personal connections to the story

- The discussion occupies the entire class period.

A discussion receiving a B will be characterized by the following:

- Each group member takes a roughly equal part in leading the discussion, although some students speak noticeably more than others.

- The discussion includes at least 50 percent of other students in the class.

- The questions posed ask for factual information only when those facts serve to help explore open-ended questions (i.e., those without a single correct answer).

- The questions include at least one from most of the following categories:

  - inferences about characters or events within the text

  - generalizations from the text to society at large

  - the effects of literary form or technique

  - the purpose of a particular event in terms of the text's meaning

  - evaluations of the literature

  - emotions that students had in response to the story

- personal connections to the story
- The discussion occupies the entire class period.

A discussion receiving a C will be characterized by the following:

- Some group members speak substantially more than others.
- The discussion includes fewer than half of other students in the class.
- The questions posed occasionally ask for factual information that does not serve to help explore open-ended questions (i.e., those without a single correct answer).
- The questions include at least one from at least four of the following categories:
  - inferences about characters or events within the text
  - generalizations from the text to society at large
  - the effects of literary form or technique
  - the purpose of a particular event in terms of the text's meaning
  - evaluations of the literature
  - emotions that students had in response to the story
  - personal connections to the story
- The discussion occupies most of the class period.

A discussion receiving a D will be characterized by the following:

- Some group members do most of the talking.
- The discussion includes no more than 25 percent of other students in the class.
- The questions frequently request factual information.
- The questions include less than half of the following categories:
  - inferences about characters or events within the text
  - generalizations from the text to society at large
  - the effects of literary form or technique
  - the purpose of a particular event in terms of the text's meaning
  - evaluations of the literature
  - emotions that students had in response to the story
  - personal connections to the story
- The discussion ends well before the class period ends.

A discussion receiving an F will be characterized by the following:

- The discussion leaders give little evidence of having read the book.
- The discussion leaders give little evidence of having prepared questions of any kind.
- The discussion ends well before the class period ends.

20 minutes: Students begin working on their preparations for leading their set of chapters.

2 minutes: Return the desks to their original positions; exeunt.

Day 24 (Thursday)

3 minutes: Attendance, housekeeping.

45 minutes: Students work in small groups preparing their questions and formats.

2 minutes: Return the desks to their original positions; exeunt.

Day 25 (Friday)

3 minutes: Attendance, housekeeping.

47 minutes: Student group leads discussion of Chapters 1–4.

Week 6

Day 26 (Monday)

3 minutes: Attendance, housekeeping.

47 minutes: Student group leads discussion of Chapters 5–8.

Day 27 (Tuesday)

3 minutes: Attendance, housekeeping.

47 minutes: Student group leads discussion of Chapters 9–12.

Day 28 (Wednesday)

3 minutes: Attendance, housekeeping.

47 minutes: Student group leads discussion of Chapters 13–16.

Day 29 (Thursday)

3 minutes: Attendance, housekeeping.

47 minutes: Student group leads discussion of Chapters 17–20.

Day 30 (Friday)

> With all the attention to process, this unit has stretched a little longer than I'd originally anticipated. It appears that we'll have to take an extra week to complete the extended definitions on a particular kind of discrimination. And we need to spend some time working on the multimedia assignments and portfolio exhibits. Because I want continuity in the extended-definition assignment, Friday appears to be a good day to work on the multimedia projects.

3 minutes: Attendance, housekeeping.

45 minutes: Provide the students the following assignment. I may also wish to bring in art supplies or be prepared to release students to other parts of the building where resources are available to work on their projects.

> You have read a number of literary works that concern the theme of discrimination. To show what you have learned through your engagement with this literature, create an interpretive text in any form of your choice: collage, painting, poetry, music, drama, sculpture, performance art, or other textual form. You are also welcome to combine forms to produce your text. Keep the following in mind when designing your text:
>
> - It should in some way depict your understanding of experiences with discrimination.
>
> - It should make some kind of reference to at least one work of literature studied during the unit.
>
> - You may produce your text individually or in a group of any size up to three.
>
> - You will have one class period in which to work on your text and must do all additional work outside class.
>
> - You must prepare a three- to five-minute presentation of your text to the class in which you explain its significance and what it shows about your understanding of discrimination and/or literature.

> Students have the remainder of the period to work on the projects, which are due the following Wednesday.

2 minutes: Return the desks to their original positions; exeunt.

Week 7

Day 31 (Monday)

3 minutes: Attendance, housekeeping.

10 minutes: Introduce the extended-definition assignment with the following handout:

> Throughout the unit we have considered the effects of discrimination. We have looked at questions of discrimination in a variety of situations, using examples from current events, from your personal experiences and observations, and from literature. In some cases, there has been disagreement on what counts as discrimination.
>
> Your task is to write an essay in which you provide an extended definition of discrimination of a particular kind, for example, gender discrimination in the workplace, racial discrimination in housing, religious discrimination in school, age discrimination in hiring, or any other sort that interests you. I encourage you to use the topic and information that you used for your webquest as the basis for this paper. To do so, provide the following:
>
> - a general *introduction* in which you include an overview for your definition
> - a set of *criteria* or rules that state clearly what discrimination is and is not
> - for each criterion, an *example* from literature, current events, or your personal experiences that illustrates the rule at work; at least half of your examples must come from the literature studied in class
> - for each criterion, a *contrasting example* from literature, current events, or your personal experiences that appears to meet the conditions of the rule yet lacks some essential ingredient; at least half of your contrasting examples must come from the literature studied in class
> - for each example and contrasting example, a *warrant* that clearly explains why the rule is or is not being met
> - for your whole argument, a *counterargument* expressing the viewpoint of someone who might disagree with you
> - conventional grammar, spelling, punctuation, and usage throughout your essay
> - evidence of having written at least one rough draft that has been submitted for peer evaluation

35 minutes: Students have the remainder of the class to work in small groups preparing outlines and rough drafts for their papers. Although they will do their preparation in small groups, they will each write their papers individually.

2 minutes: Return the desks to their original positions; exeunt.

Day 32 (Tuesday)

3 minutes: Attendance, housekeeping.

47 minutes: Students have the remainder of the period to work individually on their essays. They will bring completed drafts to class on Wednesday for peer feedback.

Day 33 (Wednesday)

On Day 33 the students will work in peer response groups to provide one another with feedback. There are different approaches you can take to doing this. The most open-ended approach is to have each student read his paper aloud to the group and have students provide feedback afterward. I have found that, particularly early in the year, students benefit from having a particular set of feedback responsibilities. In my experience, students don't spontaneously know how to provide feedback, since for many of them it's a new experience.

My approach, then, is to organize students into groups of four (obviously, some groups might be of different sizes, depending on that day's attendance). I will provide a copy of a set of three proofreading responsibilities, all derived from the assignment they are following:

1. Read the whole paper carefully. For your feedback, focus your attention on the writer's *use of criteria*. Is each criterion clearly worded? Does it outline a rule that you could apply to any kind of discrimination within the topic? In the margins of the paper, make comments about how clearly the writer has written each criterion. Then, at the end of the paper, write a brief summary of your recommendations for how to improve the paper in this regard.

2. Read the whole paper carefully. For your feedback, focus your attention on the writer's *use of examples and warrants that clearly explain how the example illustrates the criterion*. In the margins of the paper, make comments about how effectively the writer has used examples and explained their relation to the criteria with warrants. Then, at the end of the paper, write a brief summary of your recommendations for how to improve the paper in this regard.

3. Read the whole paper carefully. For your feedback, focus your attention on the writer's *use of contrasting examples and warrants that clearly explain how each contrasting example illustrates the criterion.* In the margins of the paper, make comments about how effectively the writer has used contrasting examples and explained their relation to the criteria with warrants. Then, at the end of the paper, write a brief summary of your recommendations for how to improve the paper in this regard.

Each student reads the paper of each other student in the group. The system works as follows:

1. For Round 1, each student passes her paper to the left. Students then critique the paper they receive according to the first responsibility identified above (use of criteria).

2. When students finish with this round, they again pass papers to the left for Round 2 so that they are reading a new paper, taking on the second responsibility (use of examples and warrants).

3. When finished, they again pass papers to the left for Round 3 (use of contrasting examples and warrants).

4. Following Round 3, the papers are passed once more to the left, returning to their authors. Each author now has three separate sets of feedback, each with a different focus. This feedback, along with the first draft, will get handed in along with the final copy of the paper.

This approach to critiquing, while somewhat methodical, worked quite well for my students, particularly after they'd done it a few times and understood the procedure and purpose of the activity. Like other new procedures, this one will require more careful instruction and monitoring the first time students do it.

One consideration: You could either have students writing on the same topic critique one another's papers or make sure that each group is composed of students from different webquest groups. Each approach has its own advantages. For my lesson, I'll try the more heterogeneous approach as a way to help each student get exposure to different topics.

The day's class, then, might proceed as follows:

3 minutes: Attendance, housekeeping.

45 minutes: Distribute the peer feedback tasks outlined previously and explain the peer response procedures. Remind the students that the papers will be evaluated according to the same rubric through which their music

definitions were assessed. The students have the class period to work on their peer critiques, discuss one another's papers, and begin working on their revisions. The finished papers will be due on Friday.

2 minutes: Return the desks to their original positions; exeunt.

Day 34 (Thursday)

3 minutes: Attendance, housekeeping

5 minutes: Tell students that they will devote the day to selecting good portfolio exhibits. Remind them that a good exhibit is not necessarily a good product, but a source of important learning. It could be an individually produced exhibit or something generated in groups.

10 minutes: Have students freewrite about the most important things they've learned during the class so far. Remind them that their learning could be about themselves, the topic of discrimination, their learning process, particular stories, how to read literature in satisfying ways, how to write well, or anything else that they consider to be significant learning. Have them link the learning to some artifact that they could use as an exhibit.

12 minutes: Have students volunteer to share their learning experiences. The teacher's role is to classify the experience, write a brief statement about what the student learned, and catalog the relevant exhibit.

5 minutes: Demonstrate what an exhibit would look like in a portfolio: Include the artifact, followed by a page or so of reflection on how it contributed to significant learning. Distinguish between a *summary* of how it was produced and a *reflection* on how it contributed to learning. Their freewrites could serve as the basis of their reflections for particular exhibits.

15 minutes: Provide time for students to work on their portfolio exhibits.

Day 35 (Friday)

Today we'll conclude the unit. There are a few final activities that would work well on a Friday afternoon after a lengthy unit of study. One is for the students to present their multimedia presentations to the class and briefly explain them. The other is for the students to have an opportunity to evaluate the unit. Throughout this book I've advocated the idea that you should always be assessing both your students and your own teaching. If the students have performed consistently well on their writing and discussion leading, then it's likely that your instruction was effective. If they didn't, then you need to think back on how you taught the class and consider ways that you could teach differently for the learning you seek. If it worked better for some groups of students than others, then you might need to give some thought to the question of why this happened.

  Another way to evaluate your teaching is to ask the students how they experienced the unit. We'll work today on an opinionnaire that will allow the students to share their experiences with the unit and provide suggestions on how to improve it. The day's plan, then, would go as follows:

3 minutes: Attendance, housekeeping.

27 minutes: Student presentations of multimedia projects, with time for questions and answers.

20 minutes: Students respond to the following unit evaluation opinionnaire:

Please answer each question that follows. Your comments will strongly influence my efforts to revise the unit for the next group of students, so I'd appreciate your complete honesty in responding. Keep in mind that I'm much more likely to act on thoughtful answers than those that are glib or sarcastic. *You do not need to identify yourself, though you are welcome to if you wish.*

  1. We read the following literature during the unit. Please write your honest opinion of each work of literature and recommend whether or not I should use it next year.

  Songs

  The Weavers: "Sixteen Tons"

  Vanessa Williams: "Colors of the Wind"

  Dave Matthews Band: "Cry Freedom"

  Bob Marley and the Wailers: "War"

  Johnny Clegg and Savuka: "Inevitable Consequence of Progress"

  Randy Newman: "Short People"

  The Crüxshadows: "Leave Me Alone"

  Neil Young: "Southern Man"

  Creedence Clearwater Revival: "Fortunate Son"

  song of your choice

  Poems

  Peter Blue Cloud: "The Old Man's Lazy"

Short Stories

Leslie Marmon Silko: "Tony's Story"

José Antonio Burciaga: "Romantic Nightmare"

Autobiography

Richard Wright: *Black Boy*

2. What did you learn from keeping your reading log? Did you feel that you were adequately taught how to keep one? Please explain. Do you think that keeping a reading log would be a good idea for units that we do later this year? Why or why not?

3. What did you learn from conducting your webquest? Did you feel that this was a good way to introduce the unit on discrimination? Please explain. Would you recommend using webquests in the future? Why or why not?

4. What did you learn from writing your two extended-definition essays? Did you feel that you were adequately taught how to write an extended definition? Please explain. How would you recommend that I do this next year?

5. What did you learn from leading your discussion? Did you feel that you were adequately taught how to conduct it? Please explain. How would you recommend that I do this next year?

6. What did you learn from doing your multimedia project? Would you recommend including this assignment when I teach the unit next year? Why or why not?

7. What would you recommend that I do the same if I taught this unit again to other students?

8. What would you recommend that I do differently?

9. What suggestions can you make for the way in which we learn about language, literature, and writing for the rest of this year?

With this evaluation, students can let you know what they found positive and negative about the unit. I found their feedback to be particularly useful the first time I taught a unit, because the first time you teach it you're likely to make the most errors in judgment. Your students can be good informants about the strengths and weaknesses of your unit design, the materials you selected, the adequacy of your instruction, and so on.

The Unit as a Whole

I have taken you through this unit as I might plan it for a group of hypothetical students. I have tried to employ what I understand to be constructivist principles in the unit design:

- The students will use both writing and talking for exploratory purposes.

- They will be responsible for generating the questions that will initiate the class' literary discussions.

- Their writing will be treated as a process involving several drafts and continual feedback.

- Their writing will be viewed as a social act that will have readers other than the teacher. In this class, they'll have their fellow students as readers and will have the opportunity to post their webquests on the Internet. We might also create some kind of publication, either in print or on the Internet, that will include their definitions of music and discrimination.

- Part of their job in the class will be to reflect on how they learn.

Subsequent units should build on these attitudes so that students view the class as a construction zone in which their role is to be active builders. Before concluding, I would like to emphasize that I have demonstrated *one* possible way to design a unit on discrimination. You could do it quite differently, particularly if you taught this unit to other students, with other texts available, with a different emphasis, or at a later point in the year. My intention has been to show how a unit of instruction fits in with an overall curricular context, is responsive to a variety of constraints, and is designed to meet its own stated goals.

This is where my book ends and yours begins. I hope that by offering this approach to unit design, I've helped to stimulate your thinking as you consider how to go about the complex, challenging, and ultimately satisfying work of designing instruction.

References

Adler, M., and E. Rougle. 2005. *Building Literacy Through Classroom Discussion*. New York: Scholastic.

Alvermann, D. E. 1991. "The Discussion Web: A Graphic Aid for Learning Across the Curriculum." *The Reading Teacher* 45(2): 92–99.

American Association of University Women. 1995. *The AAUW Report: How Schools Shortchange Girls*. New York: Marlowe.

American Psychological Association. 2001. *Publication Manual of the American Psychological Association*. Washington, DC: Author.

Anderson, J. 2005. *Mechanically Inclined: Building Grammar and Style into Writer's Workshop*. Portland, ME: Stenhouse.

———. 2006. "Zooming in and Zooming Out: Putting Grammar in Context into Context." *English Journal* 95(5): 28–34.

Anson, C. M., ed. 1989. *Writing and Response: Theory, Practice, and Research*. Urbana, IL: National Council of Teachers of English.

Applebee, A. N. 1993. *Literature in the Secondary School: Studies of Curriculum and Instruction in the United States*. NCTE Research Report No. 25. Urbana, IL: National Council of Teachers of English.

———. 1996. *Curriculum as Conversation: Transforming Traditions of Teaching and Learning*. Chicago: University of Chicago Press.

Atwell, N. 1989. *Workshop 1 by and for Teachers: Writing and Literature*. Portsmouth, NH: Heinemann.

———. 1998. *In the Middle: New Understandings About Writing, Reading, and Learning*. 2d ed. Portsmouth, NH: Heinemann.

Barnes, D. R. 1992. *From Communication to Curriculum*. 2d ed. Portsmouth, NH: Heinemann.

Barnes, D. R., J. N. Britton, and M. Torbe. 1971. *Language, the Learner and the School*. Harmondsworth, UK: Penguin.

Bransford, J. 1979. *Human Cognition: Learning, Understanding, and Remembering*. Belmont, CA: Wadsworth.

Bruner, J. S. 1975. "The Ontogenesis of Speech Acts." *Journal of Child Language* 2: 1–40.

———. 1986. *Actual Minds, Possible Worlds*. Cambridge, MA: Harvard University Press.

Christenbury, L., ed. 1996. An Issue on Teaching Grammar (special theme issue). *English Journal* 85(7).

Cogdill, S. 1997. "Comparison/Contrast Essays." St. Cloud, MN: Wright Place. Retrieved June 1, 2007 from http://leo.stcloudstate.edu/acadwrite/comparcontrast.html.

Connors, R. J., and A. A. Lunsford. 1988. "Frequency of Formal Errors in Current College Writing, or Ma and Pa Kettle Do Research." *College Composition and Communication* 39: 395–409.

Cotner, C. 1996. Untitled collage. *English Journal*, 85(5), 62.

Csikszentmihalyi, M. 1990. *Flow: The Psychology of Optimal Experience*. New York: Harper and Row.

Csikszentmihalyi, M., and R. Larson. 1984. *Being Adolescent: Conflict and Growth in the Teenage Years*. New York: Basic.

Daniels, H. 1994. *Literature Circles: Voice and Choice in the Student-Centered Classroom*. York, ME: Stenhouse.

Delpit, L. D. 1995. *Other People's Children: Cultural Conflict in the Classroom*. New York: New Press.

Dewey, J. 1934. *Art as Experience*. New York: Berkeley.

Dixon, J. 1975. *Growth Through English: Set in the Perspective of the Seventies*. London: Oxford University Press for the National Association for the Teaching of English.

Dyson, A. H. 1990. *Weaving Possibilities: Rethinking Metaphors for Early Literacy Development*. Occasional Paper #19. Berkeley, CA: Center for the Study of Writing. Retrieved August 3, 2006, from www.writingproject.org/downloads/csw/OP19.pdf.

Ehrenworth, M., and V. Vinton. 2005. *The Power of Grammar: Unconventional Approaches to the Conventions of Language*. Portsmouth, NH: Heinemann.

Eisner, E., ed. 1985. *Learning and Teaching the Ways of Knowing*. Eighty-Fourth Yearbook of the National Society for the Study of Education, Part II. Chicago: University of Chicago Press.

Faust, M., J. Cockrill, C. Hancock, and H. Isserstedt. 2005. *Student Book Clubs: Improving Literature Instruction in Middle and High School*. Norwood, MA: Christopher-Gordon.

Freedman, S. W. 1987. *Response to Student Writing*. NCTE Research Report No. 23. Urbana, IL: National Council of Teachers of English.

Freedman, S. W., E. R. Simons, J. S. Kalnin, A. Casareno, and the M-CLASS Teams. 1999. *Inside City Schools: Investigating Literacy in Multicultural Classrooms*. New York: Teachers College Press.

Gardner, H. 1983. *Frames of Mind: The Theory of Multiple Intelligences*. New York: Basic Books.

———. 1999. *The Disciplined Mind: What All Students Should Understand*. New York: Simon and Schuster.

Gevinson, S. 2005. "Increase the Peace: Engaging Students in Authentic Discussion and Inquiry to Help Prevent School Violence." In *Reflective Teaching, Reflective Learning: How to Develop Critically Engaged Readers, Writers, and Speakers*, ed. T. M. McCann, L. R. Johannessen, E. Kahn, P. Smagorinsky, and M. W. Smith, 207–20. Portsmouth, NH: Heinemann.

Gevinson, S., D. Hammond, and P. Thompson. 2006. *Increase the Peace: A Program for Ending School Violence*. Portsmouth, NH: Heinemann.

Graham, S., and D. Perrin. In press. "Improving the Writing Abilities of Adolescent Students: A Cumulative Meta-Analysis." In *Annual Report on Adolescent Literacy*, ed. A. Henriquez. New York: Carnegie Foundation.

Hairston, M. 1981. "Not All Errors Are Created Equal: Nonacademic Readers in the Professions Respond to Lapses in Usage." *College English* 43: 794–806.

Haussamen, B., A. Benjamin, M. Kolln, and R. S. Wheeler. 2003. *Grammar Alive! A Guide for Teachers*. Urbana, IL: National Council of Teachers of English.

Hillis, V., ed. 1999. *The Lure of the Transcendent: Collected Essays by Dwayne E. Huebner*. Mahwah, NJ: Erlbaum.

Hillocks, G. 1972. *Observing and Writing*. Urbana, IL: National Council of Teachers of English. Retrieved August 4, 2006, from www.coe.uga.edu/~smago/Books/Observing_and_Writing.pdf.

———. 1986. *Research on Written Composition: New Directions for Teaching.* Urbana, IL: ERIC Clearinghouse on Reading and Communications Skills and National Conference on Research in English.

———. 1995. *Teaching Writing as Reflective Practice.* New York: Teachers College Press.

———. 2002. *The Testing Trap: How State Writing Assessments Control Learning.* New York: Teachers College Press.

———. 2007. *Narrative Writing: Learning a New Model for Teaching.* Portsmouth, NH, Heinemann.

Hillocks, G., B. McCabe, and J. McCampbell. 1971. *The Dynamics of English Instruction, Grades 7–12.* New York: Random House. Retrieved August 4, 2006, from www.coe.uga.edu/~smago/Books/Dynamics/Dynamics_home.htm.

Hunt, B. 2006. "Whose Grammar for What Purposes?" *English Journal* 95(5): 88–92.

Hymes, D. H. 1974. *Foundations in Sociolinguistics: An Ethnographic Approach.* Philadelphia: University of Pennsylvania Press.

Johannessen, L. R. 1992. *Illumination Rounds: Teaching the Literature of the Vietnam War.* Urbana, IL: National Council of Teachers of English. Retrieved August 4, 2006, from www.coe.uga.edu/~smago/Books/Illumination_Rounds.pdf.

Johannessen, L. R., E. A. Kahn, and C. C. Walter. 1982. *Designing and Sequencing Prewriting Activities.* Urbana, IL: ERIC Clearinghouse on Reading and Communication Skills and National Council of Teachers of English. Retrieved August 4, 2006, from www.coe.uga.edu/~smago/Books/Designing_and_Sequencing.pdf.

Johnson, T. S., P. Smagorinsky, L. Thompson, and P. G. Fry. 2003. "Learning to Teach the Five-Paragraph Theme." *Research in the Teaching of English* 38: 136–76.

Johnson, W. H. 2006. "The Sentence-Structure Dilemma." *English Journal* 95(3): 14–15.

Killgallon, D., and J. Killgallon. 2006. *Grammar for Middle School: A Sentence-Composing Approach.* Portsmouth, NH: Heinemann.

Kohn, A. 2006. "The Trouble with Rubrics." *English Journal* 95(4): 12–15.

Kolln, M. 1998. *Rhetorical Grammar: Grammatical Choices, Rhetorical Effects.* 3d ed. Boston: Allyn and Bacon.

Langer, J. A., and A. N. Applebee. 1987. *How Writing Shapes Thinking: A Study of Teaching and Learning.* NCTE Research Report No. 22. Urbana, IL: National Council of Teachers of English.

Lee, C. D. 2000. "Signifying in the Zone of Proximal Development." In *Vygotskian Perspectives on Literacy Development: Constructing Meaning Through Collaborative Inquiry*, ed. C. D. Lee and P. Smagorinsky, 191–225. New York: Cambridge University Press.

Loewen, J. W. 1995. *Lies My Teacher Told Me: Everything Your American History Textbook Got Wrong.* New York: Touchstone.

Lyman, F. 1981. "The Responsive Classroom Discussion." In *Mainstreaming Digest*, ed. A. S. Anderson, 109–13. College Park: University of Maryland College of Education.

Mabry, L. 1999. "Writing to the Rubric: Lingering Effects of Traditional Standardized Testing on Direct Writing Assessment." *Phi Delta Kappan* 80(9): 673–79.

Marshall, J. D., P. Smagorinsky, and M. W. Smith. 1995. *The Language of Interpretation: Patterns of Discourse in Discussions of Literature*. NCTE Research Report No. 27. Urbana, IL: National Council of Teachers of English.

McCann, T. M., L. R. Johannessen, E. Kahn, and J. Flanagan. 2006. *Talking in Class: Using Discussion to Enhance Teaching and Learning*. Urbana, IL: National Council of Teachers of English.

McCann, T. M., L. R. Johannessen, and B. P. Ricca. 2005. *Supporting Beginning English Teachers: Research and Implications for Teacher Induction*. Urbana, IL: National Council of Teachers of English.

McMahon, S. I., T. E. Raphael, and V. J. Goatley, eds. 1997. *The Book Club Connection: Literacy Learning and Classroom Talk*. New York: Teachers College Press.

Moll, L. C. 2000. "Inspired by Vygotsky: Ethnographic Experiments in Education." In *Vygotskian Perspectives on Literacy Development: Constructing Meaning Through Collaborative Inquiry*, ed. C. D. Lee and P. Smagorinsky, 256–68. New York: Cambridge University Press.

National Council of Teachers of English. 1985. *On Grammar Exercises to Teach Speaking and Writing*. Urbana, IL: Author. Retrieved March 27, 2007, from www.ncte.org/about/over/positions/category/gram/107492.htm.

Newman, D., P. Griffin, and M. Cole. 1989. *The Construction Zone: Working for Cognitive Change in School*. New York: Cambridge University Press.

Noden, H. R. 1999. *Image Grammar: Using Grammatical Structures to Teach Writing*. Portsmouth, NH: Heinemann.

Noguchi, R. R. 1991. *Grammar and the Teaching of Writing: Limits and Possibilities*. Urbana, IL: National Council of Teachers of English.

Nystrand, M. 1986. *The Structure of Written Communication: Studies in Reciprocity Between Writers and Readers*. Orlando, FL: Academic.

O'Donnell-Allen, C. 2006. *The Book Club Companion: Fostering Strategic Readers in the Secondary Classroom*. Portsmouth, NH: Heinemann.

O'Donnell-Allen, C., and P. Smagorinsky. 1999. "Revising Ophelia: Rethinking Questions of Gender and Power in School." *English Journal* 88(3): 35–42.

O'Donoghue, M. 1971. "How to Write Good." *National Lampoon* 1(12). Retrieved November 3, 2006, from www.blueroses.com/2001_04/hwrite.html.

Parsons, L. 2004. *Grammarama! Innovative Exercises, Creative Activities, Models from Reading, Sentence Combining, Updated Rules, and More!* Ontario: Pembroke.

Pooley, R. C. 1954. "Grammar in the Schools of Today." *The English Journal* 43(3): 142–46.

Ragsdale, D. A., and P. Smagorinsky. 2005. "The Role of Play and Small-Group Work in Activity-Based Instruction." In *Reflective Teaching, Reflective Learning: How to Develop Critically Engaged Readers, Writers, and Speakers*, ed. T. M. McCann, L. R. Johannessen, E. Kahn, P. Smagorinsky, and M. W. Smith, 83–98. Portsmouth, NH: Heinemann.

Reid, L., ed. 2006a. Contexts for Teaching Grammar (special theme issue). *English Journal* 95(5).

———. 2006b. "From the Editor." *English Journal* 95(5): 12–14.

Romano, T. 1995. *Writing with Passion: Life Stories, Multiple Genres*. Portsmouth, NH: Heinemann.

Rosenblatt, L. M. 1978. *The Reader, the Text, the Poem: The Transactional Theory of Literary Response*. Carbondale, IL: Southern Illinois University Press.

———. 1996. *Literature as Exploration*. 5th ed. New York: Modern Language Association.

Safire, W. 1984. *I Stand Corrected: More on Language*. New York: Times Books.

Schuster, E. H. 2003. *Breaking the Rules: Liberating Writers Through Innovative Grammar Instruction*. Portsmouth, NH: Heinemann.

———. 2006. "A Fresh Look at Sentence Fragments." *English Journal* 95(5): 78–83.

Searle, D. 1984. "Scaffolding: Who's Building Whose Building?" *Language Arts* 61: 480–83.

Shaughnessy, M. P. 1977. *Errors and Expectations: A Guide for the Teacher of Basic Writing*. New York: Oxford University Press.

Smagorinsky, P. 1991. *Expressions: Multiple Intelligences in the English Class*. Urbana, IL: National Council of Teachers of English. Retrieved August 4, 2006, from www.coe.uga.edu/~smago/Books/Expressions.pdf.

———. 1994. "Bring the Court Room to the Classroom: Develop Civic Awareness with Simulation Activities." *The Social Studies* 85: 174–80.

———. 1995. "Constructing Meaning in the Disciplines: Reconceptualizing Writing Across the Curriculum as Composing Across the Curriculum." *American Journal of Education* 102: 160–84.

———. 2001. "If Meaning Is Constructed, What Is it Made From? Toward a Cultural Theory of Reading." *Review of Educational Research* 71: 133–69.

———. 2002. *Teaching English Through Principled Practice*. Upper Saddle River, NJ: Merrill/Prentice Hall.

Smagorinsky, P., and J. Coppock. 1994. "Cultural Tools and the Classroom Context: An Exploration of an Alternative Response to Literature." *Written Communication* 11: 283–310.

———. 1995a. "The Reader, the Text, the Context: An Exploration of a Choreographed Response to Literature." *Journal of Reading Behavior* 27: 271–98.

———. 1995b. "Reading Through the Lines: An Exploration of Drama as a Response to Literature." *Reading and Writing Quarterly* 11: 369–91.

Smagorinsky, P., and S. Gevinson. 1989. *Fostering the Reader's Response: Rethinking the Literature Curriculum, Grades 7–12*. Palo Alto, CA: Dale Seymour. Retrieved August 4, 2006, from www.coe.uga.edu/~smago/Books/FRR.pdf.

Smagorinsky, P., N. Gibson, C. Moore, S. Bickmore, and L. Cook. 2004. "Praxis Shock: Making the Transition from a Student-Centered University Program to the Corporate Climate of Schools." *English Education* 36: 214–45.

Smagorinsky, P., and A. Jordahl. 1991. "The Student Teacher/Cooperating Teacher Collaborative Study: A New Source of Knowledge." *English Education* 23: 54–59.

Smagorinsky, P., T. McCann, and S. Kern. 1987. *Explorations: Introductory Activities for Literature and Composition, Grades 7–12*. Urbana, IL: National Council of Teachers of English. Retrieved August 4, 2006, from www.coe.uga.edu/~smago/Books/Explorations.pdf.

Smagorinsky, P., and C. O'Donnell-Allen. 1998a. "The Depth and Dynamics of Context: Tracing the Sources and Channels of Engagement and Disengagement in Students' Response to Literature." *Journal of Literacy Research* 30: 515–59.

———. 1998b. "Reading as Mediated and Mediating Action: Composing Meaning for Literature Through Multimedia Interpretive Texts." *Reading Research Quarterly* 33: 198–226.

————. 2000. Idiocultural Diversity in Small Groups: The Role of the Relational Framework in Collaborative Learning." In *Vygotskian Perspectives on Literacy Research: Constructing Meaning Through Collaborative Inquiry*, ed. C. D. Lee and P. Smagorinsky, 165–90. New York: Cambridge University Press.

Smagorinsky, P., M. Zoss, and C. O'Donnell-Allen. 2005. "Mask-Making as Identity Project in a High School English Class: A Case Study." *English in Education* 39(2): 58–73.

Smith, M. W. 1991. *Understanding Unreliable Narrators: Reading Between the Lines in the Literature Classroom*. Urbana, IL: National Council of Teachers of English. Retrieved August 4, 2006, from www.coe.uga.edu/~smago/Books/Unreliable_Narrators.pdf.

Smith, M. W., and J. Wilhelm. 2007. *Getting It Right: Fresh Approaches to Teaching Grammar, Usage, and Correctness*. New York: Scholastic.

Smitherman, G. 2006. *Word from the Mother: Language and African Americans*. New York: Routledge.

Sommers, C. H. 2000. *The War Against Boys: How Misguided Feminism Is Harming Our Young Men*. New York: Simon and Schuster.

Strong, W. 1994. *Sentence Combining: A Composing Book*. 3d ed. New York: Random House/McGraw-Hill.

Thoreau, H. D. 1998. *Civil Disobedience, Solitude, and Life Without Principle*. Amherst, NY: Prometheus Books.

Topping, D. H., and S. J. Hoffman. 2006. *Getting Grammar: 150 New Ways to Teach an Old Subject*. Portsmouth, NH: Heinemann.

Underwood, W. 1987. "The Body Biography: A Framework for Student Writing." *English Journal* 76(8): 44–48.

Vygotsky, L. S. 1978. *Mind in Society: The Development of Higher Psychological Processes*. Ed. M. Cole, V. John-Steiner, S. Scribner, and E. Souberman. Cambridge, MA: Harvard University Press.

————. 1987. *The Collected Works of Lev Vygotsky, Volume 1: Problems of General Psychology (Including the Volume Thinking and Speech)*. Ed. R. Rieber and A. Carton. Trans. N. Minick. New York: Plenum.

Weaver, C. 1996. *Teaching Grammar in Context*. Portsmouth, NH: Heinemann.

Wertsch, J. V. 1991. *Voices of the Mind: A Sociocultural Approach to Mediated Action*. Cambridge, MA: Harvard University Press.

Wheeler, R., ed. 1999. *Language Alive in the Classroom*. Westport, CT: Praeger.

Wheeler, R. S., and R. Swords. 2006. *Code-Switching: Teaching Standard English in Urban Classrooms*. Urbana, IL: National Council of Teachers of English.

Wilhelm, J. D. 1997. *You Gotta BE the Book: Teaching Engaged and Reflective Reading with Adolescents*. New York: Teachers College Press.

Wilhelm, J. D., and B. Edmiston. 1998. *Imagining to Learn: Inquiry, Ethics, and Integration Through Drama*. Portsmouth, NH: Heinemann.

Wilson, M. 2006. *Rethinking Rubrics in Writing Assessment*. Portsmouth: Heinemann.

Zoss, M. 2007. *Integrating Visual and Language Arts: A Case Study of a Teacher's Experiences Composing a Curriculum*. Unpublished doctoral dissertation. University of Georgia.

Index